The Vestry Records of the Parish of
St John the Evangelist, Dublin, 1595–1658

Map 1. Extract from John Speed's map of Dublin (1610) showing Woodkey (8), Fishamble Street (24), Winetavern Street (25), Christ Church Cathedral (35), and Dublin Castle (23). St John's parish church is immediately north of Christ Church.

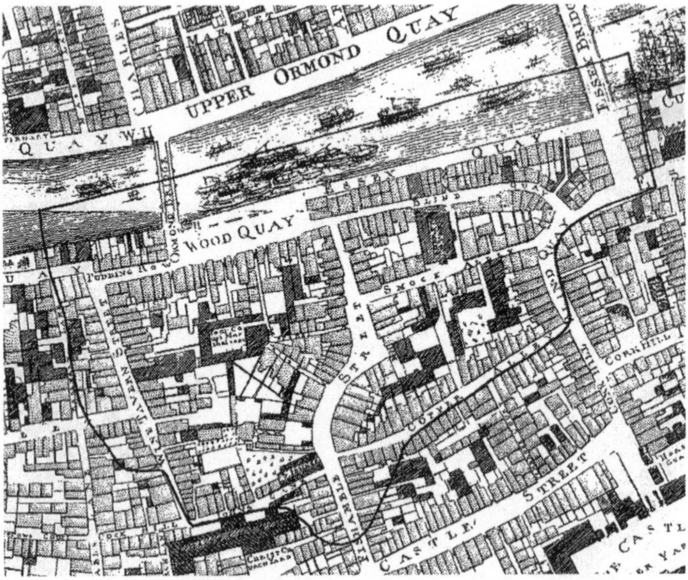

Map 2. Extract from John Rocque's map of the city of Dublin (1756) with an outline of the boundaries of the parish of St John superimposed. The parish boundaries are conjectural as they were poorly defined and gave rise to boundary disputes (ff 57, 97). Rosemary Lane was included in some cess lists but not in others.

The Vestry Records of the Parish of St John the Evangelist, Dublin 1595–1658

EDITED BY

Raymond Gillespie

FOUR COURTS PRESS • DUBLIN

in association with

THE REPRESENTATIVE CHURCH BODY LIBRARY

This book was set in 11 on 12.5pt Ehrhardt
by Carrigboy Typesetting Services for
FOUR COURTS PRESS LTD
Fumbally Court, Fumbally Lane, Dublin 8, Ireland
and in North America for
FOUR COURTS PRESS
c/o ISBS, 5824 NE Hassalo Street,
Portland, OR 97213.

A catalogue record for this title is available from the British Library.

ISBN 1-85182-623-8

This publication has received support from the Heritage Council under the 2001 Publications Grant Scheme.

AN CHOMHAIRLE OIDHREACHTA
THE HERITAGE COUNCIL

Printed in Great Britain
by MPG Books, Bodmin, Cornwall.

CONTENTS

ILLUSTRATIONS

PREFACE

This is the first volume in a new texts and calendars series to be published by Four Courts Press in association with the Representative Church Body Library and is intended to complement the Library's already established parish register series. However, unlike the register series which has concentrated on the publication of texts with a minimum of historical introduction, largely for genealogical use, the texts and calendars series will seek to provide critical editions of important Church of Ireland archives and manuscripts with substantial interpretative and explanatory apparatus.

This volume, the vestry book of the parish of St John the Evangelist, exemplifies this aspiration. The parish of St John was a high status Dublin city parish which had, from medieval times, a close association with Christ Church cathedral, of which it became a prebendal church in the sixteenth century. Its vestry book is the oldest such record to survive for the Church of Ireland just as its first register, which was re-issued as part of the Library's parish register series last year, is the oldest parish register in Ireland. The vestry book, containing not only the minutes of the vestry but also accounts of the churchwardens and records of the parish cess, the latter augmented in this edition by material from Dublin City Archives, casts light on many aspects of religious, social and economic life not only in the parish of St John but in the city of Dublin.

I am indebted to Raymond Gillespie for agreeing to edit this inaugural volume. He has brought to the task his customary enthusiasm, meticulousness and breadth and depth of knowledge. Bridget McCormack computerised a draft typescript of the vestry book and the Library of the Royal Irish Academy kindly provided facilities for Dr Gillespie to check the text. I am grateful also to the staffs of the Representative Church Body Library, Dublin City Archives and the Department of Manuscripts of the Library of Trinity College, Dublin, for facilitating Dr Gillespie's work. Bernadette Cunningham compiled the index.

Material in appendix two relating to St John's parish from Cess Books, 1647–49, (MR/16) from Dublin City Archives is reproduced by kind permission of Dublin Corporation and appendix one from Trinity College, Dublin MS 851 appears by permission of the Board of Trinity College, Dublin.

The publication of this volume has been supported by a grant from the Heritage Council.

RAYMOND REFAUSSÉ
Series Editor

INTRODUCTION

It is difficult for today's historians to appreciate the importance of the parish in the life of the early modern world, especially in the urban setting where large numbers of people living in very close proximity had to find ways of organising their everyday lives. In the early seventeenth century the parish took on an ever increasing role in such social organisation. In addition to their religious functions, the Irish parliament in the early seventeenth century demanded that parishes manage the roads which passed through them. At the same time local authorities, such as Dublin corporation, required parishes to organise local fire fighting arrangements and deal with both local and wider civic arrangements for the poor.[1] Understanding how these local administrative units adapted to their changing role is not easy since few of the records which they produced have survived. Accepted wisdom has decreed that much of this parochial material was destroyed in the 1922 explosion in the Public Record Office. This is only partly true. Five sets of parish registers containing material predating 1660 were destroyed but much of this, such as the registers of St Michan's, has survived in other forms. Eight sets of pre-1660 parish registers survived the fire.[2] While parish registers may have been destroyed in the 1922 fire the fate of the vestry records, including minute books, cess books, churchwardens accounts and parish deeds, is more mysterious. The designation of parish registers as public records after the disestablishment of the Church of Ireland in 1870 did not extend to other vestry records which were, in the main, not sent to the Public Record Office.[3] Other explanations are necessary for the lack of such parochial material. In some rural parishes, where the Church of Ireland population in the seventeenth century was small, parochial records may not have been kept. In the case of Leixlip all that survives of the work of the vestry is a few memoranda jotted down in the parish register.[4] In larger urban

1 11, 12 & 13 Jas I.c. 7; J.T. and R. Gilbert, *Calendar of the ancient records of Dublin* (19 vols, Dublin, 1889–1944), iii, pp 129, 292–3 and ff 71, 77 below. For the evolution of parochial functions Rowena Dudley, 'Dublin's parishes: the Church of Ireland parishes and their role in the civic administration', Ph.D. thesis, Trinity College, Dublin, 1995.

2 Noel Reid (ed.), *A table of Church of Ireland parochial records and copies* (Naas, 1994).

3 Gréagóir Ó Duill, 'Church records after disestablishment' in *Irish Archives Bulletin* v (1975), pp 17–18.

4 Suzanne Pegley (ed.), *Register of the parish of Leixlip* (Dublin, 2001), pp 1, 9–10, 28–9, 32–3, 36.

settings records may not have survived because of neglect or accident. A 1754 fire in St Werburgh's church destroyed at least some of the parochial records including registers containing entries from the late 1620s.[5] In other cases material was lost. The vestry records of the parish of St Audoen's from the early seventeenth century were certainly extant in the 1880s when they were used by C.T. McCready for his work on the history of the church although they are no longer among the parish archive.[6] An exception to these generalisations of destruction and loss is the parochial records of the parish of St John in Dublin. Although the parish was amalgamated with that of St Werburgh's in 1878 and the church taken down in 1884 its records form the oldest nearly complete series of parochial records in the Church of Ireland. The registers, beginning in 1619, are the oldest parish registers in Ireland and although the churchwardens' accounts for St Werburgh's are older they have significant gaps in the seventeenth century.[7]

I

The text edited here, though loosely described as a vestry book, in fact consists of three elements which later in the seventeenth century would become three separate entities in the St John's archive. The first element is the minutes of the vestry, the second the annual accounts of the churchwardens and the third the records of the parish cess. All of these elements were produced under the administrative aegis of the parish and its officials, most importantly the churchwardens. It is difficult to be precise about how parochial administration worked in Ireland in the early seventeenth century for a number of reasons. The first is certainly the paucity of evidence but a second reason is that, unlike England, the duties of churchwardens and others were not set out in canon law before the 1630s.[8] The result of this was

5 For these entries seen in the 1690s, Trinity College, Dublin, MS 851, f 107. In 1627 St Werburgh's churchwardens' accounts record 'a book for the church to write christenings and burials in' (Representative Church Body Library, P 326/1/21).

6 Marsh's Library, Dublin, C.T. McCready's notes 'The memorials of St Audoen's'. The early registers of the church which, according to the late seventeenth century notes in Trinity College, Dublin, MS 851, f. 109, dated to the 1630s may also have disappeared at this time since the earliest extant registers begin in 1672.

7 James Mills (ed.), *Registers of the parish of St John the Evangelist, Dublin, 1619–1699* (Dublin, 1906, reprint, 2000). The records are now in the Representative Church Body Library, Dublin, P 328.

8 The English canons of 1571 and 1604 set out churchwardens' duties in some detail. For the English context, N.J.G. Pounds, *A history of the English parish* (Cambridge, 2000), pp 182–6.

a wide variation over Ireland in the customs of parochial organisation. In early seventeenth-century Youghal, for instance, churchwardens were not elected by the parish. Instead one was appointed by the corporation and the other by the minister. By contrast in Crumlin, near Dublin, in the 1590s the proctors of the parish were appointed by the manor court.[9] In the case of Belfast the position of the churchwardens is unclear but the corporation certainly appointed the sexton of the parish.[10] There were equally wide divergences in what churchwardens might do. In Belfast they collected recusancy fines which were given to the corporation but elsewhere other arrangements were in place for the collection of such fines.[11] Again the body to which the churchwardens were answerable depended on the arrangements for their appointment. In Galway the accounts of the proctors were to be taken by the mayor but in Youghal the churchwardens were to bring their accounts to the town council, who were also responsible for church property.[12] The Irish canons of 1634 may have brought some order to this situation by stipulating that churchwardens were to be chosen in Easter week by the consent of minister and people. At the end of their term the wardens were to account to the parish for the money and church property which had passed through their hands. They were to preserve the church and provide necessities for preaching and administration of the sacraments. Churchwardens were also required to present to the bishop or archdeacon's court schismatics and non-communicants. From the 1630s these regulations provided the framework for the questions asked at episcopal visitations.[13]

In practice St John's parish seems to have resembled the model set out in the canons of 1634 from the late sixteenth century. The earliest entries in the vestry book record the appointment of churchwardens at Easter. From 1639 sidesmen were also appointed in what seems to have been a move to align the workings of the parish with English norms. How these wardens and sidesmen were appointed is not clear from the vestry book. The formula stipulating that the appointment was made 'by the assent of the whole

9 Richard Caulfield (ed.), *The council book of the corporation of Youghal* (Guildford, 1878), pp 52–3; Edmund Curtis, 'The court book of Esker and Crumlin, 1592–1600' in *Journal of the Royal Society of Antiquaries of Ireland* lx (1930), p. 148.
10 R.M. Young, *The town book of the corporation of Belfast, 1613–1816* (Belfast, 1892), pp 38–9.
11 Young, *Town book*, p. 4.
12 J.T. Gilbert (ed.), 'Archives of the town of Galway' in Historical Manuscripts Commission, *Tenth Report* (London, 1885), appendix 5, p. 400; Caulfield, *Council book of Youghal*, pp 12, 42, 53, 150–2.
13 Gerald Bray (ed.), *The Anglican canons, 1529–1947* (Woodbridge, 1998), pp 514–6, 525–9; *Articles to be enquired of by the churchwardens and questions of every parish in the lord primate's visitation* (Dublin, 1638).

parish' or by the 'full consent' of the incumbent 'and the assembly of the parishioners' need not be taken literally. The parish vestry in theory did comprise all those resident within the parish but the entries in the vestry book appointing the wardens carry relatively few signatures, usually about a dozen. It may be that, as in London, the practice of holding a select vestry, which confined power in the hands of a few, had emerged in Dublin by the early seventeenth century.[14] The only indication of how parish meetings were summoned comes from 1660 when a meeting had to be called to deal with the refusal of the churchwardens appointed in 1659 to take the required oath at the archdeacon's court. According to the vestry book a meeting was held 'upon warning given in the church of this parish of St John's, Dublin, the last Sabbath day for a general meeting and also upon warning given at the houses of the chief inhabitants of the said parish'.[15] The special notice given to the 'chief inhabitants' does suggest the workings of a select vestry in practice. It also seems clear from the churchwardens' accounts that a second meeting was held in the course of the year to audit the churchwardens' accounts. Where the amounts paid for wine at these occasions are stipulated it seems that this second meeting was much smaller than the first and was probably confined to the churchwardens and the auditors of the accounts appointed by the vestry. The holding of a third meeting of the vestry in one year was highly unusual and intended to deal with special problems.

The eligibility for the post of churchwarden was an ill defined area. Some, such as clergy, peers, lawyers or members of parliament, were excluded by virtue of their position but in theory all others in the parish were eligible. Whether Catholics, or those with suspect confessional allegiances, could serve is a moot point. It is difficult to test this since it is difficult to determine confessional allegiances at a low social level. At least one Catholic may have served as warden in St John's. Alderman Richard Browne was elected as one of the wardens in 1638–9 and 1639–40, yet in 1642 he was deprived of his position on the aldermanic bench for his sympathies with the Catholic rebels.[16] It also seems highly likely that William Plunkett, churchwarden in 1621, was closely related to the Catholic family of Plunkett who lived in Fishamble Street.[17] St John's, unlike many other Dublin parishes, had a substantial Protestant population and hence had little difficulty in finding Protestants to undertake the office.[18] In the 1620s two individuals were elected each year and it was rare for the same person to hold the office

14 Pounds, *History of the English parish*, pp 192–3.
15 Representative Church Body Library, P328/5/2, p. 1.
16 Gilbert (eds), *Calendar of the ancient records of Dublin*, iii, p. 393.
17 Colm Lennon, *The lords of Dublin in the age of reformation* (Dublin, 1989), p. 263.
18 Myles Ronan (ed.), 'Archbishop Bulkeley's visitation of Dublin, 1630' in *Archivium Hibernicum* viii (1941), p. 58.

twice.[19] In the 1630s a custom developed of each church warden serving two terms and retiring in rotation so as to maintain continuity between the years of appointment. The system was not perfect and collapsed in the 1640s under the stress of rapid population mobility during the rebellion. No clear pattern emerges of the sort of men who filled the office of churchwarden except that those at the extremes of the social spectrum do not appear. To judge from the assessments for the minister's stipend printed in the text below those who served as churchwardens fell in the middle of the social rank although most came from the wealthiest area of the parish around Fishamble Street. They were also drawn from a wide range of trades from merchants to chandlers and apothecaries. Most were probably interested in the office not for religious reasons but for the standing it gave them in the local community.

Churchwardens in St John's parish had a number of duties defined by custom. In the late 1630s, for instance, they were responsible for the keeping of the parish register and they signed the entries made there.[20] More importantly they were responsible for the maintenance of the church, the provision of its liturgical needs (including bread and wine for communions, bibles and prayer books and vestments) and the payment of the parish clerk. The income for this was provided by the parish estate. In the case of St John's this was composed of two parts. First there was the medieval property accumulated as a result of benefactions to the church. In particular after the Reformation the church seems to have absorbed the property of a chantry endowed in the church by John Lytill in 1434 and the property of the guild of St John the Baptist established in the church by royal charter in 1418.[21] The second element in the parochial estate was the property of the medieval parish of St Tullock's (or St Olave's) which had been merged with St John's in the early 1550s. At least some of this property was alienated from the dissolved parish but a substantial amount passed to St John's.[22] While the property was managed as part of the parish estate it was kept separate in the surveys of that property (ff 147–9, appendix 1) and in 1558 it was stipulated in a lease of part of St Tullock's land that if the parish should be restored the rents should be payable to the churchwardens of St Tullock's.[23]

The expenditure of the income derived from this estate was accounted for each year by the churchwardens in their accounts which were audited by a

19 For a list of the wardens S.C. Hughes, *The church of S. John the Evangelist, Dublin* (Dublin, 1889), pp 120–2.

20 Mills (ed.), *Registers*, pp 30–5.

21 John L. Robinson, 'On the ancient deeds of the parish of St. John, Dublin' in *Proceedings of the Royal Irish Academy* xxxiii sect C (1916–17), pp 175–6.

22 *The Irish fiants of the Tudor sovereigns* (4 vols, Dublin, 1994), Edward VI no. 1108, Philip & Mary no. 6.

23 Robinson, 'Ancient deeds', no. 170.

number of people appointed by the vestry and copied into the vestry book. These are the second element in the St John's parish archive. The resulting accounts provide a unique insight into parochial life in early seventeenth-century Dublin. The rituals of bell ringing at key moments in the political calendar, such as 5 November or the king's birthday or the return of Charles, prince of Wales, from the failed negotiations over the Spanish match, help to highlight something of the political sensibilities of the parish.

Again the liturgical life of St John's is reflected in the increasing amounts spent on bread and wine for the communion in the 1630s as communion services became more frequent. Extensive works were carried out on the church in the late 1630s, including the railing in of the communion table, to make it conform to the new ideas of worship promulgated by Archbishop Laud in England and introduced to Ireland under Lord Deputy Wentworth. No doubt these changes reflect not only the wishes of the incumbent of St John's but the fact that the church was a prebendal church of Christ Church where such changes were proceeding with some speed in the late 1630s.[24] Again the works in the 1650s, although more poorly documented, suggest that many of these innovations were undone. These, in turn, were reversed in 1661–2 when the churchwardens paid for replacing the rails in the chancel taken down in the 1650s.[25] However not all these changes were formally liturgical. The considerable sums of money spent on the porch leading to St John's Lane, which was clearly a substantial structure, point to the importance of the church as a social centre for the parish. In 1639 a merchant, Albert Skinner, was required to perform penance by sitting in the porch at St John's.[26] The importance of such public statements in maintaining social order was considerable and the function of the parish church in revealing those statements to the community was central. The churchwardens' accounts in this volume deserve close attention in reconstructing local life.[27]

The final element in the parochial archive represented by the vestry book are the cess applotments for the minister's stipend. Supporting the clergy in towns, where tithes were impossible to calculate or collect, was a continual problem. In 1616 the government had fixed salaries for the Dublin clergy to be raised by means of assessment on the inhabitants of parishes. The income of the incumbent of St John's was increased from £11 per annum, recorded

24 Raymond Gillespie, 'The crisis of reform, 1625–60' in Kenneth Milne (ed.), *Christ Church cathedral, Dublin: a history* (Dublin, 2000), pp 197–201.

25 Representative Church Body Library, Dublin, P 328/5/2, accounts for 1661–2.

26 Marsh's Library, Dublin, MS Z4. 2. 1 no. 20.

27 For some approaches to such accounts, J.S. Craig, 'Elizabethan churchwardens and parish accounts' in *Social History* xviii (1993), pp 357–80 and Beat Kumin, *The shaping of a community: the rise and reformation of the English parish, 1400–1560* (Aldershot, 1996) esp. ch. 3.

in the 1615 visitation, to £60.[28] This made St John's the second richest living in Dublin, only marginally behind St Audoen's which was rated at £66. The basis of these ratings is not clear and city-wide demographic and taxation data are lacking until the 1640s. Using the 1648 cess books (appendix 2) as a basis for the estimation of wealth, St John's was one of the poorest Dublin parishes on the basis of cess payable per head and the parish had certainly complained (f. 77) of its poverty in 1636.[29] Part of the reason for this may be that, on the basis of the poll tax returns of 1660 St John's had one of the highest population totals of all the Dublin parishes, despite its relatively small size. Its population total was only exceeded by the large parishes of St Michan's and St Catherine's.[30] In the early seventeenth century that population was growing. The cess list for 1621 recorded 164 houses which had grown to 248 houses by 1643 but the effect of war and plague caused a contraction to 192 houses by 1659. It seems likely therefore that the assessment was calculated on the basis of population size rather than overall wealth. This overall assessment was, in turn, divided among the parishioners regardless of confessional allegiance in the form of a parish cess. How the £60 was applotted by those appointed by the vestry to cess the parish is not known. It may have been related to rents or perhaps simply to local perceptions of wealth, although after 1665, according to the vestry minutes, the assessment was made on a property valuation. Cessors were usually drawn from the different streets of the parish suggesting that local knowledge was important. However it was done it seems to have caused little disagreement. The resulting cess lists, together with the other cess lists in appendices 2 and 3, provide an important body of material for any assessment of the demography and social structure of the parish in the early seventeenth century.[31]

II

In its present form the manuscript is a paper volume of 175 folios. However it has suffered a number of losses over the years. The manuscript begins with entries for 4 May 1595 and this seems to be the condition it was in during the 1880s when the last curate of St John's, S.C. Hughes, saw it.[32] However on

28 Myles Ronan, 'Royal visitation of Dublin, 1615' in *Archivium Hibernicum* viii (1941), p. 11; Representative Church Body Library, Dublin, MS C6/1/26/2, no. 9.

29 Dublin City Archives, MR/16, pp 11–14.

30 Séamus Pender (ed.), *A census of Ireland c. 1659* (Dublin, 1939), p. 373.

31 For some indications of the possibilities here, Katherine Anderson, 'The evolution of the parish of St John the Evangelist, Dublin, 1600–1700', M.A. thesis, National University of Ireland, Maynooth, 1997.

32 Hughes, *The church of S. John*, p. 16

the basis of a brown ink pagination which continues until 1657, and may therefore be of roughly that date, two pages or one folio had already been lost. How much material that represents is unclear although given that the first entry in the book is numbered '8' this suggests that seven entries are missing which cannot constitute more than two or three years business. The origins of the manuscript may be in 1593 or 1594. Why the vestry should have begun keeping records at this point is uncertain. It does not correspond to a change of minister or any other obvious shift in the life of the church. One explanation may be that the earliest folios are not contemporary entries but copies from older, more scattered papers. Despite the different dates of the entries on ff 1–1v they are all in the same hand and in the same ink and the page has been formally laid out with margins on all four sides, which only ff 1–2v have. Moreover the lacunae between the 1595 entries and the next entries for 1602, though on the basis of the brown ink pagination without any loss of pages, suggests that the real beginning of the vestry book may date from the arrival of Barnaby Bolger as prebendary of St John's in 1602 with some earlier entries being copied into the volume. In its present form f. 2 has become reversed and this is reflected in the brown–ink pagination. The original order has been restored in this edition by printing the verso of f. 2 before the recto.

The second significant gap in the manuscript is between the entries for 1606 and the incomplete churchwardens' accounts for 1618–19 on what is now f. 3. The brown ink pagination suggests only one page is missing here and that another thirteen are missing after the account. Indeed the gap may be greater than it appears for the fragmentary document of ff 4–4v does not seem to have belonged to this volume and its brown ink pagination overlaps with the pagination in this volume. From later entries in the volume, such as the reference to the 1616 act for determining the incumbents stipend being in the volume (f. 80v), more material seem to have been lost from the 1606–18 lacunae than the smaller one from 1618–22. The pagination which suggests otherwise is probably in error and this implies that the volume was already in a poor state by the time this pagination was done. From 1622 the volume seems complete. Although the cess list for 1644 appears incomplete this resulted most probably from the copyist using a faulty list rather than a loss of folios from the volume. There seems to be nothing missing from the end of the volume although it finishes in 1658 and the succeeding volume begins in April 1660.[33]

The volume is written in a large variety of hands. In the case of the churchwardens' accounts and the cess lists the accounts may well have been written by professional scribes and they are certainly not in the hands of the churchwardens. They are usually neat and in the accounts there are occasional

33 Representative Church Body Library, Dublin, P 328/5/2.

references to the payment of clerks for writing the cess or the accounts (ff 110, 137, 162v). It seems likely that the accounts were prepared on loose sheets of paper, as was the case in St Werburgh's parish, and then a fair copy was transcribed into the vestry book. In some cases an auditors' certificate was written in the same hand and then signed by the auditors but in other cases the audit certificate was written by one of the auditors themselves. The accounts of the elections at the Easter vestry, by contrast, are not written by professional scribes but by one of those in attendance. Whether the vestry had a formally appointed secretary or not is not clear but a number of hands do continue over a long period of time. The record of the Easter vestry from 1632 to 1636 and again from 1642 to 1646 are all in the hand of William Plunkett. Another unidentified hand recorded those from 1638 to 1641. Why Plunkett did not record those years is not known as he was certainly still in the parish and wrote the audit certificate for the accounts for 1639–40.

III

The vestry book of St John's parish is a unique record of parish life in early seventeenth-century Dublin. It has, however, been little used by historians. James Mills printed some of the cess lists in his edition of the St John's parish register and J.B. Leslie has written a short paper on the contents of the volume.[34] The only sustained discussion of its contents is contained in a thesis by Katherine Anderson.[35] The uniqueness of the text inevitably raises questions of its representativeness of the parishes whose records either have not survived or who never bothered to keep records at all. Such questions are impossible to answer. In some respects St John's was an abnormal parish. Its connections with Christ Church laid it open to influences which may have spread through the other city parishes more slowly. Again, together with St Werburgh's, it had the largest Protestant population in the city which made it possible to operate an administrative structure which relied on a substantial pool of people prepared to shoulder the responsibilities of churchwardens, sidesmen and auditors of the parish accounts. However in other respects it shared the problems of many parishes. The juxtaposition of rich and poor, as evidenced by the cess lists, inevitably gave rise to social tensions and religious tensions are clear from the will of one St John's

34 Mills, *Register*, pp 273–7; J.B. Leslie, 'An old Dublin vestry book' in *Journal of the Royal Society of Antiquaries of Ireland* lxxiii (1943), pp 40–9. Two copies of Leslie's extensive notes on the volume exist in National Library of Ireland, MS 1618 and Representative Church Body Library, Dublin, MS 61. 6. 16.

35 Anderson, 'The evolution of the parish of St John the Evangelist, Dublin, 1600–1700'.

parishioner, Thady Dunn, who threatened to disinherit any of those benefiting from his will if they became Catholics.[36] There were other common problems such as the care of the poor and the maintainence of some form of law and order. In this area the parish was an invaluable institution. Even when the Church of Ireland effectively disappeared in the 1650s the parish as a social and religious institution flourished and it is from this decade that parochial records of all kinds become common for the Dublin city churches. While many may not have liked the theology of the parish church it still provided a focus for community loyalties. Those who lived in the parish could be buried there at preferential rates (f. 1v) and from 1644 the poor of the parish could be recognised as being from St John's by the badges provided by the parish (f. 127v). As a micro society the parish had many functions other than purely religious ones, among which was the provision of institutions which could be used in maintaining social stability in what seemed to be a rapidly changing world. How it did that is told by the text edited here through its record of the daily round of repairing a church, proving the parish bounds, ringing bells, buying holly and ivy to decorate the church and dealing with the poor. Such were the realities of parish life and the focal point of many individual worlds.

36 National Library of Ireland, MS GO 290, p. 130.

EDITORIAL CONVENTIONS

The text presented here is a transcript of Representative Church Body Library MS P 328/5/1. The spelling has not been modernised although some punctuation has been added to make the text more comprehensible. A number of obvious contractions which have been used consistently throughout the manuscript (such as wch for which and wth for with and p^{sh} for parish) have been silently expanded. Technical terms have been explained in the notes to the text when they first occur.

The following editorial conventions have been used

[ ]	editorial matter
< >	deletions in the original
{ }	interlined in the original
Fishamble	marginal note in the original

Accounts usually indicate that sums of money are in sterling (st) and it seems highly probable that all parish accounts were kept in sterling.

TEXT

[f. 1] Quarto May 1595. Annoque Elizabethe xxxvijth
8 It is agreed upon and resolved that a vewe shalbe made [of] the debtts dewe to the saide Church and suche debtts wh[ich] adjudged separate presente order to be taken for the collection and recoverie of the same to be expended towardes the reparacon of the said Church by the Procurators [of] the same for the time being; and that a Procurator be appoynted by the parisshe and a procurator by the Bishop[s] corte at St Patricks[1] for the collecting of the same.

9 Item yt is agreed upon that Alson ffleminge late w[ife] to John Shereffe, deceased, beinge charged with rec[eiving] debtts due to the said Churche, shall without any [delay] Come before the said Proctors and parishioners on sondaie in the after noon to shewe and produce such disc[harges] <upon> as she hath touchinge the same debts Charge[d upon] her, and that in the meane time she shall have of the Charge imposed upon her late husband [MS torn]. Shee and Richard Duffe procurators of the said Church.

10 Item yt is agreed that the order concerning George [Ardglasse] his accompt dated 30 May 1595 shalbe confirmed.

11 It is agreed that Mr Walter Plunkett, Mr Bedlewe [and] Mr Longforde shalbe assistants to the proctors of the Church in the reparacons and surveying the repacons of the same.

It is agreed touching the petition of Xpofer Ussher [Ulster kin]ge at armes that he shall have a lease of a [house in Fi]shambles streete Confirmed unto him in h[MS damaged] ge th[e e]fecte of his [pe]ticion and that he [MS damaged] [tou]ching th[e] [MS damaged] before his [remainder of page damaged][2]

[f. 1v] Decimo Septium die May 1595
It is agreed by the proctors and petioners of St John the Evangeliste that everie petioner above the age of xvj years that shalbe buried in the saide Churche shall paie for the burial vj^{s} viij^{d} in the boddie of the same and x^{s} in the Chauncel and everie straunger double the valewe.

Vicesimo Quinto die May 1595. Annoque RR[eg]ine Elizabethe xxxvij^{mo}
It is agreed by the parishe meeting the daie above said to have continunce of the same untill thursdaie next being asscencon daie and then to give full answer unto Mr Jefferie ffenton his request and to admonishe allso the rest of the parishe to meete for the same and other Causes.

We have appointed for the next yere followeinge for our proctors Mr Richard Longford and Mr James Wickombe to beginne the firste of July next and to call ni for the arrearyes.

Item that theare shalbe three Lockes on the Comen Chest and the Revenues and Rents brought thereunto eache tearme and thereoute to be disbursed as neede requireth.

That the proctors for the time beinge shall af[ter the] ende of their yeeres make upp and deliver with[in a] moneth to the parish their accompts and deliver [su]ch goodes into the hands of the newe proctor [as] Inventorie.

[f. 2v] It is agreed by the assent of the wh[ole parish] the 22th day of August 1602 that Nych[olas] Lynham one of the said parishioners shall be a[ppointed to] assist the nowe proctors to levy and rec[eive] all such arerages as is due unto the church in assisting and directing them what spedy cou[rse] to hol[d] for the recovery thereof as in taking and trawell with them for getting in the same.

And farrther that the said proctors shall [bring] in to the sayd Church at the next metyng of all such matters as to the furtherance [of] the sayd church belongeth. The meting shall be on Sonday next.

Barnabee Bolger, Person of St Johns[3]

James Kellete
Wa Plunket
Edmund Nugent

Thomas Iolmay

It is agreed by the full consent of the parishioners that Mr Langford now proctor shall yeld up his accounts within xx dayes after this date unto Mr James Bedlow, Alderman Mr Blu[MS torn] & Mr bolger, person of the said parish, and that the foresaid Mr Langford shall com befor them within the forsaid 20 daies to pass his account to such audito[r] as by them shalbe appointed.

March 16 1602 Richard Langford

<it is agreed by the full consent>

The above named accompts is diferred to the first of August which day hee hath absolutlie promised to make his accomnptes.

[f. 2] the ixth of November 1606
It is agreed by the full consent of the parishioners that <hect> Richarde Proutfote & Thomas Osborne shalbe proctors & Church Wardens for one whole yeare beg[inn]ing at Easter 1606 & to contynue during pleasure for recevinge & disbursing of any rents or moneys due to the said Church that tyme and occasion shall serve.

As also the said proctors with Mr Bulger is appointed for taking the accompts of the late proctors John Bennes & Richard Browne notwithstanding a noat or Certificate given them by the parishioners (towching their accompt) to be shewed to the Counsell. And after the accompt taken which is to be done before Christmas next, the some to be mad knowen to the parishioners. Wittnes our hands

Barnabee Bolger, prebendary of St Johns
Richard brown
Nichas Lynhame
Richarde Golburne

[f. 3] The accounts of Dericke Hubbert and [Thomas] Evans late churchwardens according to an order made in July last & given in by us this xjth of [MS damaged]

A note of what rents & other monyes [we] have receyved in our time	
Imprimus Received of Mr Tho Conran[4] for a whole yeares {rent} of ij houses which he holdeth in ffishamble street due as Easter 1618	iij^{li} vij^{s}
Item Received of Doctor Usher for one whole yeares rent of a house in ffishamble street where in Mathew fford dwelleth due at Michaelmas 1617	xxxiij^{s}
Item Received of Mr Walter Usher for a whole yeares rent of a house in fish street due at Easter 1618	ij^{li} vj^{s}
Item Received of Mr Thos White for one whole yeares rent of the Priests Chamber due at Easter 1618	v^{s}
Item Received of John Good, Butcher, for a yeare & halfs rent of a house in St ffrancis street due at Easter 1618[5]	xxxvij^{s}
Item Received of John Anderson for a whole yeares rent of a house in Oxmanton due at Easter 1618[6]	ij^{li}
Item Received by the hand of John Bullock[7] from James White in Oxmanton in part of such rents & arrears as are behind to the church	xx^{s}
Item Received of the Master of ye taylors for ij yeares rent of St Johns parish ending at Midsomer 1618[8]	ij^{li}

Item Received of Amy Smooth for a half yeares rent ending at Michaelmas 1617[9]	vij^{s} vj^{d}
Item for ye buriall of Mr Backston	vj^{s}viij^{d}
Item for ye burial of Mr Eatens Child	iij^{s} iiij^{d}
For the dead tree sould out of ye Churchyard	x^{s}

[f. 3v] A note of the Moneys disbursed by the Churchwardens viz.

Imprimis paid unto Mr Hill[10] minister of ye said Church iiij^{li} str which he hath hitherto rec[eived] out of the rents of said Church	iiij^{li}
Item paid unto John Bullocke the clerk of the said parish for a year & a quarters stypend ending at Midsomer 1618	ij^{li} x^{s}
Item for making up the bible	x^{s}
Item to ye sexton for boughs & rushes for the whole summner	iiij^{s}
Item to the sherife for Langable[11]	iij^{s}
Item to the Masons that did the work of taking away the vestry & making the wall & whiting the Church	v^{li} v^{s}
Item for 32 sackes of Lyme & p[aid] p[er] sand	xxvj^{s} viij^{d}
Item for rotch lime	iij^{s}
Item for 5 barr[ells] hayr	viij^{s} viij^{d}
Item for timber bought of John Alfer to lay in the foundacion of the wall	v^{s}
Item for wood for pyles	ij^{s}
Item to a Carpenter to make them fitt	ix^{d}
Item for xij loads sand	iiij^{s}
Item to ye Sexton to buy boughs at Christmas	ij^{s}
Item to him for help to cleane the Church after the whiting	ij^{s}
Item for mending locks of ye Church dores	xij^{d}
Item for mending the service booke	xij^{d}
Item to ye sexton for ringing both ye kings dayes[12]	ij^{s}
Item for wine fetcht at Mr Bennises for the Communions	v^{s} vj^{d}
Item to the sexton for boughs & rushes & for some monyes paid to ye Smyth	v^{s}
Summ	xvj^{li}v^{d}

[f. 4][13] from tyme to tyme until his Majesty signify his pleas[ure] to the contrary may according to the same receave the fee [pa]id with all other lawful furtherance that is fytting to be deliv[er]ed so unto them in this p[ar]ticuler. Therefore upon deliberation and Mature consideracion had of the premysses forasmuch as his Ma[jes]tie hath not as yet revoked or recalled the said Concordatum of the nowe [Lord] Deputie and Counsell in accomplishm[en]t and fulfilling of the same and the true intent and meaning thereof. It is nowe ordered and determyned and decreed by the Barrons of this his Ma[jes]t[i]es Court of Exchequier; ffirst that the said proctors and parishioners of the said St Johns Church that nowe are or hereafter shall be shall only have, receave and enjoye to the use of said St Johns church all and singuler the arreradge of Rents due for the severall lands and p[ar]cells before specified and named. But also the growing rents thereof from tyme to tyme hereafter untill His Ma[jes]tie signyfie his pleasure to the Contrary yf so be his Ma[jes]tie and the late Quene have not made any graunt or grauntes to any p[er]son or p[er]sons to the Lawfull hinderance or ympedym[en]t of the same. Secondly that the proctors of the said Church of St Johns receaving the rents and the arrearadge of the said Lands and p[arcell]s at the hands of the ffermors and tenn[an]ts thereof and giving theire acquittances from tyme to tyme for the farm the said acquitt[ances] to be effectuall and of full power to Clere and discharge the said ffermors and tenn[an]ts and every of them the heyrs, execu[tors], admynystrators and assignes of them and every of them for the said Rentes and arreares thereof so paied and to be paied against his Ma[jes]tie his heires and successors proper. Thirdly, that the Audytor Clerk of the pype and other the officers of this Court to whom yt doth or shall app[er]tyne shall take notice of this order and of the said nowe Lo[rd] Deputy and Councells Corcordatum and forbeare from tyme to tyme to Levye any arreares or convey any Sup[er] ni the bookes of his Ma[jes]tes arre[ears] or in the Pype Rolles of this Court uppon any the tenn[an]ts or ffermors of the premysses p[ar]cells for such Rentes and arreradges they have paied or shall pay for the same unto the proctors of the said St Johns Church unto whome is [is] aforesaid the Rents and arreares now belong untill his highnes p[easure] be signyfyed for disannulling the said Concordatum. And [also] yt is ordered that yf any of the ffermors or tenn[an]ts of the said Landes and p[ar]cells before named out of which the forsaid Rentes [are payed] do or shall hereafter disregard the paym[en]t of their said [rents and] arreares thereof unto the said proctors of {the said} St Johns [church] [f. 4v] that nowe are or hereafter shalbe that by [MS damaged] the same known from tyme to tyme unto the [officers of] his Ma[jes]ties Court of Exchequer that now are [or shall] be pressed shall yssue against the severall p[ar]ties [MS damaged] and neglecting the paym[en]tes of there said rentes to come [and show] just cause why they or any of them so do which yf they can [they] shall not be able to alleadg and produce for themselves their ayde furtherance and assistance of this Court to be granted for the spedy levying and taking upp of the same to the use and behoof of the said St Johns Church whereby the benefites [and] good intended by the said Concordatum and this order by yt may be extended to the same.

William Meehweld[14]
John Blenerhassett[15]

[f. 5] xxvj^{to} February 1621

By full consent of the parishioners of St. Johns Parish. Wee have made choise of Mr Alderman B [MS damaged], Mr Richard Eustace, Mr Thomas Evans, Mr Christofer Graves, Mr Patrick English, Mr Hubb[ar]tes and Thady Duff {and Mr Matthew Sweetman} to Cesse the whole parish for the parsons dewties accordinge to the acte of State.[16]

Ma Forde	Wm Plunkett
Will Jewett	John Mornnig
John + Trues mark	James Bellew
Robert Clonie	Thos Ronsell
Thomas X Dongan mark	Connor ffarall
John Gilman	Richard R Tenbriges mark

[f. 5v blank]

[f. 6] xiiij^{to} die May, 1622

By the full consent of Edward Hill parson of St Johns Evangelist and the assemblie of the parishioners then p[rese]nt wee have made choise of Mr John Morrans & Edward Roodes gent to be Churchwardens of the said Church from the feast of Easter last for this whole year followinge.

Edward Hill, Prebendarye

Wm Plunkett	John Bennis
Ma Forde	Richard Eustace
Nich Carmick	Richard Golburne
William Bille	Tho Evans
Roger Smythe	Chr Grave
Will Jewett	Will hawley
Robart Usher	
Edward Edwards	

It is alsoe ordered that the late Churchwardens shall bringe in their accompts the twesday before Whitsen sonday next, and the parish hath made choise of Mr Richard Eustace, Mr Richard Goulburn, Mr Thomas Evans and Mr Christofer Graves or any two of them to give assistance to the newe Church wardens in the taking of their accompts.

Edward Hill
John Bennis

[f. 6v blank]

[f. 7] Anno Dom 1622.

Hereafter followeth the Cesse [of] the parishioners of St Johns Evang[elist], Dublin, due to the parson of the said parishe according to the act of state, cessed [and] taxed by us whose names are hereunder written, being auctho-rised by the whole Consent of the Parishe the xxvjth of Feb[ruary] 1621.

ffishamble street

Robt. Usher, merchant	x^{s}
Thady Dun, shoemaker	xiij^{s} iiij^{d}
Stephen Allen, vitler	xij^{s}
Richard Eustace, baker	x^{s}
John Gylsonans, plaiesterer	iiij^{s}
Robt Clawan, chanler	xij^{s}
Roger Smyth, vitler	x^{s}
Nichas Browne, baker	x^{s}
Sir Francis Annesley, kt	xx^{s}
John Trewe, vitler	vij^{s}
John Osmond	viij^{s}
John Hunter, baker	x^{s}
Nichs Carmick, gent	viij^{s}
Mathewe Forde, gent	xiij^{s} iiij^{d}
James Cade and his inmates	viij^{s}
Willm Jewett	vij^{s}
Widdowe Boxton	iij^{s}
John Morans, tailor	x^{s}
[idem] on his seller	ij^{s}
William Bylly, gent	xij^{s}
Sir Edward Fysher, kt	xx^{s}
John Carroll	viij^{s}
Stuly Haly, vitler	iiij^{s}
Raffe Grene, vitler	iiij^{s}
Willm Reynolds & Evans	xv^{s}
Richard Powell	viij^{s}
Widdowe Billett, Christofer Graves	xv^{s}
[f. 7v] Richard Browne	iiij^{s}
Mr Ledbetter	x^{s}
Nichas Maghery, baker, and the widdowe Whit	xij^{s}
Mr Alderman Wiggens	xx^{s}
Richard Williams	x^{s}
Thomas Sampson	viij^{s}
John Stafford, tailor	viij^{s}
Richard Cowgan, baker	vij^{s}
Richard Morgan	vj^{s}
The Currier	iiij^{s}

Thomas Osburne	x^{s}
John Gilman, vitler	v^{s}
James Bedlowe, vitler	vij^{s}
John Edgerton, girdler	viij^{s}
William Plunket, gent	xiij^{s} iiij^{d}
Peirs Roe, chandler with his inmates	viij^{s}
St Johns Lane	
John Warren, tailor	iiij^{s}
Mr Malone	x^{s}
Mr Flemyng for his seller	x^{s}
Mr Colman for the Read stagg	x^{s}
Patrick Mapas for his seller	x^{s}
Robt Fyan, chanler	vj^{s}
Thomas Jacobb, baker	viij^{s}
Thomas Keahan, tailor	iiij^{s}
Wyne Tavern street	
Alderman Plunket for his seller, Reyly the Cook	xiij^{s} iiij^{d}
Alderman Duffe for his seller	x^{s}
Widdowe Browne	xiij^{s} iiij^{d}
Mr Pennell, tailor	x^{s}
Patrick Rownsell	viij^{s}
Mr Weston for his sellar	x^{s}
Mr Sedgrave for his sellar	x^{s}
Thoms Cruse nowe Dowde	xv^{s}
[f. 8] *Cooke Street*	
Mr Allen for his seller	x^{s}
Myles Bennet	iiij^{s}
Richard Blake, cooke	iiij^{s}
John Lawles	vj^{s}
Richard Englishe	v^{s}
Patrick Savadg	v^{s}
Thomas Doyle, baker	x^{s}
Thomas Burne, tailor	iiij^{s}
Widow Vialls	vj^{s}
Patrick English, baker	xij^{s}
widdowe Browne	viij^{s}
The Merchaunt Keye	
William Worrall	viij^{s}
Walter Conran, shomaker	x^{s}
Matthew Sweetman, merchant	iiij^{s}
Thomas Flemyng, merchant	xv^{s}
Mr Leavered, gent	x^{s}
Thomas Whit, gent	xx^{s}

[blank] Gegin, merchant	x^{s}
Widdowe Russell	x^{s}
Mr Alexander	iiij^{s}
Widdowe Thomson al[ia]s Long	viij^{s}
John Blunt, vitler	x^{s}
Thomas Dongan, vitler	xij^{s}
John Brooke, esq	x^{s}
The Craner for the Crane	x^{s}
Mr Ragg	vj^{s}
Thomas Cave, gent	x^{s}
William Rawley, vitler	vj^{s}
John Bowcher, vitler	x^{s}
Mr Chambers	x^{s}
Richard Proutford, <merchant> marshall	x^{s}
Widdowe Furlong	vj^{s}
Sir William Ryves, kt	xx^{s}
[f. 8v] *The Wood Key*	
Jacobb Newman, gent	xx^{s}
[blank]Wollason for his howse and stable	xiij^{s} iiij^{d}
Mr Billett	xv^{s}
Richard Huetson, vitler	ij^{s}
Widdowe Hanmer	xv^{s}
Anthony Stoughton, gent	xx^{s}
Mr Tonbridge	x^{s}
Mr Heathe	x^{s}
Nichas Gennet, Mother Christian, William Hally	xij^{s}
Richard Ewstace, baker	ij^{s}
Richard Mathewes	iiij^{s}
George Burrowes	x^{s}
John Barry, glazier	iiij^{s}
Clerk the cobler	ij^{s}
Thomas Nevell, vitler	viij^{s}
Thomas Neyle, vitler	iiij^{s}
Thomas Woltherig, vitler	vj^{s}
Elizabeth Woods	vj^{s}
Christofer Harrison, vitler	vj^{s}
Thomas Evans, gent	xij^{s}
Mr [blank] Pecfeild	iij^{s}
Gavan, the shoemaker	vj^{s}
Phillipp Philpott	x^{s}
The Chanler or Cheesmonger	iiij^{s}
William Doyle	viij^{s}
Mr Danyell for his mill and brewhouse	<xj^{s}>xx^{s}

John Mathershewe, gent	x^{s}
Nichas Dillon, merchant	viij^{s}
Richard Golborne, merchant	x^{s}
Edward Roods, gent	x^{s}
Mr Neyle, late Clements	xiij^{s} iiij^{d}
James Kervan, baker	iiij^{s}
[f. 9] *Wyne Taverne Streete*	
John Hubb[er]ts, gent	x^{s}
Cornelyous Farroll, gent	x^{s}
Edward Edwards, vitler	v^{s}
John Anderson, gent	x^{s}
Anthony Enos, gent	viij^{s}
Mr ffloyde	x^{s}
John Turvin, vitler	x^{s}
Frauncis Dowde, merchaunt	xv^{s}
John Weston, merchaunt	xv^{s}
Nichas Keapock	vj^{s}
Widdowe Foster, [blank] Winckly	iij^{s}
John Rathborne	iiij^{s}
Judye Horne	iij^{s}
Leaven de Rosse	x^{s}
Zachary Roxbye, vitler	iiij^{s}
Sweetman for the Blackboy	x^{s}
Walter Browne, shomaker and twoe tenants	xv^{s}
John Bowthe, sargiant	vj^{s}
Thomas Corbally	iiij^{s}
Widdowe Lynneger	viij^{s}
Thomas Cruse	ij^{s}
Edward Dowdall	x^{s}
Alderman Dowde for his sellar	x^{s}
Hughe Dowde	viij^{s}
Widdowe Newgent	x^{s}
Christofer Colman, merchaunt	xv^{s}
Thomas Colman	v^{s}
Mr Geste	ij^{s}
Alderman Bennes	xv^{s}
Thomas Churchyard	x^{s}
[f. 9v] Hugh Lynnerame, cooke	iiij^{s}
Thomas Jacobb for Colmans towe howses holden by him	vj^{s}
Jaques for part of Mr Alderman Bennes howse	vj^{s}
Rose Mary Lane	
The Golden Lyon	x^{s}

Anstace Lyname ij^{s}
her neighbore ij^{s}
Sum total iij ^{xx}xj^{li} <x^{s} x^{d} ster>

Copp[*er*] *Alley*

John Dennis
Rich Eustace
Mathew Sweetman
John Hobarte
Thos Evans
Chr Graves

It was agreed amongst us (Mr Eustace excepted) that the Cook of the Colledge should pay v^{s} per annum.

Chr Graves
John Hobarte
Tho Evans

[f. 10] *The Sexton allowed 20*^{s} *per annum* <*for keeping*>
By consent of Edward Hill, parson, and the Churchwardens with the parishoners it is agreed that the Sexton for the tyme being shall have an allowance of twentie shillings str p[er] ann[um] for the keeping of gutters of the church cleane and the Church decent and clean with the church yarde and for the performing of his dutie in that behalfe

Wm Plunkett
Ma Forde
Tho Evans
Nich Carmick
Richard Golburn
Edward Hill
John Moring
Edward Rads
Chr Graves

[f. 10v] The accompte of William Plunkett and Matthewe fforde, gent., for the Rents, burialls and other reciepts receaved by them as proctors of St Johns Evangelist Dublin for one whole yeare, frome the feast of Easter in ye year of our Lord 1621 unto the feast of Easter 1622.

Imprimus Receaved of Mr Richard Eustace and Mrs Neale, late wiff of Christopher Clements,[17] Churchwardens of the said Church in p[ar]te of an arreare dewe on their accompts the some of viij^{li} ster
Receaved of Mr John Anderson for his howse in Oxmonton for one year and a half endinge Mich[ael]mas 1621 iij^{li} ster
Receaved of Mr Thomas Conran for his house in Fishamble street for one whole year endinge Mich[ael]mas 1621 iij^{li} vj^{s} viij^{d} ster
Receaved of the Masters of Taylors for one yeares Rente dewe for St Johns Chapple xx^{s} ster

Receaved of Katherine Taylor widowe for hir howse in
Oxmonton for one yeare & a half endinge Mich[ael]mas 1621 xxij^{s} vj^{d} ster
Receaved of Mr Alderman Duff for his house on the
woodkey for one whole yeare endinge M[ichaelmas] 1621 xx^{s} ster
Receaved of Amye Smoth for hir howse in Oxmonton
for one yeare endinge Mich[ael]mas 1621 xv^{s} ster
Receaved of Mr Walter Usher for his howse in ffishamble
street for one yeare ending M[ichaelmas] 1621 xlvj^{s} viij^{d} ster
Receaved of John Hunter for Mr Dongans howse in
ffishstreet for one yeare & a half ending M[ichaelmas] 1621. xj^{s} iij^{d} ster
Receaved of Mr Quyne, merchant, for his howse in
Oxmonton for one yeare & a half ending Mich[ael]mas 1621 xj^{s} iij^{d} ster
Receaved of John Baeth, Esq., for fowere years Rente endinge
Mich[ael]mas 1621 for land in Oxmonton at iij^{s} p[er] ann[um] xij^{s} ster
Receaved of Mr Thomas White for the Pristes chamber in
the Churchyard for one whole yeare endine Mich[aelm]as 1621 v^{s} ster.
[f. 11] Receaved of Mr Christopher Graves for three yeares
Rent endinge Mich[ael]mas 1621 for the priests chamber
in St Tullocks at ix^{s} x^{d} p[er] ann[um] xxix^{s} vj^{d} [ster]
Receaved of John Woode for his howse in St ffrancis Street
for one yeare ending Mich[ael]mas 1621 xxv^{s} ster
Receaved for the buriall of Mr Viance vj^{s} viij^{d} ster
Receaved for the buriall of Mr Nugent in Wynetavern street vj^{s} viij^{d} ster
Receaved for the buriall of Mr Colmans wiff vj^{s} viij^{d} ster
Receaved for the buriall of Mr Doyle on the Woodkey vj^{s} viij^{d} ster
Receaved for the buriall of Mr Osbornes wiff vj^{s} viij^{d} ster
Receaved for Mr Bettriches chyld iij^{s} iiij^{d} ster
Receaved for Mr Mattershewes chyld iij^{s} iiij^{d} ster
Sum total of the Rentes and Casualties amounteth to xxvij^{li} iiij^{s} x^{d} ster

An accompte of such monnys as the said Churchwardens have disbursed and layd out in and about the said church for necesarie used viz.

Imprimis payed for one hundred foote of hewn stone for
pavinge the Church porch, for lyme, sand & masons work
from the otter doores to the bell free, and to the carpender
for the footepace there, which amounteth in all to iij^{li} viij^{s} iij^{d} ster
Item payed for the cover of the ffonte to Eustace the joiner
the some of xx^{s} ster
Item payed for making upp and fynishinge the vestry viz
planckes, spares, nayles and joyners worke ammounteth to ij^{li} vj^{s} iiij^{d} ster
Item payed for three keyes for the Chest in the vestry
where the evidence of the Church doth remayn xviij^{d} ster

Item payed for two joine stolles and settinge upp of the shelffe in the Vestry v^{s} ster

Item payed for a carpett on the table in ye Vestry vj^{s} ster

[f. 11v] Item payed for fortie eight pound and a half of Iron for barres in the vestrie windowe at iij^{d} le pound, xv^{s} st and for fifty seaven foote of glasse for glasinge the same at eight pence the foote xxxvij^{s} st amountinge to ij^{li} xj^{s} ster

Item payed for carringe awaye a greate heape of rubbis that laye against church doore to John the Sexton v^{s} ster

Item payed to Mr Richard Gooborne for wyne at sev[er]all Communions since death of Mr Clements and charged in the accompte of Mr Eustace, the late church warden the some of x^{s} ster

Item payed for three newe Ropes for bells iiij^{s} vj^{d} for mending the clappp[er] of one of the bells j^{s} and for a new whyle for one of the bells vj^{s} amountinge in all to xj^{s} vj^{d} ster

Item payed to the Sheriffe of City of Dublin for Langable dewe on the church land iij^{s} ster

Item payed to Barthelomewe Jordan,[18] the Clearke of the parish, for his whole years wages the some of xl^{s} ster

Item payed to Quyne the Joyner for setting up the Kings Armes in the Chauncell xx^{s} ster

Item payed for three yeardes of greene brodcloth for a carpett for the Communion table besides xvij^{s} John the Sexton collected of the parishioners the some of xx^{s} ster

Item payed for a pulpett cloth of brouch vellet tawny with a silke ffrenge L^{s} ster

Item payed to the plasterer for whittinge the Arches and collornige the same x^{s} ster

Item payed for Mr Eustace to Mr P[ar]son for some moneys disbursed by him to the use of the church since the death of Mr Clement the p[ar]ticulars appeareth in a note deliv[er]ed by him x^{s} ster

[f. 12] xv^{to} Aprilis 1623

By the full consent of Edward Hill, parson of St John the Evangelist and the Assembly of sev[er]all of the Parishioners whose names are underwritten there is choyce made of John Hobarte and Albion Leverett gent to be Churchwardens of the sayd Church from the feast of Easter last for this whole yeare followinge

	Edward Hill, prebendary
T Osburne	John Morrin
Richard Golburne	Edward Reade
Roger Smythe	Tho Evans
Richard Proudfoot	Chr Grave
	William Bille
John Butcher	James Bellew

It is alsoe ordered that the late Churchwardens shall bringe in their Accompts on Thursday the xxiiijth of this present monethe of Aprill and the Parson and the Parishioners abovenamed have made choyce of Mr Thomas Evans now shirriffe of the Cittie of Dublin, Mr Richard Eustace, Mr Richard Goulburne and Christopher Grave gent or to any two of them to be assistaunts to the new Churchwardens in taking their Accompts.

Edward Hill, parson

William bille
T Osburne
Richard Proudfoot

[f. 12v blank]

[f. 13]The accompte of John Morrine and Edward Roads for the Rents, Buryalls and other receipts received by them as proctors of St Johns Evangelist Dublin for the whole year from the feast of Easter for year in the year of our Lord 1622 unto the feast of Easter 1623.

Rents

Imprimis Receaved of the last proctors in reddy money. iij^{li} iiij^{s} vj^{d}

Receaved at hands of Amis Somuth for one whole yeeres rent due unto St Johns and ending and due at Mich[aelm]as last past 1622 xv^{s}

Receaved at hands of Catterine Taylor for one yeeres rent ending and due at Mich[ael]mas last past 1622 for one house she holdeth in St Johns xv^{s}

Receaved at hands of Thomas Conran, gent, for one whole yeeres rent ending and due at Mich[ael]mas last and belonging to St Johns iij^{li} vj^{s} viij^{d}

Receaved at hands of Mr John Stafford, M[aste]r of the Taylors for that tyme, for one yeere due and ending at Mich[aelm]as last 1622 and belonging to St Johns xx^{s}

Receaved at hands of John Hunter, Baker, for one whole yeere ending and due at Mich[aelm]as last past 1622 unto St Johns vij^{s} vij^{d}

Receaved at hands of Alderman Duff for one whole yeeres rent ending and due at Mich[aelm]as last 1622 unto St Johns xx^{s}

Receaved at hands of Mr Maurice Smith, gent, for Arreares of Rent belonging to St Johns vitz. for three yeeres ending at Easter 1621 xl^{s}

Receaved at hands of Walter fflood, merchant, for three yeeres Rent ending and due at Mich[aelma]s 1622 and due unto St Johns xlv^{s}

Receaved at hands of John Good, Boutcher, for one whole yeeres rent ending and due at Mich[ael]mas last 1622 and due to St Johns xxv^{s}

Receaved at hands of John Anderson, gent, for one whole yeeres rent ending and due at Mich[ael]mas last 1622 due to St Johns xl^{s}

[f. 13v] Receaved at the handes of Walter Ussher, merchant, for one whole yeers rent ending and due at Mich[aelm]as last 1622 and belonging to St Johns xlvj^{s} viij^{d}

Receaved of Matthew fford, gent., for half a yeers rent ending and due at Mich[eal]mas last 1622 and belonging to St Johns	xvj^{s} viij^{d}
Receaved at the hands of Richard Quine, merchant, for one whole yeers rent ending and due at Mich[ael]mas last 1622 belonging to St Johns	vij^{s} vj^{d}

Burials

Receaved for the Buriall of Anne Osmond the 27th of May 1622	vj^{s} viij^{d}
Receaved for the Buriall of Mr Richard Williams Child the 30th of May 1622	iij^{s} iiij^{d}
Receaved for the Buriall of Sr Willm Ryves child	iij^{s} iiij^{d}
Receaved for the Buriall of a Stranger who died at Mr Williams house	x^{s}
Receaved for the Buriall of a man who died in George Burrowes his house the 28th of August 1622	vj^{s} viij^{d}
Suma total of the rents and casualties receaved amounted to	xxij^{li} xix^{s} xj^{d} ster

An accompt of such monies as the said Church wardens have disbursed and Layd out in and about the said Church for necessarye uses.

Imprimis disbursed to Mr Hill for his Stipent for one yeare ending and due at Christmas last past 1622	Lx^{li}
Disbursed unto Bartholmew Jordan, Clark of the said Church, for his stipent for one yeere ending at Christmas last 1622	xl^{s}
[f. 14] Paied to the Sexten for his wages for the same tyme	xx^{s}
Paied for mending of the rooffe to the Carpent[er] & masons and smithes and for other workes done about the said Church	iij^{li} vj^{s} vj^{d}
Paied to the plumber for raising the leads and mending the same and for lead and sawder	xj^{li} j^{s} vj^{d}
Paied to the hellyer for tiling and pointing the North side of the said Church and other defects aboute the rooffe	xxxv^{s}
Paied to the Glasier for mending the windowes about the said Church	xxvj^{s} viij^{d}
Paied to the Plasterer for whiting and mending decayed places of the said Church	xxx^{s}
Paied to the Sexton for rushes, cleaning of the said Church after the workmen amending the paves paving the stones and busshes, flowers and other necessaries.	xv^{s}
Paied for a Surplus for Mr Hill	x^{s} vj^{d}
Paied for the Communons untill this 23 of Aprill 1623	xxij^{s} vj^{d}
Paied for mending the Commmunon Cupp	xviij^{d}
Paied for mending the Booke of Comon prayer unto the bookebynder	iiij^{s}
Paied for Langable for all the Church land	iij^{s}

Paied for two hearses for the Beares vij^{s}
Disbursed for divers extraordinary expences and chardges in following the other affairs of the said Church. xx^{s} ster
Sum total xxj^{li} xiij^{s} viij^{d}
[f. 14v] So there Remayneth dew which the accompants have now paied over to the hands of the new Churchwardens the some of xxvj^{s} iij^{d} ster
Sum total of the whole disbursem[en]ts amounteth to xxij^{li} xix^{s} xj^{d} ster

24to Aprilis 1623

Wee have p[er]used the Accompts of John Moring and Edward Rhodes, gent, Proctors of St John Evangelists Dublin for one whole yeere which ended at Easter last past and doe allow all theire severall disbursements aforemencoed whereof wee allowe being Auditors appointed to past theire Accomptes.

Edward Hill, Prebendary St Johns
Richard Golburne

[f. 15] Quarto die Maij 1624
By the full consent of Edward Hill, Prebend of St John the Evangelist and the Assemblie of severall of the Parishioners whose names are hereunder written, is choice made of William Billey and John Anderson gent to be Churchwardens of the said Church from the feast of Easter last for this whole yeare followeing.

Edward Hill, prebendary St Johns
Wm Plunkett John Hobarte
Tho Evans Albon Leveret, Athlone[19]
John Morring
Edward Rhodes

It is also ordered that the late Churchwardens shall bring in their accomptes on Thursdaie in Whitson weeke next. And that the Parson and Parishioners of the same Parish have made choice of Mr Thomas Evans, Mr Richard Eustace, Mr Richard Golbourne and Mr Christofer Grave or anie two of them to be assistants to the new Churchwardens in takeing their accompts.

Edward Hill, Prebendary St Johns
Wm Plunkett John Hobarte
Tho Evans Albon Leveret, Athlone

[f. 15v blank]

[f. 16] The accompte of Albon Leveret, Athlone, and John Hobarte, gent, for the rents, burialls and other receipts received by them as proctors of St Johns Evangelist Dublin for the whole yeare from the feast of Easter in the yeare of our Lord 1623 unto the feast of Easter 1624.

Imprimis Received of the last Churchwardens in redy money	1. 6. 3.
Received of Mr Quyn for his Easters rente 1623	3. 9.
Received of Mr Anderson for one whole yeares rente ending at Mich[ael]mas 1623	2. 0. 0.
Received of Walter Usher for a whole yeares rente	2.6.8.
Received of Sir Thadie Duffe, Kt, a whole yeares rente	1.0.0.
Received of Amy Smoth a yeares rente	15.0.
Received of John Hunter, Baker, a yeares rente	7.6.
Received of Mr Chatham for Catherine Taylers howse for a whole yeare	15.0.
Received of Thomas Conran a years rent	3.6.8.
Received of [blank] Lyons M[ast]er of Taylers	1.0.0.
Received of [blank] Good Butcher for a yeares rente	1.5.0.
Received of Mathew fforde for his rent	1.5.4.
Item Received for Burialls vizt of Mrs Haley for husbands buriall	6. 8.
Received for the buriall of Robert Ditch	3. 4.
Received for Mr Sweetmans burial quia pauper	5. 0.
Received for the buriall of Sr William Reeves his child	3. 0.
Received for the buriall of Mrs Heathe	6. 8.
Received for the buriall of Mr Thimelbys cheild	3. 4.
Received for the buriall of Walter Dermod his wyfe	5. 0.
[f. 16v] Received for the buriall of Mr Plunkett his childe	3. 4.
Received for the buriall of [blank] Cheevers Child	3. 0.
Received for the buriall of Alderman Bennis	6. 8.
Received for the buriall of Englishe the Baker	6. 8.
Received for the buriall of Mr Morans daughter	6. 8.
Received for the buriall of Mr Peerse his wyffe	6. 8.
Sum totall of the rentes and casualtyes received amounteth to	18^{li} 17^{s} 2^{d}

An accompt of such moneys as the said Church Wardens have disbursed and layed out in and about the sayd Church for necessarye uses, vizt.

Imprimis payed the Sexton wages	1.0.0.
Payd to Mr Evans for landgable	3.0.
payed for mending the common prayer Book	5.0.
payed for tyles	1.0.0.
payed to Bartholomew Jurden	2.0.0.
payed to the Sexton for hinges for Pue dores	2.3.
payed to Bartholomewe for washing the Surplus	1.6.
payed for washing of the Communyon cloth	1.0.
payed to a Slater for pointing	8.
payed to Allen and his partner for three dayes and halfe after xx^{d} the day	11.8.

[f. 17] Itim paid to his man for a day and a half	2. 3.
paid to a laborer for thre dayes and halfe after iv^{d} the daye	1.3.
paid to another labourer the same tyme for fower days	3.0.
paid to the Lyme man for six sacks of lyme	4.6.
paid for xviij^{teene} loade of sande	4.4.
Itim to the Sexton for Rushes att Easter	3.0.
Itim to the Sexton for bowes and rushes the first of June	2.0.
Itim the Sexton received att that tyme for the Communion	1.1.
Itim the Sexton received the fifte of August for Ringing[20]	2.6.
Itim the Sexton received for setting up the timber against Mr Bennis his garden	1.6.
Itim the Sexton had for ringing the fifte of November[21]	2.0.
Itim the Sexton had for ringing the 24th of March[22]	2.6.
Itim the Sexton had for a workman that did laye the tyles in the Church that weare broken	1.6.
Itim the Clarke and the Sexton had for ringing when the Prince came out of Spaine[23]	4.0.
Itim to the Potter for the first tyles that were layed being 5 score dossen and for the carriage of them	3.15.0.
Itim for rushes and hearbs when the Lo[rd] Deputy[24] came first to the Church	2.4.
Itim payed to the Carpenter for mending the pues	1.9.
Itim layed out for lyme for mending and laying of the tyles	9.
Itim layed out for hollies for the Church att Christmas	2.6.
[f. 17v] Itim layd out for mending the lock of the Church dore and for a new key	2. 6.
Itim layd out and given to John the Sexton for tending workmen when they layed the tyles in the Church	2.6.
Itim for Candles the same tyme	4.
Itim for setting up the Lo[rd] Deputyes rails for the cloth and mending of ye pues	4.6.
Itim layd out for tyles	7.16.9.
Itim layd out for bread and wyne at Easter	14.0.
Itim more for bread	6.
Itim for necessarie expences in and about the Church and its affaires	1.0.0.
	Total 21^{li} 14^{s} 11^{d}

We have perused this Accompt and do allowe the churchwardens accordingly the sume of forte seve[n] shillings nyne pence ster. Dat[ed] the 24 of May 1624.

Tho Evans
Richard Golburn

[ff 18–19v blank]

[f. 20] the 25th day of Aprill 1625
By the full consent of Edward Hill, Prebend of St John the Evangelist and the assemblie of severall of the Parishioners whose names are underwritten is theire made of {Mr} John Anderson and Mr Thomas Cave, gent, to be Churchwardens of the said Church from the feast of Easter last for this whole yeere followinge.

	Edward Hill, Parson.
Wm Plunkett	Ma Forde
Domyngens Perseval	William Bill
John Warren	John Morring
	John Hobarte
	Will Jewett
	Roger Smyth
	John Egerton

It is alsoe agreed that the late Churchwardens shall bringe in theire accompts on the xxth day of May next. And the parson and parishioners of the same parrishe have made choyse of Mr Alderman Evans, Mr Willm Plunkett, Mr Mathewe fford, Mr John Morringe & Mr Smyth or any three of them to be assistants to the parson & newe Churchwardens for takinge theire accompts.

	Edward Hill, parson
Domynigens Perseval	Willam Bille
John Egerton	

[f. 20v blank]

[f. 21] The accompt of William Billey and John Anderson for the rentes, burialls and other receipts received by them as Proctors of Saint John the Evangelist Dublin for one whole yeare from the feast of Easter in the year of our Lord 1624 unto the feast of Easter 1625.

	li. s.d.
Imprimis received of the Earle of Cork for arrerages due to the sayd Church ended att Easter 1624	6.0.0.
Received of Mr Thomas Conran for one whole yeares rente ended the same tyme	3.6.8.
Received of Walter Usher for one whole yeares rente ended the same tyme	2.6.8.
Received of Mathew fforde for one yeares rente ended the same tyme	1.13.4.
Received of the M[aster]r of the Taylers for one yeares rente ended the same tyme	1.0.0.

Fo 21

The acompt William Dilley and John Anderson for the rentes burialls and other receipts receaved by them as Proctors of Saint John the Evangelist Dublin for one whole yeare from the feast of Easter in the yeare of our Lord 1624 unto the feast of Easter 1625

	li	s	d
Imprimis receaved of the Earle of Corke for arrerages due to the sayd Church ended at Easter 1624	06	00	00
Receaved of Mr Thomas Conran for one whole yeares rente ended the same tyme	03	06	08
Receaved of Mr Walter White for one whole yeares rente ended the same tyme	02	06	08
Receaved of Mrs Mathew Forde for one yeares rente ended the same tyme	01	13	04
Receaved of the Mr of the Taylers for one yeares rente ended the same tyme	01	00	00
Receaved of John Good Butcher for one yeares rente ended the same tyme	01	05	00
Receaved of Annis Swinge for one yeares rente ended the same tyme	00	15	00
Receaved of Sr [illegible] Lady Duffe for one yeares rente ended the same tyme	01	00	00
Receaved of John Hunter the Baker for one whole yeares rente ended the same tyme	00	07	06
Receaved of Mr Bates for three quarters rente ended the same tyme	00	09	00
Receaved of Mr Quin for one yeare and a halfe Easters rente ended as before	00	11	03
Receaved of Sr William Ryves for his La: buriall	00	06	08
Receaved of Mr Carie for the buriall of his man	00	05	00

1. The churchwardens' account for 1624–5 (f. 21)

Received of John Good, butcher, for one yeares rente ended the same tyme	1.5.0.
Received of Amis Smugge for one yeares rente ended the same tyme	15.0.
Received of Sir Tady Duff, Kt., for one yeares rente ended the same tyme	1.0.0.
Received of John Hunter, the Baker, for one whole yeares rente ended the same tyme	7.6.
Received of Mr Bathe for thre yeares rente ended the same tyme	9.0.
Received of Mr Quin for one yeare and a halfes rente ended as before	11.3.
Received of Sr William Reves for his La[dy's] burial	6.8.
Received of Mr Carie for the buriall of his man	5.0.
[f. 21v] Received for the buriall of Mr Tunbridge	6.0.
Received for the buriall of Bes woods daughters Childe	3.0.
Received for the buriall William Juettes Childe	3.4.
Received for the buriall of Bess woods son	6.0.
Received for the buriall of the Clarke of the Lord Deputyes kitchins wyffe	6.8.
Received for the buriall of Mrs Doyles Childe	3.4.
More received for the buriall of Stephen Allen his wyfe	6.0.
	Summa totall $21^{li}\ 0^{s}\ 5^{d}$

An accompt of such moneys as the said Churchwardens have disbursed and layed out in and about the sayd Church for necessarie uses, vizt

Imprimis payed to the Clarke for his years wages	2.0.0.
More payed the Sexton for his years wages	1.0.0.
More payed for wine for those weare together with the Church wardens	13.0.
More payed for ringing the bells on the Kings daye	2.0.
More payed to the glasier for mending the Church windowe	2.6.
[f. 22] More payed for 15 dossen of boardes for the house in the Churchyard	15.0.
More payed for 13 double sparrs	4.6.
More payed for 3 dozen of single sparrs	5.0.
More payed for 3 half deales	2.0.
More payed for spikes and nails	7.0.
More payed for pair of hinges for door of Ho[use] in church yard	1.4.
More payed for a locke and keye for the dore	1.6.
More payed the Carpenter for 6 dayes workė	9.0.
More payed a Laborer for 2 days worke	1.6.
More payed for 4 bags lime for pavement of the Church	3.0.

More payed for 4 loads sande	1.0.
More payed the Masons and a laborer for laying the tiles	7.0.
More payed for a lock and plate for Church dore	2.0.
More payed for a hinge and staple for the gate of the Churchyard	1.0.
More payed for a new stock locke for a pewe dore	1.6.
More payed for a brass key for the Parsons boxe	8.
More payed for another keye for the pewe next the Church dore and for nayles to sett on the plate and hinge	8.
[f. 22v] More payed for 9 baggs of lime for the for Church wall	6.9.
More payed for six loads of sand	1.6.
More payed 2 Masons for 2 dayes worcke	6.0.
More payed a Laborer for 2 dayes worcke	1.6.
More payed for Holly, Ivye and Rushes for the Church against Christmas	2.6.
More payed for slates, lyme and sand for the Church and labor for the roofe & porch	10.0.
More payed for the removing the tiles	1.0.
More payed for the ladder for St Johns Church[25]	8.0.
More payed for Ringing the bells on the kings daye	2.6.
More payed for washing the Communion clothe	1.0.
More payed for ringing the bells the daye of proclayming King Charles[26]	2.0.
More payed for 48 quarries of glass to mende the windowes in the body of the Church	4.0.
More payed for the long Caple	3.3.
More payed for wyne for the Communion	13.0.
More payed for following the Lo[rd] of Corke his busines and other necessaries belonging to the Church[27]	1.0.0.
More payed for two formes that are in the Church	6.0.
Sume totall disbursed	11.10.2.

M[emoran]d[um]wee have p[er]used this accompt. And we find that there is remayning in arreare in the last Churchwardens hands the some of nyne pounds ten shillings thre pence ster.

Edward Hill, Prebendary of St Johns Dublin
Wm Plunkett
Ma Forde
John Morring

[f. 23] The aforesayd of arrears of nyne pounds tenn shillinges was delyered unto the hands then {of them now Church wardens}beinge in the p[re]sence of Edward Hill parson of St John the Evangelist wetnes owr handes this Last of May 1625.

Edward Hill, Prebendary of St Johns Dublin

The said nyne pounds ten shillings engl. hath ben delivered to the nowe Churchwardens Mr Xpofer Graves & Robt Usher by the hand of Mr John Anderson one of the late Churchwardens for the use of the Church this first of June 1626.

Edward Hill, Parson
Thos Evans

[f. 23v blank]

[f. 24] xxv^{to} Aprilis 1626.
The parson and divers of the parishioners of St John the Evangelist Dublin have chosen Christopher Grave, gent, and Robert Ussher, merchaunt, Churchwardens from the feast of Easter last for one whole yeare ensuinge.

Edward Hill, parson of St Johns Dublin.
William Bille
John Morring

It is also ordered by the parson and the parishioners that the late Churchwardens shall bringe in their Accompts uppon the xvjth day of May next. And that Alderman Evans, Mr William Plunkett & Mr Mathew Ford or any twoe of them to be Assistaunts to the new Churchwardens in takinge their sayd Accompts.

Edward Hill, prebendary of St Johns Dublin
William Bille
John Morring

[f. 24v blank]

[f. 25] primo Septemb[er] 1626
The accompt of Mr John Anderson and Mr Thomas Cave for the rents, burialls and other receipts received by them as Proctors of Saint John Thevangelist Dublin for one whole yeare from the ffeast of Easter for year 1625 unto the ffeast of Easter 1626.

Imprimis received of the last Churchwardens in readie money	9.10.0.
Received of Mr Thomas Conran for one whole years rent end at Mych[aelm]as 1625	3.6.8.
Received of Amy Smooth for one yeares rent end ut supra	0.15.0.
Received of Mr Walter Ussher for one yeares rent end ut supra	2.6.8.
Received of the M[aste]r of theTaylors for that yeare	1.0.0.
Received of John Good, Butcher	1.5.0.
Received of Sr Thadie Duffe, knight, for one yeares rent end at Mych[aelm]as 1625	1.0.0.
Received of Mathew fford for one yeares rent end at Mych[aelm]as 1625	1.13.4.

Received of John Hunter, Baker, for one yeare end ut supra	7.6.
Received of Mr John Anderson for twoe yeares Arrear end ut supra	4.0.0.
Received for the buriall of Mr Rich Williams	6.8.
Received for the buriall of Mr Carmicks Child	3.4.
Received for the buriall of Mr Roades	6.8.
Received for the buriall of Mrs Wiggins	5.0.
Received for the buriall of Thomas Langford	6.8.
Received for James Quaytrods child	3.4.
	26.15.0.

[f. 25v] An accompte of such monies as the sayd Churchwardens have disboursed and layed out in and about the sayd Church for necessary uses, viz.

Imprimis payd to the Clearke for his yeares wages the some of	2.0.0.
Item payd the Sexton for his yeares wages	1.0.0.
Item for wyne etc at the chusinge of the new Churchwardens and in taking the ould Churchwardens Accompts	19.6.
Item for the burial of John the Sexton	12.0.
Item for 500th of slates	5.0.
Item for iiijor sacks of Lyme	2.8.
Item for iiijor load of sand	1.0.
Item for three dayes work for 2 slatters	9.0.
Item for laborers for three days	3.0.
Item for pynnes for the slates	3.
Item to the Shiriff for Langable	3.0.
Item for wyne and bread at the Comunion in Somer	2.6.
Item for ringing the bells on the kings day	2.0.
Item for holly & rushes at Christmas	2.6.
Item to the Glasier	5.0.
Item for bread and wyne at Easter	15.0.
Item for washing of ye Communion cloth	1.0.
Item for 2 Joyners for one day	2.6.
Item for one firr planke to mend the seates	1.4.
Item for a lock, hinges and nayles for the box in the Vestry	2.3.
Item for a brase & bolt to the bells	1.0.
Item for mendinge broken seates	1.6.
Item for mendinge the Clapper of ye great bell	1.6.
[f. 26] Item for for a Roape to the myddle bell	1.0.
Item for mendinge the great hearse	1.0.
Item for a new hearse to the little beare	3.0.
Item for Ringinge on the kings day	2.6.

Item for a new roape for the little bell	1.0.
Item for Rushes, etc. on Palme Sonday	2.0.
Item for mendinge the fflagon pott	3.
Item for 2 sacks of Lyme	1.4.
Item for heyliares on Easter Eve	1.6.
Item for mendinge the seats at Alderman fforsters buriall[28]	1.8.
Some totall disboursed	£8.9.3.

M[emoran]dum wee have p[er]used this Accompt and wee finde that there is remayninge in Arreare in the last Churchwardens hands (over and above the some of Nyne pounds tenne shillings by them formly del[iver]ed into the hands of Churchwardens for this present year in being) the some of eight pounds fyfteene shillings & eleven pence ster. Viz in the hands of Thomas Cave esquire & John Anderson gent primo Septemberis 1626.

Chr Grave Robart Usher
Wm Plunkett

M[emoran]d[um] the said some of Eight pounds fifteen shillings & eleven pence ster was payed unto the hands of Mr Graves & Mr Usher in the presence of us this ixth day of April 1627.

Wm Plunkett
Willm Bagnall
John Chevers

[f. 26v blank]
[f. 27] primo May 1626
By the full consent of the parishioners of St Johns Parish we have made {choise} of Mr Willm Plunkett, Mr Mathew fford & Mr John Hunter, Mr Thomas Begg, Mr Connor Ferrall, Mr John Anderson, Mr Willm Talbott, Mr John Chevers & Mr Willm Wirrall, or any six of them whereof two be out of each street {or warde}within the said parish at least. To sesse the whole parish for the parsons duties according to the Act of State.

Robert Clone Chr Grave Robart Usher
Ja Lalor Ric Wiggett
Thomas+ Dongan marke Jhon Turvyn
H. Bennis
Mathew Dillon
Chris ffield
Ra Lany
James Bellew

[f. 27v] xix^{mo} Marcij 1626
It is agreed touching the peticon of Maurice Smyth gent that uppon surrender of his former Leases of twoe several tenements in Oxmanton a new lease shalbe graunted in his owne name for the tearme of Threeskore &

one years from the feast of Easter next ensuing the date hereof, yealding & paying therefore yearely the some of Thirty three shillings iiij^{d} ster duringe the sayd tearme to the proctors of St Johns Church the Evangelist.[29]

Edward Hill, Prebendary of St Johns Dublin.
Wm Plunkett — Tho Evans
Ma fford — Ric Wiggen
John Morning

[f. 28] s[e]c[on]do April 1627

The parson and divers of the parishioners of St John the Evangelist Dublin have Chosen Mr Christopher Graves, gent, and Robt Ussher, merchant, Churchwardens from the feast of Easter last for one whole yeare ensuing.

Edward Hill, prebendary of St Johns Dublin.
Ric Wiggett
Ro Taylor — Wm Plunkett
Tho Begge — Richard Golburne
Ra Lany — John Morrnig
James Bellew

It is also agreed that the said Mr Graves & Mr Ussher beinge late Churchwardens shall bringe in their accompts on ye twentieth day of May next and that the parson and parishioners have made choyse of Mr Alderman Wiggins, Mr Willm Plunkett, Mr Mathewe fford, Mr John Morran, Mr Gooborne or any three of them to take the sayd accompts.[30]

Edward Hill, Prebendary of St Johns Dublin
Ra Lanye — John Weston
Thos Begge
Ro Taylor

[f. 28v blank]

[f. 29] Hereafter followeth the Cesse on the parishioners of St. Johns Evangelists Dublin, due to the parson of the sayd parish according to the Acte of State cessed and taxed by us whose names are hereunderwritten being authorized by the whole consent of the parish the first of March 1626.

ffishamble Street.

Robert Usher, merchant	x^{s}
The widdow Doynne & her inmates	xiij^{s} iiij^{d}
Stephen Allen	vj^{s}
John Huggart & his t[ena]nts	xij^{s}
Morgan Kinge	vj^{s}
Robert <Clawan> Clony[31]	xij^{s}
Dorrogh Moore	vj^{s}
Nicholas Browne, baker	x^{s}

Sr ffrauncis Ansloe, kt & Barronett	xx^{s}
John Trew	viij^{s}
Roger Mumford	vj^{s}
John Hunter, baker	x^{s}
Nicholas Carmicke, gent	viij^{s}
Mathew fford, gent	xiij^{s} iiij^{d}
James Cade & his Inmate	viij^{s}
Willm Jewett	vj^{s}
John Morran for the widdow Boxtons house	iij^{s}
Idem for his own house & sellar	xij^{s}
William Billy, gent	xij^{s}
Mr Dominicke Perceavall for his twoe houses & Brewhouse	xx^{s}
[f. 29v] John Gavan	iiij^{s}
Richard Clearke	iiij^{s}
Mr Bloodd and his t[ene]nts	xv^{s}
William Smyth	viij^{s}
Christopher Grave, gent	viij^{s}
His tennaunt	vij^{s}
Jeffrey the Coachman	iiij^{s}
Mr Leadbeater	x^{s}
Nicholas Maghery, baker	x^{s}
Mr Alderman Wiggins for house & sellar	xx^{s}
The widow Williams	x^{s}
Thomas Sampson	vj^{s}
John Stafford, taylor	vj^{s}
Richard Botterley & his Inmate	x^{s}
Robert Taylor & his Inmate	viij^{s}
John Gillman, victualler	viij^{s}
James Bedlowe, s[er]geaunt	vij^{s}
Thomas Lany, cuttler	viij^{s}
William Plunket, esquire	xiij^{s} iiij^{d}
Robert Usher for his warehouse	iiij^{s}
St Johns Lane	
John Warren, taylor	v^{s}
Mr Malone for his sellar	x^{s}
Mr Kennedy for the dragon sellar	x^{s}
Mr Tho Coleman for the Redd stagge	x^{s}
Mr Mapas for the redd Lyon	x^{s}
John Dillon for his house	vj^{s}
Thomas Jacob, baker	viij^{s}
Chr Coleman for house & seller	xv^{s}
Widdow Reyly	ij^{s}
James Quaytrod & Mr Colemans sister	v^{s}

[f.30] Thomas Jacob & Cotes	iiij^{s}
Mr Gouldinge for houses & sellar	xij^{s}
Mr Wm Bennys for house & Tenniscourt	x^{s}
Jaques Chemois	vj^{s}
Winetavern street	
John Cheevers, merchant	xv^{s}
The widow Browne	xij^{s}
Mr Pennell Taylor	x^{s}
Patricke Rounsell	viij^{s}
Mr Wm Weston for his sellar	x^{s}
Alderman Dowde for house & sellar	xv^{s}
Mr Segrave for the starr sellar	x^{s}
Mr Allen for his sellar	x^{s}
Melchier Bryen	vj^{s}
John Lawles	iiij^{s}
[blank] ffitzsimons	v^{s}
Richard English, baker	iiij^{s}
Mrs Horner	iiij^{s}
James Bedlow, baker	x^{s}
The widdow Vyalls daughters	vj^{s}
The widdow English	viij^{s}
Mr Dongan for the widdow Brownes house	x^{s}
William Worrall	vj^{s}
Walter Conran	x^{s}
Avery Calvert	iiij^{s}
Thomas ffleminge, merchant	xij^{s}
Mr Leverett	x^{s}
Mr Thomas Whytes house	xx^{s}
Thomas Gegin, merchant	x^{s}
Dennys Londers	ij^{s}
Chr ffield, merchant	x^{s}
[f.30v] Mr Myles	x^{s}
John Borran	x^{s}
Thomas Dongan	xij^{s}
John Brooks, esquire	x^{s}
The Craner of the crane	x^{s}
William Chamberlaine	x^{s}
William Talbott	x^{s}
John Turvyn	xiij^{s}
Mr ffrancis Dowde, shiriffe	xv^{s}
Mr John Weston	xv^{s}
Jeremy Woodworth	vj^{s}
Walter ffitzgarrald	iiij^{s}

Thomas Acheson	iij^{s}
Mychaell the Joiner	ij^{s}
Leavan de Rose	x^{s}
Raph Lany	vj^{s}
Mr Coleman for the blackeboy sellar	x^{s}
James Kervan and his Inmates	xv^{s}
The widdow Booth	vj^{s}
ffredericke Russel	iiij^{s}
Patricke Savadge	v^{s}
Mathew Dillon for his house & sellar	xvj^{s}
Wm Baggott for his stoarehouse	viij^{s}
John Butcher	x^{s}
Chr Harrison	viij^{s}
Hugh Lynname, cooke	iiij^{s}
Widdow Nugent	x^{s}
The golden Lyon	x^{s}
Anstace Lyname	ij^{s}
Thomas Bagh	ij^{s}
[f. 31] *Wood Key*	
Thomas Roach	vj^{s}
Mr Lee	vj^{s}
Robert Cunningham	viij^{s}
Ivan Davys	iij^{s}
John Anderson	viij^{s}
John Mongomery	vj^{s}
Cornelius ffarrall	x^{s}
John Hubbert	x^{s}
Thomas Neale	xiij^{s} iiij^{d}
John Beaghan, baker	viij^{s}
Richard Golborne	x^{s}
Nicholas Dillon	viij^{s}
Anthonie Gyfford	x^{s}
John Pettyford & his t[ena]nte	viij^{s}
Mr Bretterich for his brewhouse	xij^{s}
Thomas Begg	viij^{s}
{Michaell Purcell for his shop	ij^{s}}
Phillip Philpott	viij^{s}
John Hunter, Carpenter & his t[ena]nte	vj^{s}
The widdow Purcell & her Inmate	iiij^{s}
Thomas Evans, mayor	xvj^{s}
Chr Harrison	vj^{s}
Besse Wooddes	vj^{s}
Her ten[a]nt	v^{s}

Nicholas Williamson	iij^{s}
John Kettelane	vj^{s}
Thomas Neale	iiij^{s}
Clearke, the cobler	ij^{s}
The widdow Borrowes	x^{s}
John Barry, glasier	iiij^{s}
Widdow Eustace	ij^{s}
Jeremy Bowden	vij^{s}
Wm Hascotte	iiij^{s}
[f. 31v] Mr Derense	xij^{s}
Widdow Tonbridge	x^{s}
Mrs Staughton	xx^{s}
Widdow Hanmer and her te[na]nt	xv^{s}
Robert Savill	viij^{s}
Job Gilliott, esquire	xv^{s}
Creames stable	vj^{s}
Thomas Larke	xij^{s}
Jacob Newman	xx^{s}
Sr William Ryves, knt.	xx^{s}
Mr Bretterich	xij^{s}
Mr John ffoord	xij^{s}
Edward Blenerhassett	vj^{s}
Mr James Browne	x^{s}
Mr Motterseade	x^{s}
Mr Proutfords shopp	vj^{s}
Mr Proutford for his house	vij^{s}

Wm Plunkett
Willm Bagnall
John Chevers
John + Hunters m[ar]ke

[f. 32] xxviij^{o} die Aprilis 1628.
The parson and divers of the parishioners of St John thevangelist Dublin have chosen Mr Robert Clownes and Mr Thomas Cashel Churchwardens from the ffeast of Easter last for one whole year ensuing.

Edward Hill Parson of St Johns Dublin

Chr Grave
Robart Usher
John Gilman

Tho Evans
Ric Wiggett
Wm Plunkett
Ma fforde
John Morning
John ffee
Jeremy Bowden

It is also agreed that the late Churchwardens shall bringe in their Accompts on the xxixth of May next and that the parson and parishioners have made choice of Mr Alderman Evans, Mr Alderman Wiggett, Mr William Plunkett and Mr Mathew fford, Mr John Morran & Mr Richard Golborne or any three of them to take the sayd Accompts.

Edward Hill, Prebendarye of St Johns Dublin
Thos Cashell
Richard Proudfoot

[f. 32v blank]

[f. 33]The Accompte of Christopher Grave and Robert Usher for the rents, buryalls and other Receipts received by them as Procurators of St Johns Evangelist Dublin for twoe whole yeares ended at Easter 1628.

Imprimis receaved of Mr Wm Billy and Mr John Anderson late Churchwardens in readie money the some of	ix^{li} x^{s}
Received likewise in readie money from Mr Anderson and Mr Thomas Cave the succeedinge Churchwardens the some of	viij^{li} xv^{s}
Received of Mr Bath, M[aste]r of the Taylors, for one yeares rent in ano 1626 due to St Johns Chappell	xx^{s}
Received likewise of Mr Lyons,[32] M[aste]r of the Taylors, for the like rent due unto St Johns Chappell in ano 1627	xx^{s}
Received of Mr Thomas Conran for twoe yeares arreare of rent due at Mych[aelm]as 1627 out of his house in ffyshamble street the some of	vj^{li} xiij^{s} iiij^{d}
Received of Alderman Usher for twoe yeares Arrears ended ut supra	iiij^{li} xiij^{s} iiij^{d}
Received of Mr Mathew fford for twoe yeares Arrears of rent for the howse wherein he now dwelleth ended ut supra	Lxvj^{s} viij^{d}
Received of Walter fflood for five yeares arrears due out of the house wherein Sr ffrances Annslie dwelleth ended ut supra	Lxxv^{s}
Received of Mr John Hunter for 2 yeares Arreare due out of the house (wherein he now dwelleth) ended ut supra	xv^{s}
[f. 33v] *Baths ould rent*	
Received of Mr Bath of Dromconran for three yeares Arrears ended at Mych[aelm]as 1627	ix^{s}
Received of Amy Smooth for one yeare and a halfes rent for a house in Oxmanton	xxij^{s} vj^{d}
Received of Mr Maurice Smyth for an Arreare of rent due out of his house in Oxmanton	iiij^{li} iij^{s} iiij^{d}
Received of Mr John Anderson for one yeares rent of his house on Oxmanton	xl^{s}

Received of John Good, butcher, for 2 yeares rent of his house in St ffrauncis streete	L^{s}
Received of the Earle of Corke for his Arrears	Lxxviij^{s} ix^{d}
Received of Sir Thadie Duffe for 2 yeares rent	xl^{s}
received of Mr Quynne, merchant	xviij^{s} ix^{d}
56 – 10 – 08	

Buryalls	
For Edward Edwards	vj^{s} viij^{d}
For Patrick Osborne	vj^{s} viij^{d}
For Thadie Donne	vj^{s} viij^{d}
For Mrs Gyfford	vj^{s} viij^{d}
For Robte Fyans child	iij^{s} iiij^{d}
For Mr Hilton	vj^{s}
For Mrs Whyte	xiij^{s} iiij^{d}
For Mr Rudworth	vj^{s} viij^{d}
For Conans child	iij^{s} iiij^{d}
For Mrs Harris child	iij^{s}
For Mr Jackman	vj^{s} viij^{d}
For Mr Frames child	iij^{s} iiij^{d}
For John Dillon his child	ij^{s} vj^{d}
For Mr Kininghams child	iij^{s} iiij^{d}
For Mr Mongomeries child	iij^{s} iiij^{d}
For one at Mr Andersons	v^{s}
For Mr Golburnes child	iij^{s}
For Conans brother	vj^{s} vj^{d}
4–16–6	
Some Totall	lxj^{li} vj^{s} viij^{d} ster

[f. 34] An accompt of such monyes and disbursements for the Church of St Johns by Christopher Grave gent & Robert Usher merchant Church wardens of the said Church for two yeares ended at Easter 1628

Imprimis To the Clearke for his stipent for 2 whole yeares ended at Mich[aelm]as 1627	iiij^{li}
ffor mending the key of the Church doore	vj^{d}
ffor ringinge the bells the gunpowder day 1626[33]	ij^{s} vj^{d}
ffor mendinge <the> sev[er]all seats and for nayles in that yeare	ij^{s}
ffor mendinge the forme in the Chancell	ix^{d}
ffor a payre of hinges for a doore in theTaylors Chappell	vij^{d}
ffor roapes to the bells	v^{s}
ffor layinge the greate pyle of dead mens boanes in the the ground	iiij^{s}
ffor mendinge both the hearses	ij^{s} vj^{d}

ffor wyne and bread for the comunion at Mich[aelma]as 1626	ij^{s} j^{d}
ffor laying the greate stone in the North syde of the Church & for lyme & sand & layinge of tyles	ij^{s} vj^{d}
ffor Rushes and bowes at Christmas 1626	ij^{s}
ffor Longable for two yeares	vj^{d}
ffor mendinge the seats when Thadee Donne was buried[34]	xij^{d}
ffor wyne and bread on palme Sunday	iij^{s} j^{d}
ffor wyne and bread on tuesday after	xix^{d}
ffor wyne and bread on Thursday after	xix^{d}
ffor wyne and bread on Easter day	v^{s} ix^{d}
ffor wyne and bread on Loe Sonday	iij^{s} j^{d}
ffor mending the dormor window	vj^{d}
To the Sexton for two yeares stipend ending at Mich[aelm]as 1627	xl^{s}
To Mr Richard Quynne, merchant, for takeing out the order from Sr Willm Usher concerning the Concordatum	vij^{s} vj^{d}
To Mr Usher for a Chest for the Church and for two 2 lockes for the same	x^{s}
ffor a church booke	vij^{s} iiij^{d}
ffor bread & wyne on trinytie Sonday 1627	xviij^{d}
ffor mendinge of sev[er]all seats that year & for nayles	ij^{s}
[f. 34v] ffor a locke to the vestery doore	xij^{d}.
ffor a pickaxe and a spade	iij^{s} vj^{d}
ffor mending the greate hole of the Chancell and other holes in the body of the Church	ij^{s} vj^{d}
ffor bread and wyne the vjth of January	xix^{d}
ffor bowes and Rushes at Christmas 1627	ij^{s}
ffor bread and wyne att sev[er]all Comunions	iiij^{s} vj^{d}
To the helar for poyntinge the North syde of the Church	xv^{s}
To the glazier for glasse	vij^{s}
ffor bowes and Rushes at Easter last	iij^{s}
ffor wyne at Easter 1628 and the other day of the Comunion	viij^{s}
To Mr Hobart & Albion Lev[er]ett for an Arreare due unto them within the tyme of their Churchwardenshipp	xlvij^{s} ix^{d}
ffor a leather bagge	iiij^{d}
ffor certaine extraordinary disbursments in and aboute the church affaires as appeareth by a p[ar]ticular note in their accompt	xlv^{s}

Some Totall xvj^{li} xvij^{s} vj^{d} st

The totall of the Chardge and Receipts of the late Church wardens for boeth yeares amounteth to Lxj^{li} vj^{s} viij^{d} st. And their disbursements as app[ear]th by their accompt amounteth to xvj^{li} xvij^{s} vj^{d} st. Soe as their remayneth dewe on this accompt which is sealed upp in bage and deliv[ered] into the hands of

Mr Cashell & Mr Clons the nowe churchwardens to the use of the Church ye some of xliiij^{li} ix^{s} ij^{d} st

Wee have p[er]used & examined the accompt of Mr Graves & Mr Usher and they have fully discharged them selves thereof. Whereunto wee witness beinge Auditors appointed to take their accompt.

Wm Plunkett

[f. 35] x^{o} April 1632
Received of Mr Maurice Smyth in full satisfaction of all arrears due by him unto St Johns Church the full summe of five pounds ster for & Easter last past5^{li} ster

John Atherton, Prebend[35]
Wm Plunkett
Robart Barlow
Jeremy Bowden

[f. 35v blank]
[f. 36] xxj^{o} April 1629
The parson and divers of the parishioners of St John Evangelist Dublin have chosen Mr Thomas Cashell and Jacqey Shamnean, Churchwardens, from the feast of Easter last for one whole year ensuing.

Edward Hill, prebendary of St Johns

Wm Plunkett
Willm Flemynge
Robert Clony
John Morring
R Conynghame
Will Jewett
Richard Gouldinge
John Warren

xxj Aprill 1629
It is alsoe agreed that the late Church wardens shall bringe in their accompts on the Thursday next, after the terme being the xxjth day of May next and the parson and parishioners have made choice of Mr Alderman Evans, Mr Plunkett, Mr John Morran, Mr Richard Golburne or any three of them to take the sayd accompts

John Warren
Edward Hill, parson of St Johns Dublin
Jeremy Bowden
Will Flemyng
John Gilman
J Seamean
John Montgomerie

[f. 36v] 21° Aprilis 1629

By the ffull Consent of the parishioners of St. Johns parish wee have made Choise of Mr William Plunkett, Mr Richard Goulding, Mr John Morrin, Mr Connor O ffarroll, Mr Thomas Ellies and Mr Albon Liveret wheareof two of them to be out of eache streete or ward within the said parish. To Sess the whole parish for the parsons duties, accordinge the Acte of State.

Tho Cashell	Will fflemynge
J Seammean	Jeremy Bowden
Robert Clony	R Conyngham
John ffee	John Gilman
Law fullam	John Warren

[f. 37] 1629

Hereafter followeth the Cesse of the parishioners of St Johns Evangelist, Dublin, dewe to the parson of the said parish accordinge to the Act of State, Cessed and taxed by us whose names are hereunto writtine, being aucthorized by the whole Consent of the Parishe the xxiijth of Aprill 1629.

	all ster.
ffishamble strett	
Robte Usher, merchant	x^{s}
The widowe Dune & her sev[er]all tenents	xiij^{s} iiij^{d}
Phillipp Phillpott, victuler	vj^{s}
John Huggard	vj^{s}
William Conlan, baker	vj^{s}
John Huckard, buttenmaker	iiij^{s}
Murtagh Kinge, gent	vj^{s}
Robt Clony, chandler	xij^{s}
Robte Barley, vict[ler]	x^{s}
Nicholas Browne, baker	x^{s}
Sr ffraunces Annesley, kt, Barronett	xx^{s}
John Trewe	viij^{s}
Murtagh Hughes, taylor	vj^{s}
The widowe Hunter, baker	viij^{s}
Nicholas Carmick, gent	viij^{s}
Mathewe fford, gent, howse	xiij^{s} iiij^{d}
William Austine & his Inmates	viij^{s}
Willm Jewett & his Inmates	vij^{s}
John Murrins howse	x^{s}
Stevine Usher, merchant for howse & seller	xij^{s}
Sr Thomas Cary, kt, for howse and stable	xvj^{s}
John Murrine for p[ar]t of Percevalls howse	x^{s}
Edmond Lyons & his Inmattes	vj^{s}
Sr Dudley Norton, kt	xvj^{s}

John Gavan & his Inmattes	vj^{s}
Richard Clerke	iiij^{s}
Andrew Dickes, Thomas Crafford, Willm Cattelyn	xij^{s}
The Widowe Appevey	ij^{s}
Willm Smyth	viij^{s}
Mr Henry Kenney	x^{s}
Dorby Lalor, gent	viij^{s}
Jeffrey Powell	iiij^{s}
[f. 37v]Edmond Ledbeter, gent	x^{s}
Nicholas Maghery, baker	x^{s}
Mr Alderman Wiggett for his howse & seller	xvj^{s}
Willm ffleminge, gent	x^{s}
Thomas Sampson, victular	iiij^{s}
John Tafford, taylor	iiij^{s}
Richard Botterley & his Inmattes	x^{s}
Richard Lutterell, gent	viij^{s}
John Gilman	viij^{s}
James Bedlowe, s[er]gent	vij^{s}
Thomas Lanys howse nowe Osbornes	vj^{s}
Thomas Gunter	v^{s}
William Plunket, gent	xiij^{s} iiij^{d}
John Colesons, goldsmyth	vj^{s}
Mr Ushers warehowse	iiij^{s}
St Johns lane	
John Warrine, taylor	iiij^{s}
Mr Malones seller	x^{s}
The Seller called hell	x^{s}
Mr Colman for the Reade stagg	x^{s}
Patrick Mapas for the Reade Lyon	x^{s}
[blank] Conrans, the Joyner	vj^{s}
Thomas Jacob, baker	x^{s}
Christ Colman for howse & seller	xv^{s}
Widdowe Realy	ij^{s}
The widowe Cottes howse	viij^{s}
Mr Gouldin for howse, seller & Teniscourt	xvj^{s}
Jacques Chemoies	vj^{s}
John Cheevers, merchant	xv^{s}
The widowe Browne	xij^{s}
John Lynch	viij^{s}
Richard St Johns & Patr Rownsell	x^{s}
Willm Weston for his sellar	x^{s}
[f. 38] *Winetavern street*	
Alderman Dowde for howse & seller	x^{s}

Knowles for the starr seller	x^{s}
Mathewe Dillon for the shipp seller & howse	xvj^{s}
John Lawles	ij^{s}
Thomas fitz Symonds, merchant	iiij^{s}
Richard Engl[ish], baker	iiij^{s}
Richard Brasbrigg	iiij^{s}
James Bedlowe, baker	x^{s}
The Vidow Vialls daughters	vj^{s}
The Vidowe Englishes howse	viij^{s}
Thomas Dongans howse & Inmattes	x^{s}
William Worrall	vj^{s}
Walter Conran, baker	viij^{s}
John Waterhowse	iiij^{s}
Thomas ffleming, merchant	xij^{s}
Albone Leavorett	x^{s}
Thomas Cashell	xvj^{s}
James Corvane, baker	viij^{s}
Robt Savill	xij^{s}
Raphe Myles	xij^{s}
Raphe Bryde	viij^{s}
Thomas Dongan	xij^{s}
John Brooke, Councellor at Lawe	x^{s}
The Craner for the Crane	x^{s}
Willm Chamblyns howse	x^{s}
Willm Talbott, merchant	x^{s}
John Turvine	vj^{s}
ffrauncs Dowde, merchant	xv^{s}
John Weston	xv^{s}
Jeremy Woodworth	vj^{s}
Walter fitz Gerrald	iiij^{s}
Thomas Akins	ij^{s}
Michaell the Joyner	ij^{s}
Seven Garnans for howse & Tenniscourt	x^{s}
[f. 38v] Raphe Lany for ye blacke boye	vj^{s}
Mr Colman for ye seller of ye blakboy	x^{s}
James Browne, gent	xiij^{s} iiij^{d}
Redagh Geoghegan, merchant, & his Inmates	x^{s}
The widowe Russell	iiij^{s}
Patrick Savage	iiij^{s}
The Royall exchange & seller	xvj^{s}
John Butcher, merchant	xij^{s}
Hugh Lyneham	iiij^{s}
Richard Harrysson	viij^{s}

Widowe Nugent	x^{s}
Rose Mary Lane	
The golden Lyon	x^{s}
Annestace Lynhame, vidowe	ij^{s}
Thomas Baeth	ij^{s}
John Iremonger	ij^{s}
Wood Key	
Thomas Roch, shomaker	vj^{s}
John Lee	vj^{s}
Robte Cunningham	viij^{s}
Ivan Davys seller	iij^{s}
Raphe Rogers	viij^{s}
John Mongomery	vj^{s}
Cornelius ffarroll, gent	x^{s}
John Hardinge	x^{s}
John Parker	xiij^{s} iiij^{d}
James Daniell, victuler	vj^{s}
John Beaghan, baker	x^{s}
Thomas Neale	iiij^{s}
Anthony Williams	v^{s}
Richard Golborne	vj^{s}
Nicholas Dyllon	viij^{s}
William Boyle	x^{s}
Hugh Locke and his Inmattes	vj^{s}
[f. 39] Mr Henry Jones for ye brewhowse	x^{s}
Andrew Gerrott	ij^{s}
Thomas Begg & his Inmattes	x^{s}
John Anyon	vj^{s}
Michaell Purcells shopp	ij^{s}
The vidowe Purcell	iiij^{s}
Mr Alderman Evans	xiiij^{s} iiij^{d}
Christofer Harrisson	vj^{s}
Richard fframe	vj^{s}
Andrewe Reade	v^{s}
William Browns & his Inmattes	viij^{s}
Thomas Neale, yeoman	iiij^{s}
ffraunces Clerke	ij^{s}
John Barry, glaser	ij^{s}
Henry Ashborne	viij^{s}
James Catwallyder	iiij^{s}
Jeremy Bowden	vj^{s}
William Haskett	iiij^{s}
Sr Mathew Derensie, kt	xvj^{s}

Vidowe Tonsbridge	x^{s}
Mr Staughtons howse	xx^{s}
Vidowe Hamner & her tenent	xv^{s}
James Goodman, Counsellor at Lawe	xv^{s}
John Harrys	iiij^{s}
Math Bently for Mr Dermott howse & stable	xiiij^{s}
John Pollyder	x^{s}
Thomas Larke	x^{s}
Jacob Newman	xx^{s}
Sr Willm Ryves, kt	xx^{s}
Jeromy Alexander, Councellor at lawe	xiij^{s} iiij^{d}
James Donnellan, Councellor at Lawe	xiij^{s} iiij^{d}
Edward Blen[er]hassett	vj^{s}
Widowe Carter	viij^{s}
Thomas Ellys	x^{s}
Mr Proutford	x^{s}

Richard Gouldinge	Wm Plunkett
Connor fferrrall	John Morring
	Thomas Elliss

[f. 39v blank]

[f. 40]The Accompte of Mr Thomas Cashell and Mr Robert Clony for the Rents, burialls and other Receipts received by them as Proctors of St Johns Evangelist Dublin for one whole yeare for the feast of Easter 1628 unto easter 1629

Imprimis Received of the late Churchwardens in Readie money {Sealed up in a bagge}[36]	xliiij^{li} ix^{s} ij^{d} ster
Receaved of Mr Thomas Condran, gent, for one years rent ending at Michaelmas 1628	iij^{li} vj^{s} viij^{d}
Receaved of Mr Walter Usher for one years rent ending ut supra	ij^{li} vj^{s} viij^{d}.
Receaved of Mr Kinginham,[37] M[aste]r of the Taylors, for one years rent ending ut supra	j^{li} ster
Receaved of Nicholas Robocke for John Goods house in St Frauncis Streete for one years rent ending ut supra the some of	j^{li} v^{s} ster
Receaved of Ammye Smooth for one years rent ending ut supra the some of	xv^{s} ster
Receaved of Widdow Hunter for one years rent ending ut supra the some of	vij^{s} vj^{d}
Item receaved for the buriall of the Child of William Benniss in May	iij^{s} iiij^{d}

Item receaved for the buriall of the Child of John Harris in May iij^{s} iiij^{d}

Item receaved for the buriall of the Child of the Widdow Williams in May iij^{s} iiij^{d}

Item receaved for the buriall of the Child of Mr Colemans in May iij^{s} iij^{d}

Suma totall 9^{li} 14^{s} 1^{d}

[f. 40v] An accompte of such monyes as the said Churchwardens have disboursed and Layd out in and a bout the sayd Church for necessary uses for the yeare 1628.

	li. s. d.
Imprimis paid Bartill. Jurdan	2.15.0.
Item paid for Lyme, sclates pines and Laborars and Hellers wages for to meand severall places in the said Church.	5.3.
Item paid for mending the locke of the vestery doore and locke of the great doore	7.
Item paid for whitining the Church	1.13.4.
Item paid to the glazier for mending the two dermoots the west end and south side of the said Church the 9th of Aprill	8.3.
Item paid for a coat to the beadle of the poor	9.0.
Item paid for Cleaning the lane over against the Church doore	2.0.
Item paid for Langcable to the sheriffs of the Cittie	3.0.
Item paid for Cleaning the leads of the Church	9.
Item paid fo Ivie, holy and russes for Christomas	2.4.
Item paid for bread and wyne for the Communion trinity Sundaie	2.9.
Item paid for bread and wyne for the Communion the 21 daie of September	3.4.
Item paid for bread and wyne for the Communion the 11th of January	2.2.
Item paid for bread and wyne for the Communion the 8th daie of March	2.2.
Item paid for bread and wyne for the Communion at Easter 1629	14.0.
Item paid for wyne a meetting daie	<6>16.2.
Item paid for wyne a meetting daie	7.4.
Summa totall	7^{li} 17^{s} 05^{d} [38]

Their remaynes dewe on this accompt the some of xlj^{s} viij^{d} ster.

[f. 41] quarto Junii 1629

Wee have examined the accomptes of Mr Thomas Cashel & Mr Clone for one yeare endinge at the feast of Easter last 1629 & they <have> stand indebted for monys receaved by them over & above such moneys as they have disbursed to the use of the Church the some of forty one shillings & eight pence ster which is now payed over by Mr Clons to Mr Cashell nowe

Churchwardens together with fortie fower poundes & nyne shillings {& two pence}ster. founde sealed up in a Bagg to the use of the Church.

Edward Hill, Prebendary of St Johns Dublin

Wm Plunkett
John Morring

[f. 41v blank]

[f. 42] 13° Aprilis 1630
The parson & divers of the parishioners of St Johns Evangelist Dublin have chosen Mr James Browne and Mr Jaquis Shemeyn Churchwardens from the feast of Easter last for one whole year ensuing.

John Atherton, Preben de St Johan

Will Flemynge	Richd Wiggett	Tho Evans
	Wm Plunkett	R.B. Sams
	Richd Proudfoot	Nich Carmick
	John Morring	

13° Aprilis 1630
It is alsoe agreed that the Late Churchwardens shall bringe in their accompts the next thursday after the this Easter Tearme beinge the Twelveth of May next. And the parson and parishioners have made Choise of Mr Alderman Evans, Mr Willm Plunkett, Mr John Morran, Mr Willm Fleming or eny thre of them to take the sayd accompts.

John Atherton	
Rich Wiggett	R.B. Sams
Rich Proudfoot	

xij May 1630 which was extened untill 24 May & this day paid me in p[ar]te of viij^{li} x^{s} v^{d} ster right due on Mr Cashell & Mr Jaquis the said iij^{li} x^{s}. Ja Browne

[f. 42v blank]

[f. 43] The Accompte of Thomas Cashell and Jaques Semay for the Rents, Burialls and other receipts Receaved by them as proctors of St Johns Evangelist Dublin for one whole yeare begining Easter 1629 and ending Easter 1629.

	ster
Imprimis Receaved by them in Remayne of an ould Accompt due on the last Churchwardens	ij^{li} j^{s} iiij^{d}
Item from Mr Thomas Conran of Wyanston for a yeer Rent begining Mich[aelm]as1628 and ending Mich[aelm]as 1629	iij^{li} vj^{s} viij^{d}
Item Receaved from Mr Anderson for the yeres Rent ending Mich[aelm]as 1629	vj^{li}
Item Receaved by them from the master and wardens of Taylors rent for for yeer ending midsomer 1629	xx^{s}

Receaved from Mr Morish Smith for arrears of rent due on him yealding iij^{li} vj^{s} viij^{d}
Item receaved for several burialls in that year as by Examinacon appeared iij^{li} x^{s}
Item receaved from Mr Robuke for a yeers Rent ending at Mich[aelm]as 1629 xxv^{s}
Suma total xx^{li} ix^{s} viij^{d} ster

xx^{li} ix^{s} viij^{d}

[f. 43v blank]

[f. 44] The Accompt of Thomas Cashell and Jaques Semay for the disbursements by them made of the Church Revenue taken by William Plunkett & Thomas Evans, Aldermen.[39]

Imprimis The Clerke and {sexton} stipend	2.0.0.
Item for bread and wine at severall Communions that year.	1.1.10.
Item for the beadle	10.0.
Item for Langable	3.0.
Item for the poynting the church at twoe severall tymes	4.0.
Item for for mending the shade near the bell	1.10.0.
Item for Iron Worke	10.0.
Item to the healers & Laborers with for lyme & sand	14.0.
Item for a warrant for getting church money	10.0.
Item for glasing the church at severall tymes	1.0.0.
Item for mending seates at taylors Chappell	18.0.
Item for pointings the church at severall tymes	3.0.0.
Item for Extraordinaries	9.0.
More geven in reddy money to the new church warden	8.0.0.

M[emoran]d[um] this viij^{li} st is to be chardged on the next Church wardens accompt

Suma total xx^{li} ix^{s} x^{d} ster

Wee have p[er]used this accompt the xxth day of July & they have fully discharged them selves thereof. Whereunto wee witness being Auditors appoyned to take their accompt.

Wm Plunkett Thos Evans

[f. 44v blank]

[f. 45] The Accompte of James Browne and Jaques Semay for the rents, Burialls and other Receipts by them made & Receaved as proctors of St Johns Evangelist Dublin for one whole yeare begining Easter 1630 and ending Easter 1631.

	li. s. d.
Imprimis Receaved from the last church wardens in reddy money	8.o.o.
Item more in reddy money from Mr Newman app[er]tayning to the Church & left in repositie.	42^{li} 2^{s} o^{d}
Item from Sir Thady Duff for twoe yeers begining Easter 1628 ending Mich[aelm]as 1629	2.o.o.
Item from Widdow Hunter for twoe yeeres and a halfe beging Mich[aelm]as 1627 and endinge Easter 1630 at vij^{s} vj^{d} per annum	18.9.
Item from Mr Conran of Wyanston for halfe a yeere ending at Easter 1630 the som of	1.13.4.
Item from Mr Bath of DromConragh for two yeer begining Mich[aelm]as 1627 & ending Mich[aelm]as 1629	6.o.
Item from the Earl of Corke for arrear due from Mich[aelm]as 1627 ending Easter 1630. Upon condicion of restitucon if it be needful	3.6.o.
Item from the Master of the Taylors for a yeere ending Midsomer 1630	1.o.o.
Item from Mr Alderman Usher for a year & a halfe begining Mich[aelm]as 1628 & ending Easter 1630 at 46^{s} $viij^{d}$ p[er] ann[um] the som of	3.10.o.
Item for Doyles daughters buriall	3.4.
Item for buriall of Harrison the mason	6.8.
Item for Jeffrey Walshes child	3.4.
Item for Golbornes child	3.4.
Item for Ralph Rogers	6.8.
Item for Beaghgans wife	6.8.
[f. 45v] Item for John Habberly buriall	3.4.
Item for one Cookes buriall	6.8.
Item for Mr Wilsons child	3.4.
For Mr Chevers child	3.4.
For Mr Alexanders child	3.4.
For Wm Jewetts burial	6.8.
Item Received from Mr Robuck for yeeres house for one yeers Rent ending Mich[alem]as	1.5.o.
Item for Mr Carmickes burriall	6.8.
Item for another child of Mr Wilsons	3.4.
Item from Amy Smoth for twoe yeers ending Mich[aelm]as 1630 at xv^{s} ster per annum	1.10.o
Item from Mr Mathew Ford for three yeeres begining Mich[aelm]as 1629 and endinge Mich[aelm]as 1630 at xxxiiijs iiijd per annum the some of 5.o.o.	
Item from Mr Anderson for a yeeres rent ending Mich[aelm]as 1630	xl^{s} ster
Item from from Sir Thady Duff againe for a yeare ending Mich[aelm]as 1630 twenty shillings	xx^{s}
For the buriall of Mrs Eustace	6.8.
Sum total of the charge	$Lxxvij^{li}$ v^{s} ij^{d}

[f. 46] An accompt of James Browne and Jaques Semay for such disbursements as were by them made from Easter 1630 untill Easter 1631 about the parish church of St Johns Evangelist, being p[ro]ctors of the said churche.

Imprimis for a Lock and key for the great chest	1.4.
Item for Bread and wyne for Communion on Whitsunday	2.2.
Item for twoe padd lockes & keyes for the same with other things	1.0.
Item for three keyes for the chest of Evidences	1.6.
Item to the smith for setting on locks	1.0.
Item for a hinge for the porch of the church door weying three quarters of a stone	2.0.
Item for Ringing bells on princes Day	2.6.
Item for case for the chalices	6.0.
Item to Bartholmew Jordan	2.0.0.
Item for bread & wyne on Sunday 27° June	2.0.
Item to the sheriffs for Langable for the church	3.0.
Item for Ringing the generall triumphing day[40]	2.6.
Item for bread & wyne at the comunion xj August	1.2.
Item for washing Comunion Cloath	6.
Item for warrant to Sr William Ussher about Dolmans house	4.0.
Item for Expenses upon a meeting of the parishioners	19.6.
[f. 46v] Expenses about the building in the church	
Item to labourers for removing the earth in church yard	1.0.
Item for masons for erecting the stone walls in churchyard	18.0.
Item to him for mending the post under the gallery with sand and Lyme	1.0.
Gallery	
for sand to the worke	12.0.
for Lyme	1.9.0.
for double deal 5 dozen x^{s} dozen	2.10.0.
for sawing a peece of Tymber	1.0.
for spars a dozen & a halfe	6.0.
for nyne slitt deale at xvj^{d} the peece	12.0.
for eight hundred of spikes	7.0.
for carring planckes to the church	1.0.
for eight hundred more spikes	7.0.
for double spikes	8.
for half dozen dubble sparr	6.0.
for two hundred single boord nayless	8.
for twoe hundred more spikes	1.6
for hundred more spikes	9.
for twoe hundred more single boord nayles	8.
for one hundred more pikes	9.

for half a dozen deale boords	5.0.
for carring them	3.
for one hundred more single boord nayles	4.
To the Carpenters for their worcke	3.5.0.
To a plasterer for Worckes under gallery	1.10.0.
Item for a dozen of more deale bordes	10.0.
for eight slitt deal	10.0.
for carriage	4.
for three hundred single bord Nailes	1.0.
for twoe hundred spikes	1.6.
for twoe slitt deale more	2.8.
for 2^{C} single boord Nayles more	8.
[f. 47] Item for a hundred an a halfe of spikes more	1.2.
Item for more spikes	5.
Item for a ladder for the Churche	10.0.
Item for a pyn of Iron to bauyr the kinges Armes in the church	1.6.
for making the new windows in the church to the Carpenters	2.0.0.
Belfrey	
for fouer dozen dale boords	2.0.0.
for one dozen slitt dale	18.0.
for one thousand single spikes	7.6.
for half a thowsand of single board	1.8.
for one dozen duble sparrs	4.0.
for the Carring of those p[ar]cells	1.0.
to the Carpenters for theire worke there	2.0.0.
Item more for nayles & other necessaries	13.6.
Item for holly for the church	2.0.
for ringing on the gunpowder day	2.0.
Item to Barth Jordan for his stipend at Mich[aelm]as 1630	1.0.0.
Item for Comunion on Sonday xix^{o} Decemb[e]r	2.0.
for pulling down the house next the church[41]	12.0.
Item to Ralph Cotton for paynting	1.0.0.
for 33 foot new glass & mending ould glass	1.7.0.
for Coloring vestry window	9.0.
for nayles to sett upp the glass	1.0.
for Irons to hang buckett	1.4.
for lyme & Laborers	2.0.
[f. 47v] for washing the Comunion Cloath	2.0.
for a dozen of bucketts	2.8.0.
for Laborers at church yard	3.0.
for Covering the church	2.6.
for washing surplus	2.6.
for Ringing on the Coronacon day	2.0.

Item for a new howre glass and mending the Iron to hould it	2.0.[42]
Item paid to William Dyllon for 57 hogsheds and a half of lyme at xiiij ^{d} the hogshed amounteth to	3.7.1.
Item more to the said William Dyllan for 14 cartt of stones at ij^{s} the Cartt	1.8.0.
Item to Edmond Heyland for five hogsheds and a halfe of lyme at xiiij^{d} the hogshed	6.5.
Item to Philip the Carman for sand, Clay and Carriage of stones being six score and xij loade at ijd ob. the load amounth to	1.10.0.
Item to Willm Maly for the masons worke and digging the foundacion, etc.	3.0.0.
Item paid for pavenig the street, sand and removinge the stones in the Church yard the 24 of March	14.0.
Item paid for 6 baskett men for carrying the Rubbish into the Church yard	3.0.
Item paid a Carpenter for working in the Church	1.0.
Item paid a laberor for leavelling the church yard	7.
Item paid for stones in St Patricks church yard	15.0.
Item paid for 6 Choise deals for scaffelling	7.0.
Item for Carriadge	1.
Item paid for 32 load of stones in St Patricks streett & St ffrancis streett	13.0.
Item paid to a Carpenter that made the pyles & set up the seate in the Chancell and nayles for 2 days & a halfe	4.3.
[f. 48] Item paid for spickes to nayle the scaffold	3.
Item paid Mr John Gough on the key for 2 Cartt of stones and one barre at ij^{s} the Cartt	3.6.
Item paid one merchant winetavern gate for 4 carrs of stones	2.4.
Item paid Christopher Duff for 22 carts and one barroe of stones at 2^{s} the Cartt	2.4.0.
Item paid for weighing	1.6.
Item to 3 laborers for carring away the Rubbish and cleaning the Church	2.0.
Item to the lords Justice & Councells warrant for takinge down the house on the East side of the Church	x^{s}
Item for Richard Morly the plasterer for frettsiling the gallery next the Church dore he finding all materials	xxx^{s} st
Item for Pyles for the fundacion besides the timber that was in the Churchyarde	x^{s}
Item to Raphe Cotton for writting the Commandments and painting work he fynding the goulding and all Cullors	v^{li} x^{s}
Sum total of the disbursem[en]ts amounteth to	Lvij^{li} xvj^{s} st

Wee have p[er]used & examined this accompt of Mr James Browne & Jaques Chemoyes late Churchwardens for one yeare ending at our lady day 1631 & wee find that their remayneth dewe in the hands of Mr Browne the some of nyneteen pounds & fower shillings st this xxvijth day of May 1631.

Wm Plunkett   Ric Wiggett
Robart Ussher
Edm Leadbetter

[f. 48v blank]

[f. 49] xxxth of March 1631
The parishioners & divers of the parishioners of St Johns Evangelist Dublin have chosen Mr William Stoughton and Mr Edmund Leadbetter churchwardens from the feast of the Aunticion of our Lady last past for one whole year ensuing.

Tho Wilkinson	Ric Wiggett	Wm Plunkett
Ja Browne	Willm Smyth	Nicholas Dillon
		Willm Woorrall
Henry Ashbourne		Jeremy Bowden
Robart Ussher		

xxx^{o} Martj 1631
It is alsoe agreed that the late churchwardens shall bringe in their accompts the next Thursday after the this {next} Easter Tearme and the parson and parishioners have chosen and nominated Mr Alderman Wiggett, Mr William Plunkett, Mr John Anderson and Mr Robt Usher, or or any twoe of them to take the sayd Accompts.

Thos Wilkinson	Ja Browne	Wm Smyth
Henry Ashbourne	Edward Blennerhassett	
John Browne		

[f. 49v blank]

[f. 50] *6 October 1630*
Memorand[um] that the parson, Churchwardens and parishioners of this Church p[re]ferred their peticon to the Right ho[noura]ble the Lords Justices and Councell of Ireland, which peticon together with their Lo[rdshi]ps order, and all the proceedings theruppon followeth in hec verba

To the Right Hon[oura]ble the L[ords] Justice & Councell

The humble peticon of John Atherton, prebend of St Johns, James Browne & Jaques Chemoyes, churchwardens, William Plunkett, Esq & the rest of the parishioners of St. Johns Evanglist Dublin.

Most humbly shewinge that whereas in ffishamble street Dublin, towards the Easte end of the Church of St John on the Kings pavement their is built a litle tenement about halfe a storie heighe which is fastened to the said Church wall so close as by the continyuall rayne which hath falne on the said house these manie yeares past the same hath soaked so farr into the wall of the Church as ye Chauncell of the Church is like to fall if it be not prevented, there being a great wyndee of the same alreadie falne down and the rest cracked in such wise as it threatneth each hower to fall which may prove verie dangerous unto manie. Which said tenement was erected by Mr Ball upon a demise made to him from the cittie of Dublin at vs per ann[um] on the Kings pavement which ye peticioners are enformed they could not doe it being part of the Auntient Market place and it being fastned to the Church wall without the consent of the saide Prebend and parishioners or the p[re]dicessores. Maye it therefore please your L[ordshi]ps to take the same into serious consideracon and inasmuch as the saide poore tenant yieldeth litle or no p[ro]fitt to the saide Mr Ball and yet a great damage to the saide Church and is also a nusaunce to ffishamble stret having much straightned the passige of the same [f. 50v] the markett being of late much encreased by reason of Englishe Butchers that doth frequent them to the great reliefe and comfort of the inhabitaunts.[43] And further the said house being so poorlie built havinge a chimney therein which being latlye on fyer did much endanger the Church and the whole street. That your L[ordshi]ps will be pleased to give order for takeinge downe of the saide House beinge so great a nusaunce to the saide Church and the whole commonwealth of the cittie and the rather because the house beinge fastned to St Michaell Church was latlie puled downe to the great honor of the cittie. And they shall pray

6 Octo[ber] 1630
Wee require the Maior of the Cittie of Dublin calling the peticioners and the within named Ball before him to consider of the peticion and having vewed the howse in the peticon mentioned to be a nusance to the Church to certify unto us their opinions concerning the petiticoners request

	Ad Loftus Canc	R Corke
	Moore, Baltinglas	R Ranelaghe
J Dillon	Hen Dockwray	Fra Mountnorris
Ja Shurley	Cha Coote	

May yt please your L[ordshi]ps
In obedience unto your L[ordshi]ps I have called the p[ar]ties interessted in thsi peticon before me and haveing debated the matter in difference I doe find that the howse in the peticon mentioned is buylded on the kings pavem[en]t wherein auntientlie ther was a ffishmarket and that the Cittie of Dublin in Anno 1583[44] mad a lease thereof to one Cavell for the use of

Barthol Ball deceased for syxty yeares whereof thirtene yeres is unspent by which lease being p[ro]duced before me [f. 51] I find the Cittie intended only a place for a ffishamble should be errected and not a howse doth with many other inconveniences as did appear unto me upon p[er]usall so as I conceyve it were fitt that Mr Ball shold be compelled to pull downe the said howse so offensive to the said Church and yf he will have the benifitt of his Lease then to erect only a void building for a ffyshambles according theffect of his grant which will no waye offende the said Church nor p[re]judice the walls therof. All which I submitt unto your L[ordshi]ps ho[nourable] considerations

27 Octo[ber] 1630

Your L[ordshi]ps to be commanded

Thos Evans, Mayor

4 Decem[ber] 1630

Uppon Consideracion of the above certificate from the Maior of this Cittie wee have thought fitt hereby to require and authorize the saide Maior to call the within named Ball before him and to take ordr that the saide howse which is founde to be so offensive to the Church contrarie to the intention of the Lease by which the saide Ball holdes the same be pulled downe & seing it appeares that by the saide Lease that place was intended for a ffyshambles and not to errect a howse theron which should prove an nusiance to the Church wee think fitt that when the said howse shalbe pulled downe the said Ball or his Assignees maye erect a void building there for a ffishambles according to the intention of his Lease which is to be so done as it maye in no degree be a nusiance to the Church. And in the execution of this our direction the Sheriffes of this Cittie are required to be assistant.

Ad Loftus Canc — R. Cork
Hen Valentia — Montgomery
Claneboye
Erskine

[f. 51v] Acordinge to a warrant directed unto me from the Lords Justices and Counsell Theise are to will & require you the undernamed p[er]sons to take notice that on tuesday next after Twelfth daye ensuing The howse wherein you Richarde Gylman nowe dwelleth is to be pulled downe in p[ur]suaunce of the contents of the said warrant weherof you are to take notice at your p[er]ills dated the xxth of December 1630.

Tho Evans, maior Dublin

To Richard Gillman
Bartholomewe Ball &
Albon Leverett

[f. 52] A true note of such monies as Edmund Leadbetter, Proctor of St John the evangelist,[45] hath Rec[eived] of the Revenues and burialls per annum since he was chosen begining at Easter 1631 and ending at Easter 1632 viz.

Imprimis Received of Mr Conran of Wyanstowne for one yeare ending at Easter 1631 due upon John Trewws howse in ffyshamble street	iij^{li} vj^{s} viij^{d}
Item Received of Alderman Dowde for yeares Rent due by Amy Smoth at Easter 1631	vij^{s} vj^{s}
Item Received of the M[aste]r of the Taylors for a yeares Rent due at Midsomer 1631	xx^{s}
Item Received of Mr James Browne beinge due uppon his last accompt unto the Church	xix^{li}
Item Received of Ald[erman] Usher for a yeares Rent due and endinge at Easter 1631	xlvj^{s} viij^{d}
Item Received of Mr Anderson for one yeares Rent for a howse he holdeth in Oxmanton endinge at Mychaelmas 1631	xl^{s}
Item Received of Mr Bath of Drumconron for two yeares Rent endinge at Mich[aelmas] one thousand syxe hundreth thirty one	vj^{s}
Item Received of Walter fflood for fower yeares arrear due & payable upon the Right Ho[nourable] the Lo[rd] Mountnorris his howse endinge at Michaell[mas] 1631	iij^{li}
Item Received of Sr Taddy Duffe, kt, for one yeares Rent of a howse he holdeth on the wood key due & endinge at Mych[aelmas] 1631 last past	xx^{s}
Item Received of Ald[erman] Dowde for Amy Smoth for half yeares Rent endinge at Mych[aelmas] 1631 last past	vij^{s} vj^{s}
Item Received of one Rawbucke for Jo Good his rent due at Micha[elams] 1631[46]	xxvs
Item Received of Mr Conron of Wyanstown for half a yeares Rent endinge at Mych[aelmas] 1631	xxxiij^{s} iiij^{d}
Item Received of Ald[erman] Usher half a yeares Rent for a howse in ffishamble stret due and endinge Mych[aelmas] 1631	xxiij^{s} iiij^{d}
[f. 52v] Item Received of Robt Gylbert purysuivant for three halfe yeares Rent he holdeth from the Right Ho[nourable] Therle of Cork & endinge at Mychaellmas1631	xxxix^{s} iiij^{d} ob
Item Received of Wydoe Hunter for the Rent of her howse due and endinge at My[chaelmas] 1631	xj^{s} iiij^{d}
Soma totall is	xxxix^{li} vj^{s} vj^{d} ob.
Burials Received	
Imprimis Received of Mrs Champion for her ffathers buriall the 8 of June 1631	vj^{s} viij^{d}
Item Received of Mrs Graves for her husbands buriall 26th of Aprill	vj^{s} viij^{d}
Item Received for Mr Bagnes his buriall the 28 of April	vj^{s} viij^{d}

Item Received for Mrs Lockes burial	vj^{s}
Item Received for Mrs Evans her burial	vj^{s} viij^{d}
Item Received for Mr Talbotts childs burial	iij^{s} iiij^{d}
Item Received of Mr Wm Plunkett for his childs buriall	iij^{s} iiij^{d}
Item Received for Mrs Golborne buriall	vj^{s} viij^{d}
Item Received for Mr Smyths childs buriall	iij^{s} iiij^{d}
Item Received for Sir George Sextons his buriall	xiij^{s} iiij^{d}
Item Received for Mr Cheevers his buriall	vj^{s} viij^{d}
Item Received for Mr Gunters child buriall	iij^{s} iiij^{d}
Item Received for Mr Lawlors childs buriall	iij^{s} iiij^{d}
Item Received for Mrs Jacques childs buriall	iij^{s} iiij^{d}
Soma	iij^{li} xix^{s}
Soma totall Received is xliiij^{li} v^{s} vj^{d} ob	

[f. 53] A true noat of such mon[ies as have been disbursed] and paid in and about [the church of St John] the Evangelist by Edmund [Leadbetter proctor of] the same Church in the yeare 16[31]

Imprimis paid to Bartholl Jurden for breade and wynne at fyve severall tymes	xiij^{s} x^{d}
Item Paide unto Barth Jurden for his stipende 2d of July 1631	xx^{s}
Item paid for glasse that wanted in the body of the church & mortar for the wyndoes	iiij^{s}
Item paid to a Carpenter for a daies work	xviij^{d}
Item paid for bars for a wyndoe & nailes to mend seates & dores	xviij^{d}
Item paid for ij sparrs	vj^{d}
Item paid for a deale bord	xij^{d}
Item paid for mending a key of the church	iiij^{d}
Item paid to Morley for whitening the gallery and church portch	ij^{s}
a doore in St Johns Chappel[47]	
Item paid to one Cadle a Carpenter for making of a dore in St Jo[hns] Chappell	xviij^{d}
Item paid for half a hundred of spykes	v^{d}
Item paid for a payr of hok & hinges	xiiij^{d}
Item paid for lock & a key	xviij^{d}
Item paid for a newe bridge to lock for the church dore	iiij^{d}
Item paid to the Sheriff for Langcable	iij^{s}
Item paid to Edw Tyngam mason[48]	xx^{s}
Item paid the 16 Sep[tember] for tyles to mend the church that the wind stript	vj^{s} vj^{d}
Item paid for lathes and lath nailes	iij^{s} x^{d}
Item paid for bringing the tyles	vj^{d}
Item paid for Edw Tyngham 16 of Sep[tember].	iiij^{li}
Item paid for Wexforde bords to mende the Church ewsings	viij^{d}

Item paid to a plasterer for mending the belfry & plasteringe the dormer wyndoes with lathes, heare & lyme	iiij^{s}
[f. 53v] [Item paid for] two Tylers for fowre daies [work] upon the church at 18^{d} p[er] die[m]	xij^{s}
[Item] paid to laborer for the like tyme	iij^{s}
Item paid for 7 sacks of lyme at 9^{d}	v^{s} iij^{d}
Item paid for a roole of water	j^{d}
Item paid for single spykes	iij^{d}
Item paid to three laborers for carrying of Rubbish & cleaning the Church	ij^{s}
Item paid more for nayles	ij^{d}
Item paid to Edw Tyngam 24 Sep[tember].	xl^{s}
Item paid more to a glasier for mending the wyndowes and leading them that were broken by the wynde	vj^{s} j^{d}
making ye portch doore[49]	
Item paid to one Robt Seaghor Mr Tyngams man to sett him on work 1 Octo[ber] upon the portch and to buy lyme	xviij^{s}
Item paid to Edw Tyngam the same day	xx^{s}
Item paid for two sacks of lyme to supply the work for Mr Tyngam 3 Oct[ober]	xviij^{s}
Item paid for paveing the Chancel & glasing of the same.	xiiij^{s} viij^{s}
Item paid for caryage of Rubbish in vestry	xviij^{d}
Item paid for washinge the Church lynnen	ij^{s}
Item paid for a hundred and a half of great nailes to sett on the hinges of the portch dore	ix^{d}
Item paid more for great nailes in & about the church	ij^{s} vij^{d}
Item paid for Candles	j^{d}
Item paid to three Carpenters for a daies work and a half in the church	vj^{s} ix^{d}
Item paid for Great spykes & syngle bord nailes	xix^{d}
Item paid for lock & a key for the portch	ij^{s} vj^{d}
Item paid for fyve sacks of lyme & a bagg of roch lyme & a barr of of heyre	v^{s} ij^{d}
Item paid for j^{li} & ½ of lyme & nailes to sett upon the portch dore	iij^{s} ix^{d}
[f. 54] Item paid to Bar Jurdan for 3 Communions of breade & wine 13 Octo[ber]	ij^{s} vj^{d}
Item paid for glasse that the madwoman brak	ij^{s} ij^{d}
Item paid to Mr Plunkett for stones for the portch	vij^{s}
Item paid for 4 sacks of lyme 26 Octo[ber]	ij^{s}
Item paid to one Walshe a Mason by Mr Plunketts direction for Tyngam & for lyme	x^{s}
Item paid for 2 Ridge tyles	ij^{s} iiij^{d}
Item paid for Mr Banysters man for two dayes worke & for making two formes	iiij^{s}

Item paid to a mason for work done at the portch the 14 No[vember] xviij^{s}

Item paid more for red tyles & lath nailes vj^{d}

Item paid to a laborer that wrought there x^{d}

paving stones within & without ye porch[50]

Item paid to one Lee for paving stones laide within & without the portch 17 No[vember] xxij^{s}

Item paid for Paving before the portch xij^{d}

Item paid for 3 sacks of lyme & heyre to plaster within the portch 18 Nov[ember] ij^{s} vj^{d}

Item paid to a laborer vj^{d}

Item paid for Water j^{d}

Item paid for 4 foot of hewd stone for portch xx^{d}

Item paid to Edw Tyngam p[er] his wyef 19 No[vember]. xl^{s}

Item paid to Morleys man for a daies work to plaster the inside of the portch and to a laborer ij^{s} ij^{d}

Item paid for latch for the work also iij^{d}

Item paid to a glasier for mending the glasse wyndoe over the portch the 22 Novem[ber] iiij^{s}

Item paid for 6 bunches of lathes for the portch ij^{s}

Item ½ M of lath nayles viij^{d}

Item paid to a plasterer for ½ a daye ix^{d}

Item paid to a laborer vj^{d}

Item paid to two Carman that brought hewde stones for Tyngham 24 No[vember] iiij^{s} vj^{d}

Item paid for a plank to mend a dore vj^{d}

Item paid for nailes to mend the seat in the portch & the pulpitt iij^{d}

Item paid to a Carpenter for a daye ix^{d}

[f. 54v] Item paid more for heyre for the porch vj^{d}

Porch and vestry[51]

Item paid to Morleys man for plastering three daies & a laborer the like tyme for the porch and old vestry. vj^{s} ix^{d}

Item paid for 3 sacks lyme 24 Oc[to]b[er] xviij^{d}

Item paid for a 100 of spykes for the Carpenter to mende formes vj^{d}

Item paid to Bar Jurden for his stypend ending at Easter 1632 this 27 Octo[ber] xx^{s}

Item paid to a laborer that wrought with man that laid tyles in the Chappell iiij^{d}

Tiles for the chapel[52]

Item paid for ijc of smale tyles to make an end of the Chappell x^{s} viij^{d}

Item paid to one Curwen mason, 3 daies work in laying the tyles iiij^{s} vj^{d}

Item to a laborer for one day & a half xiij^{d} ob

Item paid for a sack of lyme vj^{d}

Item paid for 4 load sand	xij^{d}
Item paid for nailes to mende formes	ij^{d}
Item paid for Mr Banister for making roofe of the portch	xij^{s}
Item paid for stones to make up the side of the portch and for caryadge	x^{s}
Item paid to one Dillon by Mr Plunketts directions for 5 sacks of lyme 26 Octo[ber]	ij^{s} vj^{d}
Item for rynging on the gunpowder daye	ij^{s}
Item for j^{li} Candles	$iiij^{d}$
Item paid for 4 sacks of lyme for the portch and for paveing 8 Novem[ber]	ij^{s}
Item paid for 2 doble quarters for the portch	$viij^{d}$
Item paid for 4 loads of sand for the portch	xij^{d}
Item paid for a M of slates & for caryadge for the portch	xij^{s} $viij^{d}$
Item paid for a M of lathe nailes	x^{d}
Item paid to two masons for <two> {fower} daies & a half 18^{d} p[er] die	$xiij^{s}$ vj^{d}
Item paid to a laborer for 3 daies & a half both about the Church <dore> portch	ij^{s} $iiij^{d}$
Item paid for lath nailes for the portch	$iiij^{d}$
Item paid for bunch of laths	$viij^{d}$
[f. 55] Item paid for two hyllyars for two daies work for the portch	vj^{s}
Item paid to Mr Tyngam the 12 Decem[ber]	vj^{li}
Item paid for 6 sacks lyme 13 Decem[ber]	iij^{s}
Item paid for a seacoal blackinge & and a bar of heyre	iij^{s}
Item paid for a lock & a key & a staple for the portch in the church yarde	ij^{s} vj^{d}
Item paid to Mr Morley for 3 daies work at the portch 20 Dec[ember]	$iiij^{s}$ vj^{d}
Item paid to a laborer for two daies work	xvj^{d}
Item paid for a sack of lyme	vj^{d}
Item paid for holly and Ivy against Xpamas	iij^{s}
Item paid to Carpenter for putting in nailes into the Church dore	ix^{d}
Item paid to Bar Jorden for two Comunions in No[vember] & Ja[nuary]	ij^{s} vj^{d}
Item paid for Edw Tyngam the 4 ffeb	xl^{s}
Item paid to one Cantwell by Mr Plunketts direction for pollissing ye East windowe[53]	xx^{s}
Item paid to the bookbinder for mending a bible	vj^{d}
a stone laid in ye Chappell p[er] parish[54]	
Item paid for Mason laying a stone in the Chappell 26 March	vj^{d}
Item paid for 3 Roopes for the bells	v^{s} xj^{d}
Item paid for Ringinge on the Kyngs daye	ij^{s}

Item paid for Edw Tyngam the last March v^{li}
Item paid for extraordinaries as bread & wyne at one meteinge & for the Proctors paynes [blank]
Item paid for Bartoll Jorden for bread and wyne at severall tymes & nowe at Easter 1632 ix^{s} ix^{d}

Sum $xlij^{li}$ xix^{s} ij^{d} ob ster.

Wee have p[er]used and examined the accomptes of Mr Staughton & Mr Edmond Leadbeter late church wardens for one yeare ending at our Lady day 1632 & wee find that their remayneth dewe in the handes of Mr Leadbeter the some of vj^{s} & 4^{d} st which they have discharged them selves & so they kept nothing.

John Atherton, Prebend de St Johan
Wm Plunkett — Tho Evans
Robart Usher — Robert Cunigham

[f.55v] 3^{d} Aprill 1632
By the consent of the Prebend of St John thevangelist and manie of the parishioners of the same <is is this day> Mr Robert Barloe and Mr Jeremy Bowden are by them nominated and appoynted to be Churchwardens for this p[re]sent year foll[owing].

John Atherton, Prebend de St Johns.

Edm Leadbetter
Hen Ashburne
The marke of John \$ Stafford — Leonard Comford
George Plunkett
Jhon Turvyn — Law fullam
Thomas + Sampsons mark
Nicholas Dillon
Robert Cunigham
Richard Gallwey

It is likewise by consent of the {prebend &} parishioners agreed that Ald[erman] Evans, Mr Willm Plunkett, Mr Robt Usher and Mr Cunningham shall take the accompts of the late Church wardens upon Thursday next after Easter term or any two of them shall take the same & to give a discharge.[55]

This accompt is discharged on the other syd by the p[ar]ties nominated as appeareth[56]

It is further agreed the daie & yeare abovesaid that {Mr} Ald[erman] Evans, Mr Wm Plunkett & Edm Leadbetter & Mr Robt Usher, {Mr} ffran Dowd

{&} Mr Coleman, shall revewe the sesse at some conveynent tyme they shall appoynt betwene this and Whitsonday next [f.56] and to alter in such wyse as they shall think fytt of.

John Atherton, Prebend de St Johns
Hen Ashburne
Robart Barlow
Jeremy Bowden
John \$ Staffords mark
Nicholas Dillon
George Plunkett
Richard Gallwey
Robert Cunigham
Law ffullan

[f. 56v] vij^{o} Aprill 1632
fforasmuch as it appeareth that there wilbe dewe to Edmond Tingam, Mason, wages he hathe fynished the East end at St Johns Church according to his Covenant, besydes such moneys as Mr Leadbetter late Churchwarden hath payd him being xxvij^{li} st the some of twentie & five poundes st which wee order & think fitt to be payed by the nowe Churchwardens out of such Rent & arreares of Rent & other dewties Causalties as are anywaye dewe or to be dewe to the said Church.

John Atherton, Prebend de St Johan
Robart Barlow
Tho Evans
Wm Plunkett
Robart Ussher
Jeremy Bowden
Robert Cunigham
Edm. Leadbetter

xiij^{o} May 1633
M[emoran]d[um] there is payed unto me Willm Plunkett Esq on the behalf of the said Tyngame the some of ten poundes & ten <pounde> shilings st by the hande of Mr Barlow and Mr Bowden, Churchwardens in p[ar]t of the said xxv^{li} st & nyne pounds payd to the said Tyngam him self as appear by their accompt.

Wm Plunkett
Jo Puerfoy

[f. 57] vij^{o} April 1632
Forasmuch as we the parishioners of St Johns Church doe concieve and doubt not to p[ro]ve by good wittnesses that the ye {inhabitants dwelling in}Copp[er] Alley is of the parish of St Johns & ought to repayere to said Church to Devyne Service & to paye all dewties dewe to the parson of the said Church. Wee therefore pray & authorise Mr Atherton to commence suit for the said right of our parish against Sr Edward Bagshowe, kt, & such other

of the inhabitance of <the> Copp[er] Alley as he shall thinke fitt at the Cost & charges of the said parish.

John Atherton, Prebend de St Johan	
Robart Barlow	Tho Evans
Jeremy Bowden	Wm Plunkett
	Robart Ussher
	Robert Cunigham
	Edm Leadbetter
	Jacob Newman

[f. 57v] vijth Aprill 1632

Whereas there was heretofore an intention to buyld a howse for the mynyster of this parish by the parishioners of the same. Nowe forasmuch as by reason of dyvers ympediments the said good work could not be p[er]fected according to their intention and that such p[ro]vision of tymber & stones etc as thereunto was allotted hath bene converted unto pyos uses about the said Church. It is nowe resolved that the Mynister in tyme to come maye be furnished of a convenient habitation that such howse within <the> {his} appurtennces of the Church land <as and>. As Mr Atherton nowe Prebend of St Johns <nowe> thinketh fitt of shalbe ymedyath conveyed unto the Mynister & his successors by Lease for a thousand yeares or otherwise in such wyse as Counsall shall devise, such a conveyance to be p[er]fected upon request of the mynister by the Churchwardens, allwayes reserving the auncient rent to the Church which nowe is paide. The said estate to begin upon determination of such estate as is now in being.[57]

John Atherton, Prebend de St Johan	
Robart Barlow	Wm Ryves
Jeremy Bowden	Tho Evans
Ja Browne	Wm Plunkett
	Edm Leadbetter
	Robart Ussher
	Jerom Alexander
	Jacob Newman

[f. 58] 1632

Hereafter ffolloweth the Cesse on the parishioners of St Johns Evangelists Dublin, due to the Parson of the saide Parish according to the Acte of State. Cessed & taxed by us whose names are hereunderwritten being authorized by the whole consent of the Parish the vijth daye of Apr[il]: 1632.

ffyshamble street

Robt Usher, merchaunt	x^{s}
Darby Lawlor and his Inmates	xiij^{s} iiij^{d}
Phyllyppe Phylpott, victualer	vj^{s}
John Lyngarde	viij^{s}

Wm Conlan, baker	viij^{s}
Murtaghe Kynge, gent	vj^{s}
Robt Clony, Channler	xij^{s}
Robt Barloe	x^{s}
Nicholas Browne, baker & Inmates	x^{s}
The Lo[rd] Mounte Norris	xx^{s}
John Trewe	viij^{s}
Murtagh Hewes, taylor	vj^{s}
John Gylman, vict[uale]r	vj^{s}
The Wydoe Hunter, baker	viij^{s}
John Burren, water bayly	viij^{s}
Peter Paise for Mr ffords howse	xiij^{s} iiij^{d}
<Thomas> {James} Skelton and his Inmates	viij^{s}
Wydoe Jewett & her Inmates	vj^{s}
The Wydoe Morgan & her Inmates	x^{s}
George Plunckett for howse & seller	xij^{s}
Sr Wm Reves, kt, the K[ings] Attorney	xx^{s}
John Murren	viij^{s}
Wm Isacke & his Inmates	vj^{s}
Sr Dudley Norton, kt.	xvj^{s}
John Gavan & his Inmates	vj^{s}
Wydoe Rabone & her Inmates	xij^{s}
Wydoe Morris	ij^{s}
Wm Smythe	viij^{s}
[f. 58v] Wm Eglin	x^{s}
Mr Graves his howse and stable	viij^{s}
The next howse wherin Jeffrey Bowelles	<vij> iiij^{s}
Edmunde Leadbetter, gent	x^{s}
Wydoe Mahery, baker	viij^{s}
Ald[erman] Wigett for his howse & seller	xvj^{s}
Robert Dutton	x^{s}
Thomas Sampson	iiij^{s}
John Stafforde, taylor	iiij^{s}
Rycharde Butterly & his Inmates	x^{s}
Rycharde Lutterell, gent	viij^{s}
James Bedloe, sergant	vij^{s}
James Osborne, barbor surgeon	v^{s}
Thomas Gunter	v^{s}
Wm Plunkett, Esquire	xiij^{s} iiij^{s}
Christian Hogan, goldsmythe	vj^{s}
Mr Ushers warehowse	iiij^{s}

St Johns lane

John Warren, taylor	iiij^{s}
Patrycke Mayle	iiij^{s}
Mr Malones seller called the half moone	x^{s}
The sellar called Hell	x^{s}
Mr Coleman for the Red Stagge	x^{s}
Mr Mapas for the Red Lyon	x^{s}

Corkhill

Robt Coffy, goldsmyth	vj^{s}
Thomas Jacob, baker	x^{s}
Christopher Coleman for howse & seller	xv^{s}
Wydoe Reyly	ij^{s}
Wydoe Jaques	viij^{s}
Mr Goldinge for howse seller & teniscourt	xvj^{s}
Edwarde Browne	vj^{s}

Winetavern street.

Wydoe Chevers for howse & sellers	xv^{s}
Wydoe Browne	x^{s}
Wydoe Lee	viij^{s}
Richard St Johns and the Widoe Rownsell	x^{s}
Roger Garlande for Westons seller	x^{s}
[f. 59] Ald[erman] Dowde for howse and seller	x^{s}
Mr ffitz Garrett for the starr seller	iiij^{s}
Rychard ffitz Symonds for house & seller	xiij^{s} iiij^{s}
John Lawles	ij^{s}
Barnaby Enos, cooke	iiij^{s}
Rycharde English, baker	iiij^{s}
Wydoe Brasbridge	iiij^{s}
James Bedloe, baker	viij^{s}
Wydoe Vyalls daughters	vj^{s}
Patricke Whyte, baker	viij^{s}
Thomas Dungan for his howse & Inmates	x^{s}
Wydoe Worrall	vj^{s}
Walter Conrann showmaker	viij^{s}
Rycharde Gallwaye	iiij^{s}
Thomas ffleminge, merchaunt	xij^{s}
Albone Leverett	x^{s}
Mr Whyt	xvj^{s}
Patryck Butler	viij^{s}
Robte Savell, Esq	xij^{s}
[blank] Jackson for his shoppe	iiij^{s}
John Newel, barbor	xij^{s}
Richard Browne, taylor	iiij^{s}

Thomas Dugan for his owne howse	xij^{s}
John Browkes, Counselor & his Inmates	x^{s}
The Crane for the Crane	viij^{s}
John Browne	x^{s}
Willm Talbott, merchaunt	viij^{s}
John Turvyn	vj^{s}
Mr ffrancis Dowde, merchaunt	xv^{s}
John Weston, merchaunt	xv^{s}
Jeremy Woodward	vj^{s}
Walter ffytz Garrett	iiij^{s}
The howse wherein Thomas Akins and Mychaell the Joyner dwelt in	iiij^{s}
Stephen Garnon for howse and teniscourt	x^{s}
[blank] Sutton for the black boy	vj^{s}
The seller of the black boye	x^{s}
[f. 59v] James Browne, gent	xiij^{s} iiij^{d}
John Harris and Robt Dollard	x^{s}
Wydoe Russells howse	iiij^{s}
Patryck Savedge, taylor	iiij^{s}
The Royall Exchange & seller	xvj^{s}
John Butcher	viij^{s}
Wydoe Lynehan	iiij^{s}
Peirse Keatinge, taylor	viij^{s}
Wydoe Nugent	x^{s}
Rosemary Lane	
Peter Dyllon for the golden lyon	x^{s}
Annestace Lynam, wydoe	ij^{s}
Thomas Baghe	ij^{s}
John Iremonger	ij^{s}
Wood Key	
Thomas Roche, Showmaker	vj^{s}
Thomas Marrett, gent	vj^{s}
Robt Cuningham, gent	viij^{s}
Rychard ffitz Symonds for Ivan Davis his sellar	iiij^{s}
John Anderson and his ten[ant]	viij^{s}
John Mungumbery	vj^{s}
[blank] Thompson	x^{s}
John Collyns	x^{s}
John Walker	xiij^{s} iiij^{d}
James Donnell	vj^{s}
Rychard Luttrell, baker	x^{s}
Domynick Devoroxe	iiij^{s}
Edmunde Sprynge	viij^{s}
Thomas Plastoe for p[ar]t of his howse and seller	x^{s}

Benjamin Rob[er]ts for the other p[ar]t of that howse	vj^{s}
Martyn the bruer	vj^{s}
Nycholas Dyllon	vj^{s}
Willm Boyd	x^{s}
Heughe Lupe & his Inmates	vj^{s}
Andrewe Garrett	ij^{s}
[f. 60] Thomas Begge and his Inmates	x^{s}
John Union and Martyn Watts	iiij^{s}
Mychaell Pursell shoppe	ij^{s}
The Wydoe Pursell	iiij^{s}
Mr Ald[erman] Evans	xiij^{s} iiij^{d}
Christopher Harryson	vj^{s}
Rychard fframe	iiij^{s}
Andrewe Reade	v^{s}
George Teadie	viij^{s}
Jane Ashbrooke	iiij^{s}
Jeremy Sympson	iiij^{s}
John Barry, glasier	ij^{s}
ffrancis Clark	nil
Henry Ashburne	vj^{s}
Jeffrey Bowthe	iiij^{s}
Jeremy Bowden	vj^{s}
Josephe Sampson	iiij^{s}
Sr Mathewe Derensye, kt.	xx^{s}
Mrs Samon	x^{s}
The howse wherein Mr Staughton dwelt when the p[ar]son doth not dwell there	xij^{s}
The Wydoe Hanmer & her tenannts	xv^{s}
James Goodman, Counselor at lawe	xv^{s}
Patrycke the cook	iiij^{s}
George Bentley for Mr Dermotts howse and stable	xiij^{s}
{Sr Willm Ryves, kt	xx^{s} st}
Randolphe Aldersey, Esquier	xij^{s}
Thomas Lork, Pursyvaunt	x^{s}
Mr Jacob Newman	xx^{s}
The howse wherin Sr Wm Reves latelie dwelt in	xx^{s}
Jeremy Alexander, Counselor at lawe	xv^{s}
James Donnaloe, Counselor at lawe	vj^{s}
Edward Blennerhassett	vj^{s}
[f. 60v]Wyddoe Carter	viij^{s}
Mr John Mottershed & the shop	x^{s}
Mr Rychard Prudford	x^{s}

Wm Plunkett Tho Evans
Edm Leadbetter
Robert Usher

[f. 61] xxvij° Aprill 1632
Memorandum this day the parson & parishioners meat concerning a peticion p[re]ferred by Mr Richard Eustace Late Church warden beinge in arreare upon his accompte.[58] It is ordred with Consent of the said parson and parishioners & of the said Richard Eustace that he shall paye to the use of the said Church the some of three pounds st, viz. xx^{s} st in hand & xx^{s} st at Mich[ael]mas next & the other xx^{s} st at Easter next 1633 in full satisfaction of all arrears dewe on his accompt of ye churchwardens.

With Consente Rich Eustace

John Atherton, Prebend de St Johan
Jeremy Bowden
Tho Evans
Wm Plunkett Ric Wigget
Randall Aldersey
Robart Barlow
Robert Usher
per me Edm Leadbetter

10 ^{day} May 1632
Received of Richard Eustace the som of twentie shillinges starlen beeing the first paymentt of ye sumes a bove mencened wee say reacevid by us.

Robert Barlow
Jeremy Bowden

Received by me Thomas Donegan for arrears to St Johns Church of Richard Eustace the some of forty sh[illings] ster. 7th of May 1637.

[f. 61v] 14th March 1632
Received of Mr Jeremy Bowden one of the Church wardens of this parish to the summe of thre score pounds ster according to severall acquittances given him for the some which is for one yeares paym[en]t due unto mee from the parishioners of this parish ending at Christmas last. I say received lx^{li} ster.

John Atherton, Prebend de St Johan.

Wittnes herof
Wm Plunkett
Ja Browne

[f. 62] Ultimo April 1633
Memorandum the parson & parishioners being assembled this day have chosen Mr Jeremy Boyden & Mr Willm Smyth to be churchwardens for this whole year next ensuing & the old churchwardens is to pass their accompts uppon Munday next at two of the Clock in the afternone & Mr Willm Plunkett, Mr James Browne & Mr Edmund Leadbeter to be Auditors of the accompts or any two of them.

John Atherton, Prebend de St Johan
Ric Wiggett
Ja Donellan
Jerom Alexander
Robert Dutton
Henry Ashbourn
Tho Larke

[f. 62v blank]
[f. 63] A true note of such monies as Robert Barlowe & Jeremy Bowden Proctors of St Johns the Evangelist have received of the Revenues & burialls there for theire year begining at Easter 1632 & ending at Easter 1633 vizt.

Rents	li s d
Mr Ford for two yeres Rent ending at Mich[aelm]as last	3.6.8 ster.
Mr Anderson for one yere	2.0.0.
Mr Smith for arrears ending at Easter 1632	5.0.0.
Mr Eustace for arrears	1.0.0.
Mr Smith for halfe a yeres ending at Mich[aelm]as last	16.8.
Mr Conran for one yere ending at Mich[aelm]as last	3.6.8.
Amy Smooth for one yere ending at Mich[aelm]as last	15.0.
The Master of the Taylors	1.0.0.
Robucke the Butcher at Mich[aelm]as	1.5.0.
The widow Hunter at Mich[aelm]as	7.6.
Mr Alderman Usher at Mich[aelm]as	2.6.8.
The Lord of Cork at Mich[aelm]as	1.6.3.
Sir Tade Duffe, knt	1.0.0.
Burials	
ffor one Child of Mr Robert Elfin	3.4.
Mr <child> Darby Lawlers	5.0.
A child of John Harris	3.4.
A Child of Mr Wm Smiths	3.4.
ffor Hamlet Sankey	6.8.
A child of Mr Savilles	3.4.
A child of Mr Tho Wilsons	3.4.

Mr Alderman <wch> Evans	6.8.
Mrs Anne Vien	6.8.
The wife of John Collins	6.8.
A child of Robt Dunns	3.0.
A daughter of Mr Elfins	3.4.
A child of Mr Goldings	3.4.

Benevolence money received towards the rep[ai]ring of the Church

Imprimis Sir Wm Ryves, knt	1.0.0. ster
of Sir Jas Ware the elder, knt. dec[eased]	1.0.0.
of Alderm[an] Evans	1.0.0.
of Sir Mathew Derensey, knt.	10.0.
of Mr Alexander	1.0.0.
of Mr Donnellan	11.0.
of Mr James Browne	10.0.
of Tho Wilson, gent	13.4.
of Arland Usher, gent	5.0.
of Robt Clony	5.0.
of Mr Moris Smith	10.0.
of Mr Jo Stoughton	5.0.
Item p[ai]d by Mr Plunket to make this even	8.

Sum 7.10.0. ster
Sum totall received is 33.18.5.

[f. 63v] A true note of Mr Barlow & Mr Bowdens disbursements in theire year

	li. s. d.
Paid to Thomas Hickes, Tiler	15.0.
To Mr Gorman the smith for the ironwork for ye fane	10.0.
To Mr Cotton for gilding the fane	7.6.
To the mason that viewed Mr Tinghams worke	4.6.
ffor a staple for the Church dore	4.
To Bartholomew Jordain for his whole yeres means	2.0.0.
To Mr Tingham towards the East end of the Church	9.0.0.
To the Smith for a Clapp[er] for the litle bell a paire of hinches for the belfry doore	1.6.
To Mr Sanders the Plumer for led, Sander, workmanship & fire.	19.0.
To Hilliers & Labourers, for Lime, sand & workmanship	13.6.
To Barthol Jordaine for Turne-pillars & Railes which was left unpaid in Mr Ledbetters accompt	15.0.
To the Hillier for one daies worke	1.0.

To the Sexton for Ringing on the gun-powder Treas[on] day	2.0.
ffor holly & Rushes on Christmas day	2.6.
ffor Sand & paveing in St Johns Lane	1.5.10.
ffor John Hustes for 2 bers & Covers	1.0.0.
ffor Ringing on the Kings day	2.0.
ffor 19 foote of paveing at the Church dore	6.4.
ffor carying of Rubbish out of the Churchyard	1.8.
To a Labourer that worked with the paver	6.
ffor entring the p[re]sentm[en]t in the Archdeacons Courte	2.4.
ffor Longable	3.0.
ffor mendeing the Comunion table	3.0.
ffor washeing of the Church Linnen	2.6.
ffor mendeing the locks of the Chest & Church dore	8.
ffor 4 foote of glasse	2.0.
ffor mendeing of the broaken formes & seates	3.4.
ffor blackeing and littorring the bucketts	4.0.
ffor collouring the East doore	6.0.
ffor 7 deale boords	8.2.
To Mr Cotten for East gallery	10.0.
ffor 6 Sparrs	1.6.
ffor putting Seates in the Chauncell when The Lord Primate preached	4.0.
ffor breade & wine at 13 severall Comunions	1.3.1
ffor severall meeteings	1.6.6.
To Tingham paied by Mr Barlow	3.0.0.
More to Tingham out of the benevolence money	7.10.0
To the poore	2.
Total disbursements	£33.18.5

We have exa[mi]ned this accompt & finde that the receipts & disbursements are equall & that the said Mr Barlow & Mr Bowden, being Churchwardens, have sufficiently acquitted themselves. Witnes our handes this 13th May 1633.

John Atherton, Prebend   Wm Plunkett
Edm Leadbetter

[f. 64] 24 March 1633
Received of Mr Jeremy Bowden, one of the Churchwardens of this parish, the sume of threescore pounds ster according to severall acquittances given him for the sume which sume is for one years paym[en]t due unto mee from the parishioners of this parish at Christmas Last I say received 60li ster.

John Atherton, Prebend de St Johan

[f. 64v blank]

[f. 65] xvijo Aprill 1634
Memorandum the parson & parishioners have chosen Mr Willm Smyth & Mr Jeremy <Boyde> Sympson to be churchwardens for this next yeare ensuing. And the old church[wardens] is to pass their accompts uppon this day senigst & Mr Willm Plunkett, Mr Robt Usher & Mr Edmund Leadbeater to be Auditors of the Accompts or any two of them.

John Atherton, Prebend de St Johan
Wm Plunkett
Jermy Bowden
Jerom Alexander
Robert Usher
Robert Dutton
Edm Leadbetter
Robart Barton

M[emoran]d[um] It is ordered by the Consent of the parson & parishioners that Mr Alderman Wiggett, Willm Plunkett Esq, Mr James Browne, Mr ffrancis Dowde, Mr Edmond Leadbeater, Mr Jeremy Boyde, Mr Robt Usher, Mr Jo Trewe, Mr Henry Ashborne & Mr Willm Samon or any six of them to viewe and make the Cesse of the parsons dewties

John Atherton
Willm Smyth
Jeremy Simpson
Jerom Alexander

[f. 65v blank]

[f. 66] The accompt of Mr Jeremy Bowen and Mr William Smith Proctors of the parish of St Johns Dublin for the yeere begining at Easter 1633 & ended 1634.

Rents received

	li. s. d.
Imprimis of Mr Thomas Conran for one yeres rent of a house in ffishshamble streete ended at Mich[aelm]as 1633	3.6.8.
Item of Mr Mathew fforde for one yeres rent of a house in ffishamble streete ended at Mich[aelm]as 1633	1.13.4.
Item of Mr Alderman Usher for one yeres rent of a house in that streete ended the same time	2.6.8.
Item of the widow Hunter for one yeres rent of a house in the same streete ended the same time	7.6.
Item of the Master of the Taylors for one yere ended at Midsomer 1633	1.0.0.
Item of Mr Bath of Drumconragh for two yeeres rent of a house in Oxmanton ended at Mich[ael]mas 1633	6.0.

Item of Amy Smooth for one yeeres rent of a house there ended the same time	15.0.
Item of Mr Maurice Smith for one yeeres rent of a house there ended the same time	1.13.4.
Item of Mr Anderson for one yeere of a house there ended at the same time	2.0.0.
Item of Mr Robuck for one yeeres rent ended at Mich[alem]as 1633 of a house in St ffrancis streete	1.5.0.
Item of Earl of Cork for one yeeres Rent of a house in Castle streete ended at Mich[aelm]as 1633	1.6.3.
Item of Sir Thadee Duff, knt, for one yeres rent of a house upon the key ended at Mich[aelm]as	1.0.0.
	16.19.9.

Burials

John Dunne buriall	6.8.
Mr Manne	6.8.
Mr Montgomryes child	3.4.
Nil Mr Chievers child	3.4.[59]
Mr John Murren	6.8.
Mr Larkes child	3.4.
Mr Gilman	6.8.
Hugh Lux	6.8.
	1.16.8.
So all the mony received comes to	18.16.5.
	6.8.
	19.3.1.

Sum total xix^{li} iij^{s} j^{d} ster.[60]

[f. 66v] Money payd by the said Proctors in that yeare to the use of the Church	li s d
Imprimis to Mr Bar Jordan for his whole yeeres meanes	2.0.0.
ffor taking down the Bell	2.6.
ffor bringing it down to the Crane & weighing of it	8.
ffor carying of it to be cast	4.
ffor 2 formes	8.0.
To the bellfounder	5.17.0.
To a Smith for bew brasers of Iron & other work.	6.2.
To a Carpenter for fitting the bellstock to porters, for ropes & other necessaries	5.4.
ffor a paire of hinches for the Parsons pew-doore	8.

To the Shiriffe for Langable	3.0.
ffor morter & laying tiles	4.0.
ffor Holly, Ivy and rushes	2.6.
ffor paving in St Johns Lane	1.6.
To the hillier and for 3^{li} of lead	4.0.
ffor ringing on Kings daies	4.0.
ffor 2 yds. 1 qr. & ½ velvett	2.2.4.
ffor 3 ounces of Silke, q[uar]ter & halfe at 7 grotes the ounce	7.10.
ffor weaveing fringe & working tassells	2.2.
To the glasier	8.2.
ffor 14^{li} of feathers to fill the new & old Cushings	7.0.
ffor Linings for both the Cushings	3.6.
ffor a short ladder & mending the old	1.2.
To the p[ro]ctor at the Consistory Courte	5.0.
To the Sexton at St Owens[61]	6.
ffor 10 severall Comunions breade & wine	15.8.
At severall meetings	1.2.2.
ffor a loade of sand	3.
ffor a new wheele & brasers & other things necessary about the bells	9.3.
Two sacks of lime & 3 q[ua]rter hundred slates	1.10.
Lathes, slat nailes & pinnes	9.
ffor making the new & old Cushings	2.6.
ffor making the parsons deske	5.6.
To the hillier & his man	5.0.
ffor 13 ridging tiles for the dormant windos	3.2.
ffor 3 pair hinches & nailes	2.2.
ffor washing the Church linnen	2.6.
ffor 14^{li} iron for brasers for 2 bells at 5^{d} the pownd & for spikes & other worke	7.0.
ffor mending the pickaxe	1.6.
ffor collouring the bellstocks & brasers	1.6.
To the Plumer for 2^{li} ¾ of solder & worke	4.0.
4 ledges on the chest in the Gallery, a hook for the doore & hanging it	1.8.
iij^{li} 3^{s} iiij^{d} st for the ruffing[62]	
vij^{li} ix^{s} ix^{d} for repaires of the Bells this yeare[63]	
[f. 67] For Nails	2.
<for entering & p[er]fecting this accompt	2.0>
The totall disburs[ed] are	18.3.9.

S[u]m total xviij^{li} iij^{s} ix^{d} ster[64]

Wee have examined the accomptes of Mr Jeremey Boyden & Mr Willm Smyth, the late Church Wardens, for one yeare ending at Easter last & they have sufficiently acquitted them selves save onely they nowe stand indebted uppon this accompt the some of xix^{s} iiij^{d} st which is nowe payed over into the handes of the nowe Churchwardens. All which wee witnes being Auditors to this Accompt.

Wm Plunkett
Robert Usher
Edm Leadbetter

[f. 67v blank]

[f. 68] Hereafter followeth the Cesse on the parishioners of St Johns Evangelists due to the parson of the saide parish according to the act of the state. Cessed and taxed by us whose names are Subscribed authorized by the whole consent of the parishioners the fower and Twentyeth daie of Aprill Anno dm 1634.

Fishamble St

Robert Usher, merchant	x^{s}
Mr Robert Dunn his house and tenn[ant]s	xiij^{s} iiij^{d}
Phillippe Philpott, victualer	vj^{s}
Mr Huggard	viij^{s}
Willyam Conlon, Baker	viij^{s}
Mr Murtagh Kinge	vj^{s}
Robert Clony, Chandler	xij^{s}
Robert Barlow, gent	x^{s}
Mr Browne, Baker and his Inmates	viij^{s}
Morris Eustace, Esq	xx^{s}
John Trew	vj^{s}
Turlow Hughes, Taylor	vj^{s}
Widdowe Gilman	iiij^{s}
Patrick Russell	viij^{s}
Mr Burrame, water baily	x^{s}
Mr Drewes	xiij^{s} <iiij^{d}>
Mr Skelton and his Inmates	viij^{s}
Thomas Quine & his Inmates	vj^{s}
Edward Marginer and his Inmates	x^{s}
Mr Georg Plunkett his house	xij^{s}
Willyam Vasquyle	xx^{s}
[blank] Rayneer	viij^{s}
Georg Teder, Taylor and his Inmates	vj^{s}
Sir Dudley Norton knight	xvj^{s}
Laurence Robinson	vj^{s}
Willyam Stevens	ij^{s}
Widdowe Rabone & her Inmates	xij^{s}

Johan Morris	ij^{s}
Mr John Pitte	viij^{s}
Mr Willyam Eglin	x^{s}
Widdowe Hardinge	viij^{s}
Arthur Chad	iiij^{s}
Mr Edmond Leadbeater	x^{s}
Patricke Cleere	viij^{s}
Mr Wiggett his house and seller	x^{s}
Mr Robert Dutton	x^{s}
Thomas Sampson	iiij^{s}
Mr John Stafford	iiij^{s}
[f. 68v]Richard Butterby and his Inmates	x^{s}
Widdowe Luttrill	viij^{s}
Mr James Bedlowe	vij^{s}
Mr James Osborne	iiij^{s}
Mr Thomas Gunter	v^{s}
William Plunkett, Esquire	xiij^{s} iiij^{d}
Mr Christian Hogan	vj^{s}
Mr Kempte	viij^{s}
Mr Edward Kerney for p[ar]te of Kempes howse	iiij^{s}
St Johns Lane	
John Warren, Taylor	iiij^{s}
Patrick Male, <Taylor> gent	iiij^{s}
Mr Malons seller calle the halfe moone	x^{s}
John Dockett	viij^{s}
Mr Coleman for the Redd Stag	viij^{s}
Mr Patrick Dowd, redd Lyon	vj^{s}
Mr Coffy, Goldsmyth	vj^{s}
Thomas Jacob, baker	x^{s}
Mr Coleman for his howse and seller	xij^{s}
Widdow Reyle	ij^{s}
Symon Cardiffe	x^{s}
Mr Goldinge his howse, seller & Teniscourt	xij^{s}
Edward Browne	<xj^{s}> vj^{s}
Wine Tavern Streete	
Widdowe Chever her howse and seller	xv^{s}
Widdowe Browne	<xj^{s}> x^{s}
Widdowe Bathowse	viij^{s}
Mr St John and his tenen[ts]	x^{s}
Mr Roger Garlon for Weston seller at black boy	x^{s}
Mr Alderman Dowd his howse & seller	vj^{s}
ffitz Garrold for the Starr Seller	iiij^{s}
Patricke Warren for his howse and Seller	xiij^{s} iiij^{d}

John Lawlis, Baker	ij^{s}
Barnabey Annis, Cooke	iiij^{s}
Richard English, Baker	iiij^{s}
Widdowe Brasbrige	iiij^{s}
James Bedlowe, baker	vj^{s}
Widdowe Vials daughter	vj^{s}
Patricke White, baker	viij^{s}
Robt Wiggett, Shoemaker	viij^{s}
Thomas Dungan house to be let	viij^{s}
James Tully, Apothegary	vj^{s}
Water Conran, Shoemaker	viij^{s}
Mathew Browne	vj^{s}
Mr Thomas ffleamin, merchant	xij^{s}
Mr Leoverit	x^{s}
Mr White and his Tennant Mr March	xvj^{s}
Patrick Butler	viij^{s}
Mr Robert Savill	xij^{s}
[f. 69] Mr Willyam Briggis his shop	iiij^{s}
Mrs Dalle	xij^{s}
Mr Browne, Taylor	iiij^{s}
Mr Dungas	xij^{s}
Mr Brookes and his Tenantes	x^{s}
Mr Browne for the Crane	vj^{s}
Mr Wraye	x^{s}
Widdowe Talbott	viij^{s}
Mr Georg Lambert	viijs
Mr Dowd, merchant	xiij^{s} iiij^{d}
Mr Patricke Moore & James Carvane, baker	xv^{s}
Jeremy Woodworth	vj^{s}
Walter ffitz Gerald	iiij^{s}
The next little howse	iiij^{s}
The next unto yt	iiij^{s}
Mr Stephen Garlan	x^{s}
Mr Sutton for the black boy	vj^{s}
The Seller of the black boy	x^{s}
James Browne, gent	xiij^{s} iiij^{s}
Mr Robt Dallard	v^{s}
Mr Robt Dollart {tenent}	v^{s}
Edmond Hegges	vj^{s}
Patrick Savage, Taylor	iiij^{s}
The royal exchange and seller	xvj^{s}
Mr Willyam Browne	iiij^{s}
Mr John Butcher	viij^{s}

Mr Keatinge, Taylor	viij^{s}
Widdowe Newgent	x^{s}
Rosemary Lane	
Mr John Chevers for the golden Lyon	x^{s}
Anstar Lyames, widdowe	ij^{s}
Thomas Bagges	ij^{s}
Robert Jackson, Chaundeler	ij^{s}
Wood Key	
Robert Dee, Shoemaker	vj^{s}
Margarett Wilkinson	vj^{s}
Robert Cuningham	viij^{s}
Samuell Samesons	iiij^{s}
Mrs Edwards	viij^{s}
John Mungumery	vj^{s}
Mr Leonard Tompson	x^{s}
Mr Thomas the vintner	x^{s}
Obett Williams	xiij^{s} iiij^{s}
John ffitz Symond	vj^{s}
Richard Luttrill, Baker	viij^{s}
John Harris	iiij^{s}
Mr Browne	viij^{s}
[f. 69v] Mr Valentyne Waight	x^{s}
Mr Benjamin Roberts	vj^{s}
Mr Martyn the Brewer	vj^{s}
Nicholas Dillon, merchant	vj^{s}
Willyam Boy	x^{s}
The Widdowe L[upe] & Inmates	iiij^{s}
Robert Prentize with the gate	ij^{s}
The Widdowe Beging and her Inmates	viij^{s}
John Vnyon and Martyn Watt	iiij^{s}
Michaell Purcell his shopp	iiij^{s}
Widdowe Purcell	ij^{s}
Mr Willyam Smyth	xij^{s}
Christopher Harrison	vj^{s}
<Mr Richard ffrancis his howse	iiij^{s}>
Andrew Reade	v^{s}
Henry Jordan & his tennants	viij^{s}
Adam Madrell	iiij^{s}
Mr Jeremy Sympson	vj^{s}
ffrancis Clarke	nil
John Barry, glazier	ij^{s}
Henry Ashbarne	vj^{s}
Stephen Bowers	iiij^{s}

Mr Jeremy Bowden	vj^{s}
Joseph Sampson	iiij^{s}
Sir Mathew Dernisie, Kt	xx^{s}
Mr Sammon	x^{s}
Mr Atherton his house when he lives {not there}	xij^{s}
Mr Lewys Jones	ij^{s}
Widdowe Hanmore and her Tenants	xv^{s}
James Goodman, Esquire that was	xij^{s}
Patricke Connor, Cooke	iiij^{s}
Mr George Blundell	viij^{s}
Mr Rayner his stable	vij^{s}
Mr Bentley his stable	vj^{s}
Mr Gilberts stable	vj^{s}
Mr Randall Aldersie	xij^{s}
Mr Thomas Larke	x^{s}
Sir Willm Rives, Kt, the kings Attorney gen[er]all	xx^{s}
Mr Jacob Newman	xx^{s}
Mr Lowther and Mr Sanbridge	xx^{s}
Mr Jeremy Alexander	xv^{s}
Mr James Dannellan	xv^{s}
Edward Blennerhassett	vj^{s}
Mr Francis Kinge	2^{s} [65]
[f. 70] Mr Greens	viij^{s}
Mr George Proudfoot his howse	x^{s}
John Mattersett	x^{s}
Mr [blank]	

Wm Plunkett

Ric Wiggett
Robart Ussher
Edm Leadbetter
Jeremy Bowden

[f. 70v] octavo May 1634

The choise of 2 bedles & their wages

M[emorandum] that the parishioners of the parish of St Johns the Evangelist Dublin have assembled themselves togeather by vertue of a warrant to them directed from the right worthy Robert Dixon nowe Maior of the said Cittie of Dublin, and have made choyse of Jeffrey Walsh and Morris Bray to execute the office of Beadles within the said Parish untill the ffyve & Twentith day of Aprill nexte.[66] And we have agread for to pay them for the Execucon of the said office the some of fortie shillings sterl a peece. And the said Beadles is to be p[resen]tly furnished with Coatte & staves for which the Churchwardens & overseers of the poore are to have allowance out of ther wages.

Willm Smith & Jeremy Simpson, Guardians
Ric Wiggett   Wm Plunkett
Robart Ussher
Edm Leadbetter

xxvij° Martij 1635
Receaved the day and yeare abovesaid of Willm Smyth and Jeremy Sympson Churchwardens of the parish of St John the some of Threscore poundes ster English money according to several acquittances given them for the same, which said some is for one whole yeres payment due unto mee from the parishioners of the said parish Ending at Christmas last past. I saie received sixtye poundes ster 60li

John Atherton

[f. 71] 25 Aprillis 1634
By the Maior, Recorder and Aldermen at their ffrydaie meetinge fforasmuch as it appeareth that the number of poore within this Citty is likelie everie daie to encrease unlesse some p[re]sent order be to prevent yt and that an order of state hath alreadie bene published to that purpose for the better puttinge of that order or act of State into execucon it is ordered that the Churchwardens of the sevrall parishes within the libertyes of this Citty within one fortnight after the date of this order, notice hereof beinge given unto them shall assemble the parishioners of the sevrall parishes and Choose and elect some one inhabitant or more as they or the greatest number of such parishioners as shall meet together shall thinke fitt to oversee and governe the poore and beggers within the parishe and to put in execution the said Act of State that none be suffered to begg within the said parishe wherein he is Beadle but such as are licensed by the lawes of the kingdome or the Act of State. And if the saide Churchwardens shall faile to assemble the saide parishioners within the tyme afforesaide or the saide Churchwardens and parishioners shall fayle to elect a Beadle according to this Order that then the said churchwardens and parishioners that soe make defaulte shall forfeite for their defaulte the ffyne of ffive poundes English to be levyed by distresse of theire goods by warrant from the Mayor or Recorder, or eyther of them, for the use of the poore, provided alwaies that this Order shall not anie waies give libertie to the constables of anie wards to neglect his office but if that he be carelesse or negligent in his office hee shall be punished accordinge to the lawes of the lande and the saide Act of State and the Beadle to be mayntayned at the chardge of the parishe.

And it is further ordered tht if anie within this citty shall demise or lett anie house, chamber or shopp to anie tenaunt, inmait or gueste that if such Tenaunt, inmate or gueste shall by himself, his wife or children begg or demande almes within the saide citty the saide inhabitantes that shall make such demise shall mayntaine and keep at his proper Coste and Chardges everie such tenaunt, inmate or gueste upon the paine of ffive pounds to be levyd of theire Goods by distresse in manner aforesaid. This Order to continewe for a Twelvemonth and soe to be altered or continwed as shall be thought fitt.

To the Churchwardens of St Johns parish

[f. 71v blank]

[f.72] Ultimo Martij 1635
Memorand[um] that the parson & parishioners of St John the Evangelist Dublin have chosen Mr Symon Kerdiff and Mr Thomas Dongan to be Churchwardens for this next yeare ensuing. And the old Churchwardens are to pass their accompts upon munday next come fortnight. And Mr Willm Plunkett, Mr Robert Usher, Mr Edmund Ledbettar and Mr Bowden or any two of them are to be auditors of there accomptes.

John Atherton, Prebend de St Johan
Stephen Colma[n] Wm Plunkett
Jeremy Bowden Edm. Leadbetter
Vall Wayte James Bellew
Willm WB Bings marke

It is ordered by the consent of the parson & parishioners aforesaid that

[f. 72v blank]

[f. 73] The accompt of Mr William Smyth & Mr Jeremy Simpson, Proctors of the parish of St John Dublin for the year begining at Easter 1634 & ending at Easter 1635.

Rents Receaved

	li s d
Imprimis of Mr Conran for one whole yeares rent of a howse in fishshamble street ending at Mich[aelmas] 1634	3.6.8.
Item of Edward fforeside for Mr Andersons howse in Oxmantown for one whole yeares rent endinge the same tyme	2.0.0.
Item of Sir Thady Duff, kt, for one yeares rent of an howse on the wood key endinge the same tyme	1.0.0.
Item of Maurice Smyth for one yeares rent of a howse in Oxmantown endinge the same tyme	1.13.4.
Item of Alderman Dowde for one yeares rent of a howse in Oxmantown endinge the same tyme	15.0.

Item of Patrick Russell for one yeares rent of a howse in ffish shanble streete endinge the same tyme	7.6.
Item of Mr Mathew fford for one yeares rent of an howse in ffish shamble streete endinge the same tyme	1.13.4.
Item of Mr <Robt> Gilbert for one yeares rent of an howse held by the Earle of Cork endinge the same tyme	1.6.3.
Item of the Master of the Taylors for one year endinge at Midsomer last	1.0.0.
Item received of Mr Alderman Usher for one yeares rent of a howse in ffish shamble streete endinge at Mich[aelmas] last	2.6.8.
Item received of late Churchwardens uppon the foote of their accompte remayneing as app[ears] p[er] book	19.4.
Mr Robock for one yeares rent of a howse in St ffrancis streete ending at Mich[aelm]as last	1.5.0.
Totall	17.13.1.

Burialls

Mr Savills Child his Buriall	3.4.
Andrew Reade	6.8.
Mr Cuningham	6.8.
Thoas Jones	6.6.
Mr Brookes his Child	3.4.
Mr Somers Child	3.4.
Mr Alexanders two Children	6.8.
[blank] at Dunns	6.8.
Mr Martine	6.8.
Capt Mervins ground	13.0.
Mr Larke	6.8.
Mr Esmonde	13.4.
Mr Osbornes Child	3.4.
Mr Obett Williams Child	3.4.
Mr Clinches buriall died at Brookes	6.[8.]
	4.15. [MS damaged]

Sm total $xxij^{li}$ $viij^{s}$ xj^{d} *st*

[f. 73v] Moneyes disburst by Willm Smyth & Jeremy Simpson proctors of the parish of St John in Dublin for the yeare begyninge at Easter 1634 & ending at Easter 1635.

ffor the Expence at two severall meeteinges	1.0.0.
ffor the Beadles Coates and staves	1.0.0.

ffor keeping & burying the child found in parish	8.0.
ffor Langable	3.0.
ffor sixe sacks of Lyme	5.0.
ffor three Loads of sand	9.
ffor twoe hundreth of Slates	3.0.
ffor a helliar fower dayes	5.8.
ffor a Labourer ffyve daies	3.4.
ffor twoe deals to mend seates	2.8.
ffor nayles	1.10.
ffor a dayis worke & other worke awhile after	2.7.
ffor tape to bynd up the wrytinges	4.
ffor a paire of hindges to a pew door	6.
To Walter Dermott & John Nolan, witnesses p[ro]duced to prove the parish bounds	3.6.
To Mr Hilton for swearing them	2.6.
To Mr Eustace p[ro]duced for same bounds j^{s} & to a ffoote man that went into ye Cuntry to him ij^{s} toto	3.0.
To Joane Kelly produced for same	1.0.
ffor twoe affadavites in ye prerogative Court	8.
To Bartholomew Jordan for his yeares meanes	2.0.0.
ffor a shovell & a spade	1.6.
ffor twoe ropes for the bells	1.6.
ffor holly ivy and rushes for the church	2.6.
ffor ringing on the kings days	4.0.
ffor wine at severall Communyons & bread	12.6.
ffor two damaske napkins	10.0.
ffor a Claspe for the Challices case	2.
Allowed to Mr Jeremy Bowden for the buriall of a decayed parishioner of this parish	6.8.
Allowed to Mr Robert Usher toward maintenaunce of his suite with St Warboroughs parish	10.0.
Paid to Mr William Plunkett the some of ffyve poundes & <ffyve> Tenne shillings in full discharge of the moneys laid out by him for the parish of St Johns to one Edward Tyngame masone	5.10.0.
S[u]m	xiiij^{li} vj^{s} ij^{d} st.

[f. 74] Memorand[um] wee have examined the accompt of the late Church wardens Mr Smyth & Mr Sympson & wee fynd that they have Receaved of the Rents & Casualties of the Church the some of xxij^{li} viij^{s} xj^{d} & that they have disbursed to the use of the Church the some of xiiij^{li} vj^{s} ij^{d} st. soe as their remayneth dewe uppon this accompt the some of eight poundes two shillings and nyne pence ster which they have now payed over to the handes of Mr Kerdiff & Mr Dongan the newe Church wardens. All which wee wittnes being Auditors to this accompte.

Wm Plunkett
Robart Usher
Edm Leadbetter
Jeremy Bowden

18th of ffeb[ruary] 1635
Receaved the daye and yeare aforesaid of Symon Kerdiff and Thomas Dungan, Church Wardens of the Parish of St John, the some of Three skore poundes ster English money according [to] severall acquittances given them for the same, which said some is for one whole yeres payment due unto mee from the parishioners of the said parish ending at Christmas last past. I say received sixtye pounds.

John Atherton

[f. 74v blank]

[f. 75] The accompt of Mr Symon Kerdiff & Thomas Dungan, Proctors of the Parish of St John Dublin, for the yeare begining at Easter 1635 & ending at Easter 1636.

Rentes Receaved

{Receaved at the handes of ye Late Churchwardens uppon their accompt 8.2.9.}

	li. s. d
Imprimis Receaved of Mr Thomas Conran for one whole yeares Rent for an house in ffishamble street ending at Michellmas last 1635	3.6.8.
Receaved of Alderman Doude for one whole yeares Rent of an house in Oxmantowne ending the same tyme	15.0.
Receaved of Sir Edward Winkfield for one whole yeares Rent for an house in Oxmantown ending the same tyme	2.0.0.
Receaved of Mr Maurish Smith, esq, for one whole yeares Rent of an house in Oxmantown ending the same tyme	1.13.4.
Receaved of Mr Roback for one whole yeares Rent for an house in St ffrancis streete ending the same tyme	1.5.0.
Receaved of Sir Thady Duff, kt, for one whole yeares Rent for an house one the wood key ending the same tyme	1.0.0.
Receaved of Alderman Usher for a yeares Rent for an house in ffishamble streete ending the same tyme	2.6.8.
Receaved of Patrick Russell for a yeares Rent for an house in ffishamble streete	7.6.

Receaved of the Master of the Taylors for one yeare ending at Midsumer last	1.0.0.
Receaved of Matthew fford for one yeares Rent for an house in ffishamble streete ending at the same tyme	1.13.4.
{Receaved of Robert Barlow for 4 yeares Rent ending at M[ichaelmas] last for Walter ffloods house in ffishamble streete}[67]	3.0.0.
<Burials>	
Imprimis Hugh Lock his Child	3.4.
Mr Harrison his wiffe	6.8.
One that died at the 3 pigeons	6.8.
Mr Thomas Johns his Child	3. 4
Mr William Balife	13.4.
Mr James Osborne	6.6.
Mr Christopher Collman	6.8.
Mr Alexander his Child	3.0.
Mr Thomas Cha	6.8.
Ann Warren	6.8.
Mr Carpenter his Child	3.4.
Catheren Doyle	6.8.
One that died at Mr Smith his house	6.8.
Of Bartholemew Jordan for 2 burialls	13.4.

Suma total of all their charge is xxxj^{li} ij^{s} ix^{d} ster

[f. 75v] Moneyes disburst by Symon Kerdiff & Thomas Dungan, proctors of the parish of St John Dublin, for the yeare 1635 & ending at Easter 1636.

	li. s. d.
Imprimis ffor Ringing one the kings dayes	4.0.
ffor five hundred & a half of slates	5.6.
ffor carrying the said Slates from the keye	4.
ffor Lathes & boordes	8.
ffor Nailes	2.
ffor two barreles of lime	1.4.
ffor two lodes of sand	6.
ffor a hellier	5.0.
ffor wodden pines	6.
ffor Holly, Ivy & Rushes for the Church	2.6.
paid Henry Taylor for woork in the Church {& wanscoting in the Chauncell}	16.0.0.
ffor a booke of Cannons	2.0.
ffor two sakes of lime to laye the tyles	1.4.
paid a heller for one dayes woork & for tyles	2.0.
paid John Barry, Glasier, for work done in the Church	7.5.

To Bartholemew Jordan for his years meanes	2.0.0.
paid for mending the Clapper of the bell	4.
paid for mending the Communion pott	4.
ffor washing the Communion Cloth	1.0.
ffor Longable	3.0.
disburst uppon the accompt & meetings at two severall tymes	19.8.
ffor two herses	1.0.
ffor bread and wine for the communion	1.1.6.
makinge ye stepps of ye chancell & tyling	
to James O Leyne Mason for the stone work of both the steppes in the Chancell and the stone work about the comunion table	1.12.0.
ffor 57 doz of tyles at ij^{d} p[er] dossen	1.15.0.
to 3 Massons for laying the tyles & removing the great stonnes in the Chancell	10.0.
ffor lime and sand	5.0.
ffor a great pice of Tember for a Grouncell in the Chancell	3.0.
To a laborer for bringing of earth to Raise the Chancell	7.0.
for a warrant from the Lo[rd] Chacellor	3.6.
Item payed to Mr Plunkett in full discharge of all such money as he layd out about the repares of ye church	1.4.9.

xxvij^{li} xv^{s} iiij^{d} st
26. 10. 7

[f. 76] Decimonovo Aprilis 1636
Memorand[um] that the parson & parishioners of St John the Evangelist Dublin have Chosen Mr Thomas Dongan & Mr Edmond Hunt to be churchwardens for this nexte yeare ensuing. And the old Churchwardens are to pass their accompts upon mundaie next come fortnighte and Mr Willm Plunkett, Mr Robert Ussher, Mr Edmond Ledbeter and Mr Jeremy Bowden {Willm Smyth & Jeremy Sympson} or any two of them are to be auditors of their accomptes.

	Hu Cressy, Prebend St Johns[68]
Jeremy Simpson	Willm Smyth
John March	Edward Blennerhassett
Jermy Bowden	Edm Leadbetter
John Dockett	John Aninon
	John Barrany
	Georg Sadert
	Richard Browne

[f. 76v] *Edmund Ledbetter & Jerymy Simbson overseerers for ye poor*
According to a p[ar]tie bearing date the xxijth daie of October 1633 wee the Alderman of the Ward and parson of the parish of St John {the Evangelist}

Dublin have chosen and nominated Mr Edmond Ledbettar and Mr Jeremy Simpson two substantial howseholders of the s[ai]d parish to be overseers of the poor of the said parish untill Easter nexte. Witnes our hands and seals the nynteenth daie of Aprill Anno dm 1636. Per Mr Alderman Arthur & Mr Cressey.

Memorand[um] wee examined the accomptes of the late Church wardens Mr Symon Kerdiff & Mr Thomas Dongan & <wee> they have Receaved of the Rents & Casualties of the Church the some of xxxj^{li} ij^{s} ix^{d} st. And they have disbursed to the use of the Church the some of xxvij^{li} xv^{s} iiij^{d} st. soe as their remayneth dewe uppon this accompt the some of three poundes seaven shillings & fyve pence ster which they have nowe payed over to the handes of Mr Knott & Mr Dongan ye nowe Church wardens. All which wee wittnes being Auditors assigned for this accomptes

Wm Plunkett
Willm Smyth
Robart Usher
Jeremy Simpson

3^{li} 7^{s} 5^{d}
Mr Dungan hath rec[*eived*] *ye monie above said*[69]

[f. 77] 19th day of Aprill 1636
Answer {to} the mayor and Recorders order concerning the poor of ye Parish of St Johns

According to your wor[ships] order of the 4th day of this p[rese]nt Aprill unto us driected, we have formerly certified your wor[shi]pps of ye poor of our parish of St Johns ye Evangelist Dublin. And wee doe alsoe Certifie your wor[shi]pp that wee assembled ye parishioners of ye said parish togeather and have concluded to maytaine ye said Poor of our parish which is as much as wee find our selves any way able to doe by reason that ye parishioners doe consist of many very poore howseholders and are ashamed to begg. And wee do further cerify your wor[shi]pp that according to an Act of state bearing date ye 22th day of October 1633 The Alderman of ye warde and parson of ye said parish have under their handes and seales nominated two substantiall householders of ye said parish to be overseerers of ye poor of ye parish until Easter next. And wee have also appointed beadles to attend in ye same parish and wee doe humbly desire to be eased of all strange beggers and thus wee humble take our leave

Copia vera Edmd Hunt

25th of May 1636.
Answer to ye Mayor and ye Commissioners order concerning ye Cessing of ye parishioners of the parish of St Johns for ye poore.

May it please your wor[shi]pps according [to] your wor[shi]pps order to us directed wee have made a Cess on ye Inhabitants of ye parish [of] St Johns Dublin and with much difficultie have concluded to allowe ye poor of ye said parish after ye rate of twenty pounds ster p[er] ann[um], which is as much as wee find ye parishioners are wery able to beare by reson that grett p[ar]te of ye said Inhabitants are verry poor and not able to pay or allow any thing towards ye said sess but rather fitting to receave releif from ye said parish. All which wee humbly certify to your wor[shi]pps witnes our hands of date abovesaid

Copia vera　　　　Edm Hunt

[f. 77v]16th day of June, 1636
Memorand[um] it is ordered by the Consent of the parishioners of St Johns Dublin that Willm Plunkett, Esq., Edmond Ledbetter, deputie Alderman, Willm Smyth, deputie Alder[man], Symon Cardiffe, merchant, Henry Ashburne, gent, Jerymy Bowden, ffrancis Dowde, merchant, Thomas Jacob, <merchant> {baker}, Richard Goulding, merchant, & Patrick Gough, {gent} or any six of them to veiw and make ye Cess of ye parsons duties.

Edm Hunt	Jeremy Simpson
Thomas + Dungan his marke	John Butcher
John March	Patrick Russell
Jo Dockett	John Montgomerie
Georg Sadert	Valltine Wayte
	The marke of John PI Parker

[f. 78] Hereafter followeth the Cess on the parishioners of St Johns Evangelist due to the Parson of the said parish according to the act of the state. Cessed and taxed by us whose names are here subscribed authorised by the whole consent of the parishioners the two and twentieth day of June Anno dom 1636

ffishamble streete

Robertt Usher, Mauchant	x^{s}
Robertt Dune, shoemaker and the Widdow Leleor and the Tenement	$xiij^{s}$ $iiij^{d}$
Gyles Capener, victler	vj^{s}
John Huggard and his Inmats	xvj^{s}
Mortagh Kinge, gent, and his Inmats	$viij^{s}$
Robertt Cloynie and his Inmats	xij^{s}
Thomas Lee	$iiij^{s}$
Edmond Buttler and his Inmats	xij^{s}
Nicholas Browne and his Inmats	$viij^{s}$
Robertt Barlowe, vintner	xij^{s}

John Trew	vj^{s}
Sylvanus Glegg, gouldsmith	x^{s}
Patrick Russell, baker	viij^{s}
John Borran, water bayly	x^{s}
Widdowe Drew	vj^{s}
Georg ffernsley, victailer & and Andrew Bird	<iiij^{s}> ix^{s}
[blank] Knight, Tayler	iiij^{s}
{Thos. McGwyer and his Inmates	vj^{s}}
Edmond McGwyer, gent.	iiij^{s}
Charles Hornsby, silk weaver	x^{s}
George Plunkett <Inhoulder> In houlder	xij^{s}
William Crispe, vintner	xx^{s}
Reyner Vandever, brewer	viij^{s}
Morris Killwalter, Inholder	iiij^{s}
George Teader, Tayler	vj^{s}
Robertt Guile, sayler	iiij^{s}
Edmond Hunt, gent	xij^{s}
John Singleton, boatman	vj^{s}
William Stevens	ij^{s}
John Kendingham	ij^{s}
Widdow Rawbone and George Boye	xij^{s}
Richard Williams <marchant>	<x>ij^{s}
Thomas fformby, sayler	x^{s}
Henry Lemand, marchant	x^{s}
xiij^{li} viij^{s} iiij^{d}	
<13^{li} 13^{s} 4^{d}>	
[f. 78v]Widdow Hardinge	vj^{s}
Arther Charde	iiij^{s}
Richard White, stabler	iiij^{s}
Edmond Ledbetter	x^{s}
Charles Johnson, tayler	iij^{s}
John Mallouce, tayler	iij^{s}
Alderman Wiggott and John Michell	xv^{s}
Widdowe Dutton	x^{s}
Widdowe Sampson	ij^{s}
Thomas White	iiij^{s}
Richard Buttler, baker & his In mats	x^{s}
Widdow Lutterrell	iij^{s}
Richard Dermond	iij^{s}
James Bedloe	viij^{s}
Widdow Osborne	iiij^{s}
Thomas Gunter	vj^{s}
Willm Plunkett, Esq.	xiij^{s} iiij^{d}

Anthony Mediase	vj^{s}
Kemps house	viij^{s}
St Johns Lane	
John Warren, tayler & his In mats	vj^{s}
The halfe Moone sellar <& his In mats>	xs
John Doggett and his In mate	viij^{s}
Thomas Coleman for ye Red Stagge	viij^{s}
Patrick Dowde, marchant	iiij^{s}
Robert Coffie, Gouldsmith	iiij^{s}
Thomas Jacobb, Baker	viij^{s}
Thomas Coleman and Nicholas Gennet	xij^{s}
Manny Reyley	ij^{s}
Symond Cardiffe, marchant	viij^{s}
<Edwa> Edward Waker, gerdler	iiij^{s}
Richard Goulding, marchant his house and the Tennis Court	x^{s}
John Halle	iiij^{s}
Winetavern street	
Widdow Cheevers and In mats	xvj^{s}
Widdow Browne	x^{s}
Widdow Elliott	viij^{s}
Widdow St Johns and Inmats	x^{s}
John Doggett att {the} blacke doge	viij^{s}
Honor Lewes	vj^{s}
John fitz Gerrald	iiij^{s}
Cook street	
Patrick Warren for the ship tavern	xiij^{s} iiij^{d}
xiiij^{li} *v*^{s} *viij*	
<16. 11. 8>	
[f. 79] John Callan	iiij^{s}
Joane Camance	ij^{s}
Barnaby Ennos	iiij^{s}
Patrick English	iiij^{s}
Widdow Brasbridge	iiij^{s}
James Bedlow, Baker	vj^{s}
Marry Vialls	vj^{s}
Nicholas Barnewall	ij^{s}
Patrick White, baker	vj^{s}
Wintavern street	
Robert Wiggett, shoomaker	viij^{s}
Francis Dillon, gent	viij^{s}
Patrick Galbelly	viij^{s}
Walter Curane	vj^{s}
George Chamberlaine	vj^{s}

Thomas ffleming, marchant	x^{s}
Albion Leverett	xij^{s}
John Marche, Innkeeper	xvj^{s}
Patricke Buttler, boatman	viij^{s}
Robertt Savill, Esq	<x>xiij^{s} iiij^{s}
Robertt Bridges	iiij^{s}
Widdowe Dole	xij^{s}
Mr Browne, tayler	iiij^{s}
Thomas Dungane	x^{s}
Mr Brookes and his tenants	x^{s}
Henry Browne for ye Crane	<vj^{s}> iiij^{s}
Thomas Clerke, victler	x^{s}
{Doctor ffairfax	viij^{s}}
Edmond Smith, gent	x^{s}
Widdow Duffe	viij^{s}
ffrancis Dowd, marchant	xiij^{s} iiij^{d}
Pierce Moore, clerke	xij^{s}
James Carven	iiij^{s}
Jeremy Woodward	vj^{s}
Walter ffitz Garratt	ij^{s}
Thomas Lymbey	iiij^{s}
Stephen Garland	v^{s}
The sellar under the Blacke boy	viij^{s}
John Quatemies and his Inmats	vj^{s}
Widdow Rawson	xvj^{s}
The Common seller for Mr Gibson	x^{s}
Robert Dollard	viij^{s}
Patricke Gough, gent	viij^{s}
James Begg, smith	vj^{s}
Patricke Savadge	ij^{s}
Widdow Kenningham and her Inmats	xvj^{s}
Willm Balldricke, gent	viij^{s}
John Butcher	viij^{s}
Peirce Keiton	viij^{s}
Patricke Dowd for a Celler under the gate	ij^{s}
Widdowe Nugent	xs

xviij^{li} xix^{s} viij^{d}

<18 – 12 – 7>

[f. 79v] *Rosemary Lane*

The tennant of ye Goudling Lyon	x^{s}
William Oaker	ij^{s}
Allexander Hesley	ij^{s}
William Bee	ij^{s}

Wood Key

Robertt Dee, shoomaker	viij^{s}
William Browne, Inkeeper	vj^{s}
Francis Anger, gent	x^{s}
Thomas <Gayt> Gayton	viij^{s}
John Mongomery	vj^{s}
Leonard Thompson	x^{s}
Henry Withers	viij^{s}
Obitt Willms	xiij^{s} iiij^{d}
John Browne	vj^{s}
Richard Lutterrell	viij^{s}
Peter Lemond Inmate	iiij^{s}
Clement Martin Inmate	viij^{s}
William Atkinson	x^{s}
Benjamine Robertts	viij^{s}
Roger Gernon Inmate	vj^{s}
Nicholas Dillon	vj^{s}
William Boy	x^{s}
Rob Maxwell in ye Widdow Laxills house	vj^{s}
John Blake	iiij^{s}
John Johnson	iiij^{s}
Widdow Begge	vj^{s}
Walter Doyle, sayler	iiij^{s}
John Bartlett, sayler	iiij^{s}
John <Baran> {Onion}	iiij^{s}
Richard Ball	ij^{s}
Michall Pursell, marchant	iiij^{s}
Widdow Pursell	ij^{s}
William Smith, deputie Alderman	xij^{s}
Christopher Harryson	vj^{s}
[blank] Kinge	vj^{s}
Widowe Read	iiij^{s}
Adam Maddrill	iiij^{s}
Henry Jordane	viij^{s}
Jeremy <Simson> Simpson	viij^{s}
John Barry	ij^{s}
Henry Ashborne	vj^{s}
Steven Bowers	iiij^{s}
Jeremy Bowden	vj^{s}
Peter Watson	iiij^{s}
xiij^{li} j^{s} iiij^{d} st	
[f. 80] The house next to Watsons house	iiij^{s}
Sir ffaithfull ffortescue	xx^{s}

William Salmon	x^{s}
The Bishopp of Waterford	<x>xiij^{s} iiij^{d}
The house under ye Bishops house where Lewis Jones dwelt	ij^{s}
TheWiddow Davies	x^{s}
John Rymer	ij^{s}
William Thimblebey	x^{s}
[blank] Ordame	iiij^{s}
The Barker	ij^{s}
The house where ye Widdow Davies did dwell	viij^{s}
Mr Bentleys stables	xij^{s}
Thomas Curran	<vj>iiij^{s}
Mr Gilbertts stables	<xj>vj^{s}
Patrick Connor	ij^{s}
The two houses belonging to {Rayneere Vandever}	iiij^{s}
Randall Aldersey, Esq	<xij^{s}> xij^{s}
Barker, Innholder	x^{s}
Sir William Rives	xx^{s}
Widdow Newman	xx^{s}
Mr Samdbich	xv^{s}
Mr Lyne	xij^{s}
John Parker, {boatman}	vj^{s}
Jeremy Alexander, Esq	xvj^{s}
James Donollane, {Esq}	xvj^{s}
Edward Blennerhassett and his Inmats	vj^{s}
Mr Greene	viij^{s}
Valentine <Wt> Waite and his Inmats	x^{s}
George Proudffoott and his Inmates	x^{s}

xiij^{li} xiiij^{s} iiij^{d}.

Sum total	lxxiij^{li} ix^{s} iiij^{d} st
Richard Goulding	Wm Plunkett
Patr Gough	Willm Smyth
Thomas TI Jackob his marke	Edm Leadbetter

[f. 80v] xxviij^{o} Junij 1636

Whereas by Act of State dated in ffebruary 1616 their is dewe to the Parson of this Church the some of threescore poundes st p[er] ann[um] to be payed him qu[ar]terly as by the said Act of State entered in this Booke more at Lardge maye appear.[70] Nowe forasmuch as wee nowe made a Cesse on the inhabitants & parishioners for paym[ent] therof, And wee have to the end the said parson maye be dewely payed the said some made an overplus of xiij^{li} ix^{s} iiij^{d} st in regard that some of the inhabitants maye hereafter dep[ar]t out of the parish before payem[ent] & that their howses maye lye voyde. It is therefore nowe ordered & agreed uppon that whensoever hereafter the saide parson shalbe payed the some of three skor poundes st as aforesaid the overplus of the said Cesse & whatsoever p[ar]te or p[ar]cell therof that the Church wardens shall Receave & Collecte the Church wardens for the tyme being shall hereafter accompte for the same at such tyme as the accompt for the Revenues to be disposed off by the parishioners for the use of the parish.

Patr Gough — Wm Plunkett
Richard Goulding — Willm Smyth
Thomas TI Jackob his m[ar]ke — Edm Leadbetter

[f. 81] duodecimo die Apris 1637
Memorand[um] that the prebend & parishioners of St John the Evangelist Dublin have chosen Mr John March & Mr Richard Browne to be churchwardens for this nexte yeare ensuing. And the old Churchwardens are to pass their accompts upon Monday next come seaventh nighte and <Mr William Plunkett> Mr William Smyth {William Plunkett}, Mr Edmund Leadbeter and Mr Jeremy Bowden & Jeremy Sympson or any twoe or more of them are to be auditors of their accomptes.

Willm Smyth — John Michell
Jeremy Simpson — Nicholas Symons
Edm Leadbetter — Henry Jordan
John Browne
John + Blake his mark

Jeremy Bowden & Patrick Russell overseerers for ye poore
12 Apr[il] 1637
According to a p[ar]tie bearing date the xxijth day of October 1633 wee the Aldermen of the ward & parson of the parish of St John the Evangelist Dublin have chosen and noiated Mr Jeremy Bowden & Mr Patrick Russell two substantiall howseholders of the said parish to be overseers of the poore of the s[ai]d parish untill Easter nexte. Witnes our hands & seals the twelveth day of Aprill Anno dm 1637 p[er].

[f. 81v] xxxiiij^{o} April 1637
Forasmuch as Mr Huntt & Mr Dungan the late Church Wardens haveth humbly desired a further daye to yeald their accomptes wee have therefor appointed this day fortnight being the 8th day of May next to passe their accompts for the revenues & Casualties of the Church & to yeald an accompt of the monys receaved to the use of the poor and the overplus of the Cesse for the parson of this Church of St John Evangelists.

John March — Wm Plunkett
Richard Browne — Edm Leadbetter

Jeremy Bowden Jeremy Simpson
Patrick Russell

[f. 82] A note of such monies as Mr Edmund [Hunt] and Thomas Dunngan, Church wardens for St Johns, hath receaved since Easter 1636 till Easter 1637 as followeth of the Churches Rentes and Revenues

Imprimis Thomas Conran for a house in the ocupacon of John Trew p[er] ann[um]	3.6.8.
Dockter Usher, Lo[rd] Bishop of Meath,[71] for a house in the ocupacon of Mathew fford gent, p[er] ann[um]	1.13.4.
Walter Usher, merchant, for a house in the ocupacon of Nath Cormick p[er] ann[um]	2.6.8.
Walter Dungan, gent, for one house in the ocupacon of John Hunter, baker, p[er] Ann[um]	7.6.
The Master of the Taylers for there geald in St Johns Chapple p[er] Ann[um]	1.0.0.
Amy Smooth for a house late in the ocupacon of James White p[er] Ann[um]	15.0.
Morris Smith, gent, for a house late in the ocupacon of John Allin p[er] Ann[um	13.4.
John Anderson for a house in Oxmantowne lat the ocupacon of Paul Heringe p[er] Ann[um]	2.0.0.
Sir Thady Duffe kt, for house one the Wood key	1.0.0.
Mr Gilbert for the ye Earle of Corks rent	1.6.3.
Mr Robuck the Bucher	1.5.0.
Mr. Eustace for arrears of the revenues upon ye accompt of the Churchwardens	2.0.0.
for the ffees of a writte against Mr Eustace	[blank]
	17.13.9.
[f. 82v] Burials	4.3.0.
Totall	21.16.9.
A note how much of the Church revenues Thomas Dongan hath receaved the some of	17.13.9.
The disbursement amount to	16.9.1.
So resteth due one this accompt	8.15.1.

A note of such moies as Mr Dongan hath receaved for burialls since 1636 to Easter 1637

Imprimis The buriall of Symon Esmond	13.0.
The burial of Richard Gouldings child	3.4.
ffor the burial of Mr Staughtons Child	3.4.
ffor the burial of Silvanus Leggs Child	3.4.
ffor the burial of Luke Doyle Child	3.4.
ffor the burial of ye M[aste]r of ye Roles man	6.8.
ffor the burial of ffrancis Gibson	13.4.
ffor the burial of ye Widow Lallors Child	3.4.
ffor the burial of Margrett Blackburne Widdow	6.8.
ffor the burial of Oliver Elliot, gent	6.8.
ffor the burial of Jeffrey Welsh Child	3.4.
ffor the burial of Clement Martins Child	3.4.
For Mr Francis Angers wifs buriall	6.8.
ffor Cusack buriall Crips man	6.8.
	4.3.0.
ffor the Burial of Richard Egelstons child	3.4.
ffor the Burial of Mr Marchs child	3.4.
	4.9.8.

[f. 83] A note of such monies as Mr Thomas Dungan Church warden of St Johns hath layd out from Easter 1636 till Easter 1637

Imprimis ffor one new Surplus	3.10.0.
ffor a wrest band to ye old Surpluse	1.0.
To Hallardes and labourers	1.2.4.
ffor slates and sand	5.0.
ffor Lyme	9.0.
ffor a bord and Nayls for ye halleards	6.
ffor mendinge Clapp[er] of ye Bell howse	3.0.
ffor mendinge the Church Lock	6.
ffor two Doshetts[72] for ye Comunion table	8.
ffor two Dosen of sparrs	8.0.
ffor two Dosen of sawn boards	12.0.
ffor spikes and Nayles	4.0.
ffor the Carpenters	12.0.
ffor a spade	1.0.
To Bartholl Jordan for his stipend	2.0.0.
To the Woman of ye Church one ye K[ings] day	2.10.
ffor Rushes and Holly at Xpemas	2.6.
To ye Glasier for Glasinge ye windowes	4.0.

ffor buringe of 2 men by Mr Leadbetter	5.0.
ffor mending two Dishes for ye Comm[union] table	6.
ffor whitening & mending ye crach of ye Church	1.0.0.
Paid for two Joyne stools	3.0.
ffor two hinges to ye seate dore one ye North side of the Chancell	8.
ffor a small hasp & staple for ye same	3.
ffor a lock and key to the dore & fitting one	1.2.
ffor pulling Downe ye house & office in the church yard	1.6.
ffor a Mason for laying all the lose tyles in the Church	2.6.
To the Register in the in the Arch Deacons Court for his apparance upon ye attachme[n]t	10.0.
In the highe Comisson Court his apparance	10.
[f. 83v] more To the Register of same court for his Discharge, being about the house of office	10.0.
ffor Langable to the Citie	3.6.
ffor Carving ye l[ett]res upon ye stools	2.
ffor a Dore Lock and key and Ironwork for a pew in the chancell	11.6.
ffor mendinge a pew dore belonging to the S[er]gant at Arms wifie	1.4.
ffor mending the church Cushen	3.0.
ffor Washing ye Comunion Cloth and Napkins, 3 tymes	1.0.
ffor Washing Surpluse 7 times	3.6.
ffor Wyne for the Comunion	1.9.4.
ffor 2 severrall meetings of the parish to Mr Crespe for wyne	1.12.0.
	17.0.2.

More Layd out by ye Instructions of the Buishopp of Waterford after pulling downe and reparing the former sheed as followeth

ffor one Dosen of sparrs for a shead for ye ladders and hooks for ye church	6.0.
ffor one Dosen of bords	8.0.
ffor 2 Carpenters 2 day and a halfe	4.6.
ffor ringing bells one the Kings day	2.4.
ffor Cleaning the wenskott and sweepinge ye church after ye plastering	1.0.
for mending a windfall one ye North syde of the Church	1.6.
ffor mendinge a window one the North syde of the Church	1.6.

[f. 84] xxv^{o} May 1637

Memorand[um] wee have examined the accomptes of Mr Edmund Huntte & Mr Thomas Dongan, late Churchwardens of this Church, for one year endinge at the feast of Easter last 1637 & wee fynd that they have Receaved of the Rents & Casualties of the said Church the some of xvij^{li} xiij^{s} ix^{d} st & that they have disbursed as appeareth by their accompt the some of xvj^{li} xj^{s} x^{d} st. Besydes iiij^{li} ij^{s} viij^{d} for Burialls that year. Soe as their is nowe remayning dewe in the handes of the said late churchwardens Mr Hunte & Mr Dongan the some of viijli xviijs st which some of viij^{li} xviij^{s} st the late Church wardens have payd over into the handes of the nowe Church wardens Mr John March & Mr Richard Browne. All which wee wittnes being Auditors assigned for the passing of this accompte.

Wm Plunkett
Edm Leadbetter
Jeremy Bowden
Jeremy Simpson

[f. 84v blank]

[f. 85] xxvij^{o} Marcij 1638
Memorand[um] that the prebend & parishioners of St John the Evangelist Dublin have chosen Mr Richard Browne & Mr John Michaell to be churchwardens for this next yeare ensuing. And the old Churchwardens are to pass their accompts upon this day seaventh night and Mr. Wm Plunkett, <Mr Wm> Alderman Wm Smyth, Mr Edmund Leadbeter and <Mr John March> Mr Jeremy Bowden & Mr Robt Cloney or any two or more of them are to be auditors of their accomptes.

Edw Dunstervil,[73] Cur[ate] by authoritie by Mr Cressie

Willm Smyth
Jeremy Simpson

Wm Plunkett
John March
Edm Leadbetter
Jeremy Bowden
Robert Clony
James Bellew

27 M[ar]ch 1638
According to an act of state bearing date the xxijth day of October Ano dm 1633 wee the Aldermen of the ward & parson of the parish of St John the Evangelist Dublin have chosen and noiated the Churchwardens for the tyme being for this p[rese]nt year ensuing Mr Robt Cloney & Mr Robt Dee two substantiall howseholders of the said parish to be overseers of the poore of the s[ai]d parish untill Easter nexte. Witnes our hands & seals 27 of M[ar]ch 1638.

[f. 85v blank]

[f. 86] A note and just Accompt of all such summes of moneyes and yearely revenewes belonging to St Johns Church Receaved by Mr Richard Brown and John March, Church wardens, from Easter 1637 until Easter 1638 as followeth.

	li. s. d.
Imprimis Thomas Conran for a howse in the possession of John Trew {ending at Micha[alem]as 1637	3.6.8.
Item receaved from Mr Harrison for Walter Bloods howse in ffishamble streete for arreares of rent ending at Mich[aelm]as last the sume of	1.10.0.
Item Doctor Usher, Lord Bishopp of Meath, for a howse in the occupacon of Mathew Ford p[er] Ann[um] {ending as aforesaid}	1.13.4
Item for the howse of Walter Usher, merchant, possessed by John Burran p[er] Ann[um] {ending at }	2.6.8.
Item Walter Dongan, gent, for the howse on the possession of Patrick Russell Baker p[er] Ann[um]	7.6.
Item the M[aste]r of the Company of Taylors for their Guild in St Johns Chappell p[er] Ann[um]	1.0.0.
Item Katherine Kelly for the howse lately possessed by Amy Smooth belonging to James Whyte p[er] Ann[um][74]	15.0.
Item Morish Smith, gent, for a howse lately held by Katherine Taylor p[er] Ann[um]	1.0.0.
Item the said Morish for another howse late in the occupacon of John Allen p[er] Ann[um]	13.4.
Item John Anderson for a howse on Oxmanton late in the occupacon of Paul Hearing and now possessed by the widdow fforseed p[er] Ann[um]	2.0.0.
Item from Mr Rabucke, the Butcher, in Saint ffrances streete belonging to John Good p[er] Ann[um]	1.5.0.
Earle of Corkes house in Castle streete[75]	
Item Mr Gilbert for the Earle of Corkes rent for the howse in Castle streete	1.6.3.
Item Sir Thady Duffe, knt, for a howse on the wood key	1.0.0.
Item receaved from Thomas Dongan, late Church warden the sume of 5^{li} st	5.0.0.
Item by Bill appearing sum of	3.18.0.
	27.1.9.

[f. 86v] A note of such moneys as were receaved from Church burials since the tyme within menconed

	li. s. d.
Imprimis for a child of the widdow Harrison	3.4.
Item for the buriall of Mrs Thomson	6.8.

Item for the buriall of Mr Willsons child that dyed in Backe lane	6.8.
Item for the buriall of Mr Blake a Country gent that dyed at Thomas Gunters	12.0.
Item for the buriall of Mr Mountgomery his child	3.4.
Item for the buriall of one of Mr Walter Whytes daughters in Cooke streete	13.4.
Item for the buriall of Child that dyed at Clement Martin, the Brewers house on wood key	3.4.
Item for the buriall of Alderman Smiths mother	6.8.
Item for the buriall of < … > {Mr} Plunketts mother	6.8.
Item for the buriall of Mr Willm Cripps	6.8.
Item for the buriall of Mr Cookes wife, the Goldsmith	6.8.
Item for the buriall of a gent[leman] stranger that dyed at the howse of Richard Browne	6.8.
Item for the buriall of Mr Mountgomeryes daughter.	3.4.
Item for the buriall of Mr Perceivall	6.8.
Item for the buriall of Mr Byrds wife	6.8.
Item for the buriall of M[ist]ris Byars Child	3.4.
	5.2.0.

S[u]m total amounteth to xxxij^{li} iij^{s} ix^{d} st

[f. 87] The disbursements of the Church wardens

	li. s. d.
Imprimis spent at two severall meetings	1.10.0.
Item laid out for apparance two Court dayes	1.8.
Item for mending the Comunion table	3.0.
Item for mending the boorded Gutter of the Church	3.0.
Item for binding two service bookes and mending the Bible	7.0.
Item for Langable	3.0.
Item for paving within the Church	3.0.
Item for settling, finishing and workemanshipp belonging to the ffont stone and other matterialls befitting the same	1.0.0.
Item for Cover of lead over the ffont	2.0.0.
Item paid to the Clearke for his stipend	2.0.0.
Item for laying a stone at the porch doore	1.6.
Item for a peece of tymber adjoyning to the same	1.0.
Item for paving the lane adjoyning to the said Church	5.0.
Item for Sand	1.6.
Item for double Dale to make a back doore to the porch	7.0.
Item for spikes & nails to it & the Bellfree	4.0.
Item for Lock to the doore with two smale hinges	2.3.

Item for hinge to the great doore	6.0.
Item for two smale hookes	4.
Item for the Carpenders worke	8.0.
Item for lyme towards the reparacon of the Church	11.6.
Item for Sand	3.6.
Item for Slates	19.0.
Item for carriage thereof	1.0.
Item for Slate pinns	1.0.
Item for lathes and Nailes	1.6.
Item for Ridge tylles	1.6.
Item for repairing the glasse windows at severall tymes	19.3.
Item paid the sleatier for his work	1.10.0.
Item for green bushes & Rushes at Christmas	2.6.
	13.18.6.
[f. 87v] Item for mending one of the Candle sticks	1.0.
Item for mending the Roofe of the Church	15.0.
Item for Ringing the Bells on the Kings day	2.6.
Item for 12 tymes washing the surplises	6.0.
Item for washing Table Lynnen	2.6.
Item for bread and wine on Comunion dayes at severalll tymes	1.16.3.
Item for bread & wine on Low Sunday for the Comunion that day	3.9.
	3.7.0.

The Charge in building the vestry

Imprimis for double dale boards	2.5.6.
Item for slitt dale	14.0.
Item for sparrs	15.0.
Item for Carriage to the Joiner to & fro	3.6.
Item for all sorts of Nailles	9.6.
Item for hinges and staples	2.6.
Item for a Locke and key	2.0.
Item paid to the Joiner for his worke	1.10.0.
Item for a Chair to the vestry	7.6.
Item for a Table	6.6.
Item for a fforme	4.0.
Item for a man to attend the workeman in the Church from tyme to tyme	4.0.
	7.4.0.
Sum total of ye whole disbursment amounteth to	xxiiij^{li} ix^{s} vj^{d} st

[f. 88] xij° die Aprilis Ano dm 1638
Memorand[um] that wee have Examined the accompts of Mr John March and John Browne, late Church wardens of this church, for one yeare ending at the ffeast of Easter last past. And wee fynd that they have receaved of the rents and casualties of the said Church ye some of Thirtie and Twoe pounds three shillings & nyne pence sterling and that they have disbursed as appeareth by their accompt the some of Twentie and ffower pounds Nyne shillings & sixe pence sterl soe as there is now remayneing in their hands dewe seaven pounds fowerteen shillings and three pence sterl in the handes of the late Church wardens Mr March & Mr Browne which some of vij^{li} 14^{s} 3^{d} the said late Church wardens have payed over into the handes of the now churchwardens Mr Richard Browne & Mr John Michaell. All which wee witnes being Auditors assigned for the passing of this accompte.

Wm Plunkett
Edm Leadbetter
Jeremy Bowden

xii° May 1638
I doe hereby acknowledge that I have received whatsoever was due to me by Act of State as prebend of St Johns out of that parish from my entrance thereunto untill Easter last. As witnesse my hand subscribed hereunto.

Hu Cressy

[f. 88v blank]

[f. 89] Hereafter followeth the Cesse on the parishioners of St. John Evangelist due to the Parson of the same parish according to the Act of the State. Cessed & taxed by us whose names are heere subscribed authorised by the joint and unanimous consent and agreement of all the parishioners and inhabitants of the said parish the eighth and twentieth day of Aprill Anno dom[ini] 1638.

	ster
ffishamble streete	li s d
Robert Usher merchant	10.0.
Robert Dunn	6.8.
Widow Lawlor	6.8.
Barnard Bussana	4.0.
John Hargrave the younger	6.0.
John Knott	6.0.
John Huggard & his imnates	10.0.
Richard Coffy, shoemaker	6.0.
Wiliam Holland	2.0.
Robert Cloney	12.0.

Thomas Lee	4.0.
Thomas Hill	12.0.
Nicholas Browne	4.0.
Lawrence ffullam	4.0.
John Harris	16.0.
John Trew	6.0.
Sylvanne Glegge	8.0.
Patrick Russell	8.0.
John Barran	10.0.
John Bushfeilde	6.0.
William Taylor	6.0.
Andrew Byrde	3.0.
John Mullins	2.0.
John Knight, taylor	4.0.
Francis Alllin	6.0.
Widdow Sampson	2.0.
8–10–4	
[f. 89v] Thomas Guin	6.0.
John Harrison	12.0.
George Plunkett	12.0.
The widdow Cripps	1.0.0.
The widdow Vandodvere	8.0.
Morris Killidere	3.0.
George Tedder	6.0.
Robert Prentice	4.0.
Thomas Lymbery	4.0.
Edmond Hunt	12.0.
John Syngleton	6.0.
John Kenningham	2.0.
George Boyde	8.0.
Anne Rabone	2.0.
John Leman	4.0.
Symon Hunter	2.0.
Johnn Knight	4.0.
Bartholomew Joardan	10.0.
Nicholas Baker	6.0.
Arthure Chadsey	4.0.
Thomas Connor	2.0.
Edmond Leadbetter	10.0.
Charles Johnson	3.0.
Richard White	6.0.
John Michell	15.0.
The widdow Dutton	10.0.

[blank] Bermingham	4.0.
Richard Butterly	10.0.
Mathew Nolan	3.0.
The widdow Lutterell	3.0.
James Bedloe	8.0.
Nicholas Osbourne	6.0.
Thomas Gunter	6.0.
William Plunkett, Esq	13.4.
Anthony Metdcalfe	6.0.
Henry <Kinge> Kempe	8.0.
12 – 8 – 4	
[f. 90] *Johns Lane*	
John Warren	6.0.
[blank] Tappley	10.0.
John Harris	3.0.
Theodora Skout	4.0.
Nicholas Symnods	3.0.
{John Kettle	4.0}.
Thomas Sparnell	6.0.
George Russell	8.0.
Thomas Jacob	8.0.
Thomas Colhnan	6.0.
Nicholas Synnott	6.0.
Thomas Weston	2.0.
Peter Kay	12.0.
John Kay	4.0.
Richard Goldinge	10.0.
<Lawallin Newgent	00.00>
Christopher Barnewall	4.0.
Wine Taverne Streete	
The widdow Cheevers	16.0.
The widdow Browne	10.0.
The widdow Elliott	8.0.
Patrick Lawnder	10.0.
John Dockett	8.0.
Anthony Kirck	6.0.
Thomas Attkins	4.0.
Lawrence Hollywood	13.4.
Barnaby Ennos	4.0.
Patrick English	4.0.
Widdow Brassbridge	4.0.
John Worrall	6.0.
Mary Vailes	6.0.

Nicholas Barnewall	2.0.
Patrick White	6.0.
Robert Wiggett	8.0.
[blank] fferrall	8.0.
11 – 0 – 4	
[f. 90v] Patrick Galballe	8.0.
Richard White	6.0.
Widdow Browne	6.0.
George Chamberlaine	10.0.
Albion Lewerett	12.0.
John March	16.0.
Patrick Buttler	8.0.
Robert Savill, Esq	12.0.
Widdow Bridges	4.0.
Widdow Dale	12.0.
Richard Browne	4.0.
Thomas Dongan	10.0.
John Brookes	10.0.
Henry Browne	4.0.
Jacob The baker	10.0.
{Doctor ffairfaxe	8.0.}
Thomas Richardson	10.0.
Widdow Duffe	8.0.
ffraunces Dowde	13.4.
Peirce Moore	12.0.
James Kerwan	4.0.
Jeremy Woodworth	6.0.
Thomas Taylor	4.0.
Stephen Gernon	5.0.
{Walter ffitz Gerrald	2.0.}
Henry Perice	6.0.
Thomas Burnell	6.0.
Thomas Windall	16.0.
{The Comon Cellar	10.0.}
Robert Dollan	8.0.
Patrick Gogh	6.0.
Philip Conran	6.0.
James Begge	8.0.
Patrick Savage	2.0.
George Keradder	16.0.
Wm Baldaricke	8.0.
John Butcher	8.0.
Peirce Keatinge	8.0.

Widdow Nugent	10.0.
Patrick Dowde	2.0.[76]
[f. 91] *Rosemary Lane*	
Willm Bee	2.0.
Nicholas Whittey	4.0.
Thomas Waker	2.0.
John March for the Golden Lyon	6.0.
Wood Key	
Cornelius Johnson	10.0.
James Eager	10.0.
Robert Dee	8.0.
Thomas Gayton	8.0.
Michael ffitzGarrett	2.0.
John Montgomery	6.0.
Leonard Thomson	<0.0>10.0.
John Pooley	8.0.
Obid Williams	13.4.
John Browne	6.0.
Richard Luttrell	8.0.
Clement Martin	8.0.
Peter Leman	4.0.
George Gossney	8.0.
Benjamine Roberts	10.0.
Roger Gernon	6.0.
Nicholas Dillon	6.0.
William Boy	10.0.
Widdowe Maxfeild	4.0.
John Blake	4.0.
John Johnson	4.0.
Guy Sanderson	2.0.
Widdow Begge	6.0.
Peter Akyin	2.0.
James Scott	4.0.
Walter Doyle	4.0.
Ann Legge	4.0.
John Vinon	<6>4.0.
Richard Balle	4.0.
Michael Pursell	<6>4.0.
9 – 19 – 4	
[f. 91v] Wm Smith, Alderman	12.0.
Christopher Harrison	2.0.
John Read	4.0.
Widdow Read	4.0.
Robert Gill	4.0.

Henry Gordon	4.0.
John Cheevers	2.0.
Jeremy Simpson	<8>6.0.
John Barry	2.0.
Henry Ashborne	<8>6.0.
Stephen Bowers	4.0.
Jeremy Bowden	6.0.
Peter Watson	4.0.
Wm Atkinson	4.0.
Oates Crowder	4.0.
Sir ffaithful ffortescue	1.0.0.
James Luttrell	10.0.
B[isho]pp of Waterford	13.4.
Robert Blowre	10.0.
Wm Cooke, Goldsmith	12.0.
{[blank]Evans, silkweaver	2.0.}
John Dermott	8.0.
Robert Wade	8.0.
Thomas Corran	4.0.
Rice Williams	4.0.
Thomas ffowles	2.0.
Thomas Bingham	2.0.
Thomas Richardson	2.0.
Josias White	2.0.
Wm Cooke, ye player	4.0.
Widdow Thomas	4.0.
Patrick Poore	4.0.
The widdow Aldersey	12.0.
ffrauncis Barker	10.0.
Sir Richard Osbalideston	1.0.0.
The widdow Newman	1.0.0.
Serjeant Sambach	16.0.
[blank] Lynn	12.0.
13 – 9 – 4	
[f. 92] John Parker	8.0.
Jerom Alexander	16.0.
Justice Donnelan	16.0.
Edward Blennerhassett	6.0.
[blank] Wayte {for greenes house}	10.0.
Valentine Wayte	10.0.
George Proudfoott	10.0.
3 – 16 – 0	
Totalis som	75.8.0.

Richard Browne — Wm Plunkett
John Michell — Edm Leadbetter
Jeremy Bowden
Robert Clony
Jeremy Simpson
John March
John Reade
John + Blake
his marke

[f. 92v blank]

[f. 93] xvij° Aprilis Anno Dm 1639
Memorandum that the Prebendary & parishioners of St John the Evangelist Dublin have chosen Mr Richard Browne and Mr William Cook to be Churchwardens for this next year ensuing. And the old Churchwardens are to passe their accompts uppon this day fortnighte and Mr William Plunkett, Ald[erman] William Smyth, Edmond Leadbetter and Mr Jeremy Bowden, Mr John Michell & Mr Robert Cloney, or any two or more of them are to be auditors of their accompt.

Dud Boswell,[77] prebendarie of the parish
Edm Hunt — Jeremy Simpson
Joh Michell — Jeremy Bowden
James Bellew — John Barran
Robert Deey
John Warren
Anthony Gayton
Geor Studdart
Nicholas Osbourne
John Fetlowe

30 Apr[il] 1639
I doe hereby acknowledge that I have received whatsoever was due to me by act of State as prebendarie of St Johns out of that parish from my entrance thereunto untill Easter last. As witnesse my hand subscribed hereunto.
Dud Boswell

[f. 93v] xvij° April 1639
Memorand[um] it is ordered by the consent of the parishioners of St John Dublin that William Plunkett, Esq, Alderma[n], William Smyth, Edmond Ledbetter, John March, Robert Cloney, Jeremy Bowden, John Michell, Robert Dee & Jeremy Sympson or any sixe of them to view and make the cess for the parsons duties.

Also it is ordered by the consent aforesaid that Barnard Bugany, Richard White, baker, <John …> {Richard White shoomaker}, and Oates Crowder shalbe sidesmen for ye saide year.

Dud Boswell, prebendarie of ye parish

Edm Hunt
Jeremy Simpson
John Michell
James Bellew
George Studdart
Nicholas Osbourne

Richard Browne
William Cooke
Jeremy Bowden

[f. 94] A noate of all such as doe willingly contribute towards the building of a steeple & getting upp a ring of bells fitting for the same in ye parish of St John in Dublin 17 Apr[il], 1639.

	li s d
Imprimis Mr Boswell, prebendary[78]	15.0.0.
<Item Mr Willm Cook	10.0.0>
Item Mr Richard Browne	2.0.0.
Item Jeremy Sympson	5.0.0.
Item James Bedlow	5.0.0.
Item John Michell	3.0.0.
Item John March	5.0.0.
Item George Studdart	3.0.0.
Item Robert Cloney	3.0.0.
Item John Warren	1.0.0.
Item Barthol Jordan	3.0.0.
Item George Prowdfoot	3.0.0.
Item John Bonns	1.0.0.
Item John Tetloe	1.0.0.
Item Anthony Gayton	1.0.0.
Item John Borran	1.0.0.
Item George Boyd	10.0.
Item Valentine Wayt	2.0.0.
Item John Reade	1.0.0.
	65.10.0.

[f. 94v blank]

[f. 95] A note and just accompt of all such sommes of monies and yearelie revenewes belonginge to St Johns Church Receaved by Mr Richard Browne & John Mitchell, Churchwardens, from Easter 1638 untill Easter 1639 as followeth

Imprimis receaved of Mr James Bath for five yeares arrers of a plott of ground in Oxmonton belonginge to St Johns ye Evangelist, three shillings per annum	15.0.[79]
More receaved of Mr James Bath for the same in fine of a new lease	2.10.0.
Receaved of Mr Thomas Conran for a house hee holdeth in ffish shamble streete for a whole yeares rent endinge att St Michaels last	3.6.8.
Receaved of Mr Harris of ye Swan Taverne in ffish shamble streete for a yeares rent	15.0.
Receaved of Patricke Russell for a house hee holdeth in ffish shamble streete	7.6.
Receaved of Katherine Kelley, wife to John Cruse for a house in Oxmonton for half a yeare accordinge to the old rent	7.6.
More receaved of Katherine Kelley wife to ye sayde John Cruse for half a yeares rent receaved att St Michaells last in fine of a newe lease accordinge to the rent of foure pounds per annum[80]	2.0.0.
Receaved of Mr Morrice Smith for twoe houses hee holdeth in Oxmanton from ye parish of St Johns the Evangelist	1.13.4.
Receaved of Nicholas Rawbucke for a house hee holdeth in St ffrancis streete which belongeth to St Johns the Evangelist	5.0.
Receaved of the widdowe fforesight for a yeares rent due to St Johns the Evangelist the house being in Oxmonton	2.0.0.
Receaved of Mr Robert Gilbert for a house [he] holdeth in Copper Allie belonginge to St Johns the Evangelist	1.6.3.
Receaved of Mr Walter Usher for a house hee holdeth in fish shamble streete belonginge to St Johns the Evangelist	2.6.8.
Receaved of the M[aster] of ye Taylors for ye geeld of St Johns the Evangelist	1.0.0.
Receaved of Sir Thadie Duffe for a house he holdeth in St Johns parish	1.0.0.
[f. 95v] Receaved of Mr ford for doctor Ushers house in fish shamble streete	1.13.4.
Receaved of Sir William Usher for framinge of timber in St John the Evangelist Churchyard to builde his house in ffish shamble streete	1.0.0.
Receaved from the last churchwardens in stocke when they went out	7.14.3.
Some	29.7.2.

A note of what burialls hath bin since Easter 1638 untill Easter 1639 within St Johns Church the Evangelist in Dublin.

Imprimis receaved for the burial of Mr Raneare	6.8.
for the burial of Widdowe Ranears Child	3.4.
for the burial of Mr Walshe his Child	3.4.
for the burial of Mr Raven	6.8.
for the burial of theWiddowe Newgent	6.8.
for the burial of Sir Richard Osburstons Child	3.4.
for the burial of the Lady Osburston	6.8.
for the burial of Robert Don his brother	6.8.
for the burial of Mr John Mitchells child	3.4.
for the burial of Mr Biddle	13.4.
for the burial of Mr Mitchells children	3.4.
for the burial of Mrs Widdowes	6.8.
for the burial of a Gentleman out of ye Castle	13.4.
for the burial of Sir Wm Reeves daughter	13.4.
for the burial of Rice Williams Child	3.4.
for the burial of John Reads Child	3.4.
for the burial of Walter Conran	6.8.
for the burial of Mr March his child	3.4.
for the burial of Mr Mongomeries Child	3.4.
for the burial of Mr Plunketts maide	6.8.
for ye burial of Nicholas Osbons Childe	3.4.
Some	6.6.8.
Suma totalis	37.7.2.

[f. 96] A note and just accompt of all such summes of monies as have bine disbursed by Mr Richard Browne & John Mitchell Churchwardens of St Johns the Evangelist from Easter 1638 untill Easter 1639 as followeth

Imprimis castinge the small bell	3.15.0.
for weighinge, carringe, takinge downe & and hanging up the sayd bell	5.0.
for a bell Rope	1.0.
for plates of iron that wanted for ye bell stock	4.0.
for mendinge the gutters of ye church & all ye materialls thereto belonginge as boards <nail> nailes, slates, slate pinnes & woorkemanshipp	4.0.0.
for hookes & hinges for ye barthelment doore	1.0.
for oiling & coulouringe the long Ladder	3.0.
for plasteringe, whiting & couleringe of the body of the church & pillers	3.0.0.
for clening of the Church	3.0.
for the Clerkes stipend	2.0.0.

for mendinge the locke of ye west doore	1.6.
for a staple to bear the Kings Armes	1.6.
for pointing the East porch & part of bodie of the Church	2.0.0.
for ye plummers wages to mend the leads	4.0.
for Soder that wanted to mend ye leads	12.0.
for fire to heat the plummers Irons	2.0.
for mendinge ye glasse windowes att severall tymes	15.0.
paving the Lane	
for paving the Church Lane & other materialls thereto belonginge	8.0.
for carring of rubbish out of ye churchyard	10.0.
for mendinge the brasse candlestickes	4.0.
for mendinge the Chest & Ironworke to it	4.0.
for twoe boxes to put the writinges in	2.6.
for Langable due from ye church to ye Cittie	3.3.
for a paire of hinges to the parsons pew doore	1.0.
for ringing ye bells upon powder and treason daye	2.6.
for rushes & bowes ag[ains]t Christmas	2.6.
for the topp of one of the pinnacles of the porch	3.0.
[f. 96v] More for pointinge, slatinge & slates and other necessaries	12.0.
for flagon pott of a potle for the comunion table	9.0.
for a new service booke	10.0.
for mendinge ye locke of ye East doore	1.0.
for deliveringe the p[re]sentments 2 visitacions	1.8.
for new spade & platinge a shovell	2.0.
for examininge the church writings to a Councellor	1.0.0.
for ringinge the bells uppon ye Kinges Coronation daye	2.6.
More payde to the woman which was left unpaide upon the last accompte for ringinge the bells	2.6.
for washing the surplices and the Communion table Lynnen	8.0.
for writing the tenn commaundements in golden letters	1.16.0.
for taking upp & mendinge ye board & cuttinge ye board on which Jehova is written[81]	2.0.
for bread & wine for the yearlie comunion	2.2.2.
for the expenses att the choosinge of the new Churchwardens	1.0.0.
for expenses at three severall meetings by the parishioners & Churchwardens	1.1.6.
Some totall disbursed	27.16.3.

xiij° May 1639

Wee have Examined the accompts of Mr Richard Browne & Mr John Michell, late Churchwardens of this Church, for one yeare ending at ye feast of Easter last past and wee find that they have receaved of ye rents and casualties of the said Church the some of thirty seaven pounds seaven shill[ings] & twoe pence & that they have disbursed as app[ear]eth by their accompt ye some of twentie seaven pounds sixteen shill[ings] & seaven pence soe as there is now remayneing in their hands dewe the some of nyne pounds tenne shill[ings] and seaven pence which they have paied over into the handes of the now Churchwardens Mr Richard Browne & Mr Willm Cooke. All which wee wittnes being auditors assigned for passing this accompte under our handes ye day & yeare above s[ai]d.

Willm Smyth
Wm Plunkett
Jeremy Bowden

[f. 97] Hereafter followeth the Cesse on the Parishioners of St Johns Evangelists due to the Parson of the sayde parish according to the Act of the State. Cessed and taxed by us whose names are here subscribed authorized by the joint & unamimous consent & agreement of all ye parishioners & inhabitants of the sayd parish.

ffish shamble Steete

Robert Usher merchant	x^{s}
Robert Dunn	vj^{s} viij^{d}
Widowe Lawler	vj^{s} viij^{d}
Barnard Bussana	iiij^{s}
John Hargrave the younger	vj^{s}
John Knott	vj^{s}
John Huggard	xvj^{s}
John Cardey & Edward Wilson	vj^{s}
William Holland	iiij^{s}
Robert Cloney	xij^{s}
Thomas Lee	iiij^{s}
Thomas Hill	xij^{s}
John Harris	xvj^{s}
{Laurence fullam	viij^{s}}
John Trew	vj^{s}
Sylvanne Glegge	viij^{s}
Patrick Russell	viij^{s}
John Barran	x^{s}
Willm Boyce	viij^{s}
Martin Nicolls	vj^{s}
Andrew Birde	iij^{s}
John Mullens	ij^{s}
John Knight, Tayler	
[blank] Clapton	iiij^{s}
Walter Poore	ij^{s}

<Thomas> Widowe Quin	vj^{s}
[f. 97v] John Harrison	xij^{s}
George Plunkett	xij^{s}
<The Widdow Cripps> John Harris at the three tonnes	xij^{s}
Mr Geeton	viij^{s}
Morris Killidere	iij^{s}
George Tedder	vj^{s}
Robert Prentice	iiij^{s}
Edmond Hunt	xij^{s}
John Syngleton	vj^{s}
John Tetloe	ij^{s}
John Kenningham	ij^{s}
Mr Bloods house voide	viij^{s}
Anne Rabone	ij^{s}
John Leman	ij^{s}
Randolph Terrer	ij^{s}
John Knight	iiij^{s}
Bartholomew Jordan	x^{s}
Nicholas Baker	vj^{s}
Arthure Chadsey	ij^{s}
Thomas Conner	ij^{s}
Edmond Leadbetter	x^{s}
Richard White	viij^{s}
John Mitchell	xv^{s}
The widdow Dutton	x^{s}
Adam Bragham	xij^{s}
Edward Bermingham	iiij^{s}
Richard Butterley	x^{s}
Mathew Nolan	vj^{s}
<The Widdowe Lutterell>	
James Bedloe	x^{s}
Nicholas Osborne	vj^{s}
Thomas Gunter	vj^{s}
William Plunkett, Esq	xiij^{s} iiij^{d}
Anthonie Medcalfe	vj^{s}
<Henrie Kempe> {Richard Coffee}	viij^{s}
St Johns Lane	
John Warren	vj^{s}
Charles Tapley	x^{s}
John Harris	iij^{s}
Theodora Scout	iiij^{s}
Nicholas Synnod	iij^{s}
[f. 98] John Ketle	iiij^{s}

Thomas Sparnell	vj^{s}
George Russell	x^{s}
Thomas Jacob	viij^{s}
Thomas Coleman	vj^{s}
Nicholas Synnott	x^{s}
Robert ffrench	ij^{s}
Peter Key	xij^{s}
Richard Plonkett	iiij^{s}
Richard Goldinge	x^{s}
Christopher Barnewall	ij^{s}
Wyne Taverne Streete	
The widdowe Chevers	xvj^{s}
The widdowe Browne	x^{s}
The widdowe Elliott	viij^{s}
Patrick Launder	x^{s}
John Dockett	viij^{s}
Anthonie Kerke	iiij^{s}
Charles Kensulah	vj^{s}
Laurence Holliwood	xiij^{s} 4^{d}
Barnabie Ennos	iiij^{s}
Patrick English	iiij^{s}
Widdowe Brassebridge	iiij^{s}
John Worrall	iiij^{s}
Mary Viales	vj^{s}
Nicholas Barnewall	ij^{s}
Patrick White	vj^{s}
Robert Wiggett	viij^{s}
Mr Tayler	x^{s}
Patricke Galballie	viij^{s}
Widdowe Conran	ij^{s}
Richard White	vj^{s}
<Widdow Browne>	
George Chamberlaine	vj^{s}
Albion Leverett	xij^{s}
John March	xvj^{s}
Patrick Butler	viij^{s}
Robert Savile, Esq	vij^{s}
<Widdowe Bridges>	
[f. 98v] Widdowe Dale	x^{s}
Richard Browne	iiij^{s}
Thomas Dongan	x^{s}
John Brookes	x^{s}
Henrie Browne	iiij^{s}

Richard Mulleneux	vj^{s}
<Jacob the baker >	x^{s}
Doctor ffaireffax	viij^{s}
Hunter	
Thomas Richardson	x^{s}
Widdowe Duffe	viij^{s}
Francis Dowde	xiij^{s} iiij^{d}
Peirce Moore	xij^{s}
James Keran	iiij^{s}
Jeremie Woodworth	vj^{s}
Thomas Taylor	iiij^{s}
Stephen Gernon	v^{s}
Walter ffitzgarrett	ij^{s}
Henry Perce	vj^{s}
Thomas Burnell	vj^{s}
Thomas Windall	xvj^{s}
Comon Seller	x^{s}
Robert Dollan	viij^{s}
Patricke Gogh {& Mr Evers}	vj^{s}
Phillipp Conran	vj^{s}
James Begg	viij^{s}
Patricke Savadge	ij^{s}
George Keradder	xvj^{s}
William Balldarch	viij^{s}
John Butcher	viij^{s}
Peirce Keating	viij^{s}
Widdowe Newgent	x^{s}
RoseMarie Lane	
William Bee	ij^{s}
Nicholas Whitey	iiij^{s}
John Oaker	ij^{s}
John March for ye Golden Lyon	<vj>ij^{s}
Wood key	
Cornelius Johnson	x^{s}
James Eager	x^{s}
[f. 99] Robert Dee	viij^{s}
Thomas Gayton	viij^{s}
Michaell ffitzgarrett	ij^{s}
John Mountgomerie	vj^{s}
John Perrie	x^{s}
John Pooley	viij^{s}
William Clerke	xiij^{s} 4^{d}
John Browne	vj^{s}

Richard Luttrell	viij^{s}
Clement Martin	viij^{s}
Peter Leman	iiij^{s}
John March for Gosney	viij^{s}
Benjamin Roberts	x^{s}
Widowe Dillon	vj^{s}
William Boye	x^{s}
Widdowe Maxfeilde	iiij^{s}
John Blake	iiij^{s}
John Johnson	iiij^{s}
George Boye	viij^{s}
Widdowe Begg	vj^{s}
Walter Doyle	iiij^{s}
Ann Legg	iiij^{s}
John Anion	vj^{s}
Richard Ball	iiij^{s}
Michaell Pursell	vj^{s}
William Smith, Alderman	xij^{s}
Christopher Harrison	ij^{s}
John Reade	iiij^{s}
Widdowe Reade	iiij^{s}
Henry Jordan	iiij^{s}
Robert Gill	iiij^{s}
John Cheevers	ij^{s}
Jeremie Simpson	viij^{s}
John Barrie	ij^{s}
Henry Ashborne	vj^{s}
Stephen Bowers	iiij^{s}
Jeremie Bowden	vj^{s}
[f. 99v] Peter Watson	iiij^{s}
Oates Crowder	iiij^{s}
Sir ffaithful ffoscue	xx^{s}
Mr William Kadogan	[blank]
Mr ffellys	x^{s}
Robert Bloare	x^{s}
William Cooke, goldsmith	x^{s}
Willm Evans	iiij^{s}
John Bonos	iiij^{s}
Robert Wade	viij^{s}
Thomas Corran	iiij^{s}
Rece Williams	ij^{s}
Thomas Powell	ij^{s}
Thomas Bingham	ij^{s}

Thomas Richardson	ij^s
[blank] Rawson	ij^s
Obid Willims	ij^s
Widdowe Thomas	ij^s
Richard Pellam	iiij^s
The widdow Aldersey	xij^s
Sir {Richard} Osbaldston	xx^s
The widdowe Newman	xx^s
ffrancis Barker	x^s
Serjant Sambach	xvj^s
Marmaduke Lynn	xij^s
John Parker	viij^s
Mr Martin Esq	xvj^s
Justice Donnelan	xvj^s
Jefferie Welch	vj^s
[blank] Widdow	ex^s
Valentine Wade	x^s
George Proudefoote	x^s

Willm Smyth — Wm Plunkett
Jeremy Bowden — Jer Simpson
Edm Leadbetter
John Michell

[f. 100] 6th of Aprill Ano dm 1640
Memorand[um] that the prebendary & parishioners of St John the Evangelist Dublin have chosen Mr William Cooke & Mr Clement Martyn to be churchwardens for this nexte yeare ensuing. And the old Churchwardens are to passe their accompts upon this day fortnight and Willm Plunkett Esq, Alderman Wm Smyth, Mr Edmund Hunt, Mr John Michell, Mr Jeremy Bowden, Mr Robert Cloney, Mr Jeremy Sympson & Mr Nicholas Osborne or any two or more of them are to be Auditors of their accomptes.

Dud Boswell, prebendarie of St Johns

Jeremy Simpson	Wm Plunkett
Jeremy Bowden	Edm Hunt
Patrick + Gabally his mark	Thomas + Dongan his mark
Thomas TI Jacob his l[ett]res	Nicholas Osbourne
John Worrall	John Warren
John Powley	Vallintine Wayte

Sixth of Aprill 1640
I doe hereby acknowledge to have receaved whatsoever was due to me by act of State as Prebendary of St Johns out of that parish fro[m] my entrance

thereunto untill <Easter> {Christmas last}. As witnesse my hand subscribed thereunto.

Dud Boswell

Witnes hereunto & that the word Christmas was interlyned before the signing hereof

Wm Plunkett
Jeremy Sympson

[f. 100v] sixth April 1640
Memorand[um] it is ordered by consent of ye parishioners of St John Dublin that William Plunkett, Esq., Alderman,Wm Smyth, Mr Edmond Hunt, Mr John Michell, Mr Jeremy Bowden, Mr Robert Cloney, Mr Thomas Dongan, {Mr Nichas Osborne} & Mr Jeremy Sympson or any sixe of them to veiwe & make ye Cesse for the parsons duties for this ensuing yeare.

It is also ordered by the consent aforesaid that Anthony Gayton, Thomas Hill, John Worrall & Patrick Moore shoemaker shalbe sidesmen for the said year.

Dud Boswell, prebendarie of St Johns
Nicholas Osbourne
Jeremy Bowden
Patrick + Galbally his mark
Thomas TI Jacob his l[ette]res

Wm Plunkett
Edm Hunt
Jeremy Simpson
Thomas + Dongan his marke

f. 101 blank]

[f. 101v] A Note and Just accompt of all such somes of monies and yearly Revenues belonging to St Johns Church Receaved by Mr Richard Browne and Mr William Cooke, Churchwardens, from Easter 1639 until Easter 1640 as followeth

	li s d
Imprimis Receaved of Mr Thomas Conran for a house hee houldeth in fishamble street for a whole years rent endinge at St Michals past	3.6.8.
Receaved of Mr Harris of the Swan taverne in ffishamble street for a yeares rent	15.0.
Receaved of Mr Mathew fford for a wholl years rent for a house in ffishamble street	1.13.4.
Receaved of Walter Usher merchant for a wholl years rent for a house in ffishamble street	2.6.8.
Receaved of John Hunter, baker, for one house that hee dwelleth in in ffishamble street	7.6.

Receaved of Mr ffrancis Bath for a whole years rent for a house which hee houldeth in Oxmonton	2.10.0.
Receaved of Kathering Cannell als. Kelly <for> widdow for on house in Oxmonton	4.0.0.
Receaved of Mr Morrise Smith for two howses hee houldeth in Oxmonton	1.13.4.
Receaved of John Anderson for his house in Oxmonton {for halfe a years rent}	1.0.0.
Receaved of Nicholas Rawbuck for a house which he houldeth in St francis street	1.5.0.
Receaved of Robert Gilbert for a house which he houldeth in Copper allie	1.6.3.
Receaved of Sir Thadie Duffe for one house belonging to St Johns parrish	1.0.0.
Receaved of the M[aste]r of the Companie of taylors for their geald in St Johns Chappell	1.0.0.
[f. 102] Receaved of Mr Richard Browne <which> in mony which was left in his hands of the last accompt the sum of	9.10.7.
Sum total	31.14.4.

A note of such burialls as hath bin since Easter 1639 untill Easter 1640 within St Johns Church the Evangelist Dublin

Imprimis Receaved for the buriall of Mr Thomas Quin	6.8.
Receaved for <the> {a} buriall of Mr Dunn	6.8.
Receaved for the buriall of Mr Gunters Child	3.4.
Receaved for the buriall of Mr Core	6.6.
Receaved for the buriall of Mr Stewards Child	6.6.
Receaved for the buriall of Mr Spicke	6.8.
Receaved for the buriall of Mr Brian Jones Child	6.8.
Receaved for the buriall of Mr Stewards Child	6.8.
Receaved for the buriall of John Harris Child	3.0.
	2.12.08
Sum totall	34.7.0.

[f. 102v] A Note and Just accompt of all such somes of monies as have bin disbursed by Mr Richard Browne & Mr Will Cooke Churchwardens of St John the Evangelist from Easter 1639 untill Easter 1640 as followeth.

	li s d
Imprimis for a Counsellors fee for a hearinge before my Lord of Derrie[82]	1.0.0.
for Copyinge two breviats	5.0.
for attendance to the ould woemans sonn	1.0.
for Hollie and Evie	2.6.
for expences cominge hom from My Lord of Derries	3.4.
for a sommons to Bradford	1.4.
for mending the pwes in the Church	4.0.
for mendinge the leads to the plumer	13.4.
for mendinge a Candelsticke and pott	1.10.
for Counsellors fee for the last herring that should have bin in the Church beefore my Lord of Derrie	1.0.0.
for attendance to widdowes sonn	2.6.
for expences att the chusing Churchwardens	18.0.
for Bartholmew Jordains wages	1.0.0.
for wine	1.6.0.
for Breade	4.2.
for Copyinge out the burialls and Christnings & mariages for the court	4.0.
for Changinge the Comunion Cups into one[83] and for the Case	7.14.0.
for expence for chusinge the <first> Churchwardens	1.0.0.
for expence for the second meetinge	7.6.
for a Register Booke	1.10.0.
for the p[re]sentments in Court	10.
for two new hearses	13.0.
for Langable to the Sheriff	3.3.
for writing the ould register into the new Register booke[84]	1.10.0.
for a boord to set the act of State on	6.
for ringing the bells one powder treason	2.6.
[f. 103] for the Clarke towards his stipand	1.0.0.
for a petion to bee p[re]sented att the Councell table	11.0.
for washinge the Surplases and Church lininge	8.0.
for repairinge the church in the yeare	3.0.0.
for ringinge the bells one the kings Corronation day	2.6.
Som totall	25.10.1.

xiij° May 1640

Memorand[um] wee have examined the accompts of Mr Richard Browne & Willm Cooke, Church wardens of this Church, for one yeare ending at the feast of Easter last past. And wee fynd that they have Receaved of the Rents & casualties of the said Church the some of thirtie fower pounds & seaven shillings. And that they have disbursed as appeareth by their accompt the some of twentie five {pounds} one shilling & one penny soe as there is now remayning in their hands which is nowe payed over into the handes of the said Mr Willm Cooke. All which wee wittnes being Auditors assigned for the passing this accompte. Which some nowe remayning in his hands is eight poundes sixteen shillings & eleaven pence st.

Wm Plunkett — Willm Smyth
Nicholas Osbourne
Robert Clony
John Michell

[f. 103v blank]

[f. 104] Hereafter followethe the Cesse one the parishioners of St John Evangelist due to the parson of the same parrish according to the Act of the State. Cessed and taxed by us whose names are here subscribed authorized by the joint and unamimous consent & agreement of all the <Con> parishioners & Inhabitants of the said parish the therteenth day of May 1640.

	li s d
fishamble stret	
Robert Usher, merchant	10.0.
Robert Dunn	6.8.
Widdow Lawlor	6.8.
Barnard Bussana	4.0.
Thomas ffretlie	2.0.
John Hargrave the younger	6.0.
John Brage	2.0.
John Knott	6.0.
Mrs Bond	2.0.
John Huggard	16.0.
John Cardie & Edward Wilson	6.0.
Morgan ffullam	4.0.
William Holland	[blank]
Mrs Goddin	2.0.
Roger Moore	6.0.
Robert Clonie	12.0.
Thomas Lee	4.0.
Thomas Hall	12.0.
John Harrison	2.0.
Lawrence ffullam	8.0.
$5^{li} - 17s - 4^{d}$	
[f. 104v] Patrick Garrett	4.0.

Clapton att the Swan taverne	16.0.
John Trew	4.0.
Silvanus Glege	8.0.
Patrick Russell	8.0.
John Borron	10.0.
William Boyce	8.0.
Martin Michells	6.0.
Andrew Bird	2.0.
Mr Smith	4.0.
Thomas Powell	4.0.
John Mullens	2.0.
Wallter Poore, {taylor}	2.0.
John Knight, Taylor	4.0.
Mary Elliott, Widdow	2.0.
Willan Roe	2.0.
Widdow Guin	6.0.
<John Harris at the	>
William Eldrege	10.0.
Peter Leamon, Taylor	2.0.
George Plunkett	10.0.
John [blank] a Tapster	4.0.
John Harris at the 3 tonnes	16.0.
Anthony Gayton	8.0.
Maurice Killedere	2.0.
Mr Eagers	6.0.
Robert Gill	2.0.
Robert Prentice	4.0.
Richard Doore	2.0.
Thomas Write	2.0.
Edmund Hunt	12.0.
John Singleton	4.0.
$3^{li} - 16^{s} - 00^{d}$	
[f. 105] John Tetloe	2.0.
John Keningham	2.0.
James Clench	2.0.
Heugh Gwin	2.0.
Ann Rabone	2.0.
John Moore	2.0.
Walter Roberts	2.0.
John Leamon	2.0.
Richard Bald	4.0.
Widdow Knight	4.0.
Bartholmue Jordaine	10.0.

Nicholas Baker, Clement the tapster	6.0.
Arthur Chadsie	2.0.
Rice Williams	4.0.
Edmund Leadbetter	10.0.
Richard White	8.0.
John Rotch	2.0.
John Michell	15.0.
Oliver Devorex	6.0.
James Gillsent	4.0.
Adam Beagham	12.0.
Edmund Bremigham	4.0.
<John Cotton	>
Richard Butterlie	10.0.
<Patrick the Glasier	>
Gillies Robertson	8.0.
James Bedloe	10.0.
Nicholas Osborne	6.0.
Thomas Gunter	6.0.
William Pluncket, Esq	13.4.
Anthony Midcase	6.0.
Richard Coffie	4.0.
$8^{li} - 00^{s} - 4^{d}$	
[f. 105v] *St Johns Lane*	
John Warren	4.0.
John Neale, taylor	2.0.
Mr Parrie for the Marshalsea	10.0.
Bartholl Leamon	2.0.
Theodora Scout	6.0.
Nicholas Sinott	4.0.
John Kettle	4.0.
Thomas Parnell	6.0.
George Russell	10.0.
Thomas Jacob	8.0.
Thomas Coleman	6.0.
Nicholas Sinott	10.0.
Robert ffrench	2.0.
Peter Keys	12.0.
Richard Plunket, taylor	4.0.
Richard Goulding	10.0.
Christopher Barnewall	2.0.
Wine taverne streete	
Widdow Cheevers	16.0.
William fferrie & Barthol Quoyle	2.0.

Edward Brooke	4.0.
The widdow Browne	10.0.
Patrick Landers	10.0.
John Dockett	8.0.
Nicholas Luttrell	8.0.
Anthony Kerke	4.0.
Charles Kensalagh	4.0.
Lawrence Holliwood	13.4.
Barnabee Ennos	4.0.
Patrick English	4.0.
Widdow Brasbrige	4.0.
John Worrall	4.0.
Mary Vialls	6.0.
Nicholas Barnewall	2.0.
Patrick White	6.0.
Thomas Magan	10.0.
$11^{li} - 01^{s} - 4^{d}$	
[f. 106] Mr Doungans house	10.0.
Patrick Galbally	6.0.
Patrick Moore	8.0.
The Widdow Conran	[blank]
Richard White	6.0.
Widdow Chamberlin	6.0.
Albion Leverett	12.0.
John Martch	16.0.
Patrick Scorlocke	8.0.
Thomas McGuier	2.0.
Mathew Nowell	12.0.
Widdow Dalle	10.0.
Widdow Browne	2.0.
Thomas Dongan	10.0.
Robert Savill, Esq	12.0.
Henry Browne	4.0.
John Stanlie	6.0.
Thomas <Clarke> Clarke	6.0.
Mr Hunter	10.0.
Widdow Duff	8.0.
ffrancis Dowde	13.4.
Perce Moore	12.0.
James Kerran	2.0.
Jeromie Woodworth	6.0.
Thomas Taylor	4.0.
Stephen Gernon	6.0.

Walter ffitz Garret	2.0.
The black boy	6.0.
Thomas Windall	16.0.
Common Sellar	12.0.
Robert Dollard	8.0.
Patrick Goth and Mr Evans	6.0.
Phillipe Conran	6.0.
James Begge	8.0.
{Patrick Sav{a}ge	2.0.}
George Kerrader	10.0.
James Daniell	2.0.
George Crowder	2.0.
Richard Birford Connell	10.0.
John Willson	2.0.
$14^{li} - 9^{s} - 4^{d}$	
[f. 106v] William Baldrack	8.0.
John Bucher	8.0.
Pearce Keating	6.0.
Widdow Newgent	10.0.
Rosemary Lane	
William Bee	2.0.
Thomas Booreback	4.0.
John Oker	2.0.
Oliver Bushope	2.0.
Wood key	
Mr Mazonas	10.0.
James Eager	10.0.
Robert Dee	8.0.
Roger Warren	8.0.
John Mountgomery	6.0.
James Johnson	10.0.
John Pooly	8.0.
William Clarke	13.4.
John Browne	6.0.
Richard Luttrell	8.0.
Clement Martin	8.0.
Patrick Doyle	4.0.
William Shee	2.0.
Rowland in Peter Leamons house	2.0.
Robert Wentsford	4.0.
John March for Gosney	8.0.
John James	4.0.
Benjamin Roberts	10.0.

Widdow Dillon	6.0.
William Boyd	10.0.
Widdow Maxfild	4.0.
John Blake	4.0.
John Johnson	4.0.
John Kevanagh	2.0.
George Boyde	8.0.
Widdow Begg	6.0.
John Benson	4.0.
Guy Sanders	4.0.
James Scote	2.0.
Edward fleminge	2.0.
Ann Legg	4.0.
John Union, Martin Waits	6.0.
11^{li} – 13^{s} – 4^{d}	
[f. 107] Thomas O fforeman	4.0.
Michell Purcell	6.0.
William Smith, alderman	12.0.
Captaine Bartelet	10.0.
John Reade	4.0.
Widdow Reade	4.0.
William Bell	2.0.
Henry Jordaine	4.0.
John Cheevers	2.0.
Jeremy Simpson	8.0.
John Barry	2.0.
Henry Ashborne	6.0.
Stephen Bowers	4.0.
Jeromy Bowden	6.0.
Peeter Watson	2.0.
Oates Crowder	4.0.
Robert [blank], a shoemaker	2.0.
Sir ffaithfull fortscue	1.0.0.
Mr William Kadogan	1.0.0.
Edward Henlie	10.0.
John Singleton	10.0.
Richard Osbee, upolsterer	4.0.
William Cooke, Gouldsmith	10.0.
Will Evans	4.0.
John Briscoe	6.0.
Robert Wade	8.0.
Thomas Corren	4.0.
Edmond [blank], a taylor	2.0.

Thomas Beaton	2.0.
Robert Bingham	2.0.
Thomas Richardson	2.0.
Thomas Rawson	2.0.
Ann Williams	2.0.
Ann White	2.0.
Richard Pellam	2.0.
Richard Dall	4.0.
*9^li^ – 18^s^ – 00^d^*	
[f. 107v] Robert Wimberlie	4.0.
John Ratelife	2.0.
Widdow Aldersie	12.0.
Doctor Bott	1.0.0.
Sir Richard Osbaldston	1.0.0.
the widdow Newman	1.0.0.
Sir Will Sanbech	16.0.
Marmeduke Linn	12.0.
John Parker	8.0.
Mr Martin, Esq	16.0.
Justice Donnelan	16.0.
Jefffrey Welsh	4.0.
Mr Hewett	2.0.
Will Wooddall	4.0.
Mr Ducarraway	8.0.
Vallintaine Waite	10.0.
George Prowdfoote	6.0.
Lawrence Hannes	2.0.
ffrancis March	2.0.
Peeter Thomson	2.0.
*9^li^ – 10^s^ – 00^d^*	

Wm Plunkett — Willm Smyth
Jeremy Bowden
Nicholas Osbourne
Robert Clony

[f. 108] 26° Aprilis 1641
Memorand[um] that the Prebendary and Parishioners of St John the Evangelist Dublin have chosen Mr Clement Martyn & Mr Anthony Geaton to be Churchwardens for this next yeare ensueing and the old Churchwardens are to passe theire accompts uppon the seaventeenth of May next. And William Plunkett Esq, Alderman William Smyth, Mr Edmond Hunt, Mr Jeremy Bowden, Mr Robert Cloney, Jeremy Sympson, Mr John Browne & Mr Nicholas Osborne or any two or more of them are to be Auditors of their accompte.

Dud Boswell, prebendarie of St Johns.

	Wm Plunkett
Robert Clony	Edm Hunt
Jas IE Eyers his mark	Jeremy Bowden
Mathew Noell	John Browne
Jeremy Simpson	Nicholas Osbourne
Thomas Bitfel	Jo Johnson

26º April 1641
I doe hereby acknowledge to have received whatsoever was due to mee by act of state as Prebendary of St John the Evangelist Dublin out of that parish from my entrance thereunto untill our lady Day last. As witnes my hand subscribed hereunto the day & year above written.

Dud Boswell

Witness herunto
Wm Plunkett
Edm Hunt
Jeremy Simpson

[f. 108v] Aprilis Ano dm 1641
Memorand[um] it is ordered by consent of the parishioners of St John the Evangelist Dublin that William Plunkett, Esq, Alderman William Smyth, Mr Edmond Hunt, Mr John Michell, Mr Jeremy Bowden, Mr Robert Cloney, Mr Thomas Dongan, Mr Nichas Osborne & Jeremy Sympson or any sixe or more of them shall veiwe & make the cess of the parsons dutyes for this ensueing year.

26 Apr[il] 1641
Memorand[um] that it is ordered by consent of the parishioners of the parish of St John the Evangelist Dublin that that John Briscoe William Evans, James Egar & Matthew Nowell shalbe sidesmen for this present yeare.

Dud Boswell	Wm Plunkett
Robt Clony	Edm Hunt
Jeremy Simpson	William Hook
Jo Johnson	John Browne
Clement Martyn	Nicholas Osbourne
	Jeremy Bowden

[f. 109] A Note and Just accompt of all such somes of monies and yearly revenues beelonging to St Johns Church Receaved by Mr William Cooke & Mr Clement Marten, Churchwardens, from Easter 1640 untill Easter 1641 as followeth

	li. s. d.
Imprimis Receaved of Thomas Conran for one house now in the occupacon of John Trew for a wholl years rent ending att Michallmas last past	3.6.8.
Receaved att the Swan Tavern for one wholl yeares rent	15.0.
Receaved of Mathew Ford for one wholl yeares rent for one house	1.13.4.
Receaved of Walter Usher, merchant, for one house in ffishamble street	2.6.8.
Receaved of John Hunter, baker, for one wholl yeares rent	7.6.
Receaved of {M[aster] of the}Companie of taylors	1.0.0.
Receaved of James Bath of Dromconrath for land in Oxmonton	2.10.0.
Receaved of Kathering Cannall als Kelly for one house	4.0.0.
Receaved of Kathering Taylor for one house	1.0.0.
Receaved of Mr Maurice Smith for one house	13.4.
Receaved of John Anderson for one house in Oxmonton	2.0.0.
Receaved of John Good, Bucher, for one house	1.5.0.
a house in Copper Ally[85]	
Receaved of Robert Gilber for one house in Copper Alley	1.6.3.
Receaved of Sir Thadie Duff for one house one the wood key	1.0.0.
Sum totall	23.3.9.

[f. 109v] A Note of the burialls as hath bine since Easter 1640 untill Easter 1641 within St Johns Church the Evangelist Dublin

Imprimis for the buriall of Mistres Ratcliffe	6.6.
Item for the buriall of Mr Baldroes sonne	3.4.
Item for the buriall of Mr Bowdens kinsman	6.8.
Item for the buriall of Mr White	13.4.
Item for the buriall of the Kings Attornie[86]	13.4.
Item for the buriall of Steven Bowers	5.8.
Item for the buriall of Mr Linch	13.4.
Item for the buriall of Mr Simsons Mane	6.6.
Item for the buriall of Wimberlies Child	3.0.
Item for the buriall of Rice Williams Child	3.4.
Item for the Buriall of Mr Samon	6.8.
Item for the buriall of a young gent[leman] that lay att George Plunketts	6.8.
Item for the buriall of Mathew Nowells Child	3.4.
Item for the buriall of Mr Baldro the attornie	6.8.
Item for the buriall of Reads wife	6.8.
Sum totall	5.4.8.

[f. 110] A Note and Just accompt of all such somes of monies as have bin disbursed by Mr William Cooke and Mr Clement Martin, Churchwardens of St <John> Johnes the Evangelist, from Easter 1640 untill Easter 1641.

Imprimis spent att the meeting for the making up the accomptes	4.4.
Item for writing the sesse in the booke	4.0.
Item for bayes and tape for parsones pew	4.10.
Item for mending 2 lockes on the Church doores	2.6.
Item for mending pewes in the gallerie	1.4.
Item for the mending the pewes att my Lord of Waterfords buriall[87]	9.0.
Item for putting in the p[re]sentments	3.0.
Item to Mr John Michell for wine	1.9.0.
Item for bread	4.8.
Item for paving the Church	2.10.
Item for ringing one the Kings day	2.6.
Item for glasier	10.7.
Item for glasing more	5.0.
Item for slating and repaire of the Church	3.2.5.
Item for one Cushen	2.10.0.
Item for Bartholmue Jordaines wages	2.0.0.
Item for hollie & Eivie	2.6.
Item for ringing the bells one the Kings day	2.6.
Item for washing the Church lining	9.0.
Item for for a warrent to gather the ses	1.0.
Item for writing the ses for the poore	2.6.
Item for proces & putting in p[re]sentments	3.10.
Item for the Shreeves for the long Cable	3.3.
Item spent att the Chusing of the Church wardens	1.10.0.
	15.00.7.

[f. 110v] xvij° May 1641
Memorand[um] wee have examined the accompts of Mr William Cooke & Clement Martyn Church wardens of this Church for one yeare ending at Easter last past. And wee find that they have receaved of the rents & casualties of the said Church the some of thirtie & seven pounds ffyve shillings & fowre pence ster. And that they have disbursed as appeareth by their accompts the some of fifteen pounds & seaven pence soe as there is now remayneinge in their hands which is nowe paid over into the handes of Clement Martyn aforesaid & Anthony Gayton now Churchwardens {the some of twentie & two poundes four shillings and nyne pence sterling}. All which wee witnes being Auditors assigned for passing this accompte, there remaines in the handes of the nowe churchwardens the said some of twentie & twoe pounds four shillings & nyne pence sterlinge.

Dud Boswell	Wm Plunkett
Jeremy Bowden	Edm Hunt
	Jeremy Simpson
	John Browne
	Nicholas Osbourne

[f. 111] xij° April 1642
M[emoran]d[um] It is ordered by consent of the parson & parishioners of St Jones the Evangelists Dublin & have chosen Mr Anthony Gaydon & Mr John Browne to be Churchwardens for this next yeare ensuinge and the old Church wardens are to passe their accompts uppon the xix^th^ day of this instant Aprill and Willm Plunkett, Alderman Smyth, Jeremy Bowden, Robt Cloney, Nicholas Osborne & John Michell or any two of them.

Dud Boswell, prebendarie of St Johns

	John Powley
Wm Plunkett	John Butcher
Jeremy Bowden	William Clark
John Michell	Clement Martyn
Thomas Curwen	

I doe acknowledge to have receaved whatsoev[er] was due unto me by Act of State as Prebendary of St Johns Dublin out of the parish from my Entrance thereunto untill the feast of the Nativity [of] our blessed saviour last past. Wittnes my hand the 12 th day of Aprill 1642. I say received 60^{li}.

Dud Boswell

[f. 111v] M[emoran]d[um] It is ordered by the Consent of the parishioners of the parish of St Johns that William Clarke, Willm Etheridge & James Johnson shalbe sidesmen for this ensuing yeare. Wittnes our hands the 12th of Aprill 1642.

Dud Boswell
Wm Plunkett
Joh Michell
Jeremy Bowden
Clement Martyn
John Butcher
John Powley
Anth Gayton

[f. 112 blank]

[f. 112v] A note of all such Monyes as hath been disbursed by Clement Martyn & Anthony Gayton, Churchwardens of St John the Evangelist, Dublin, from Easter 1641 until Easter 1642.

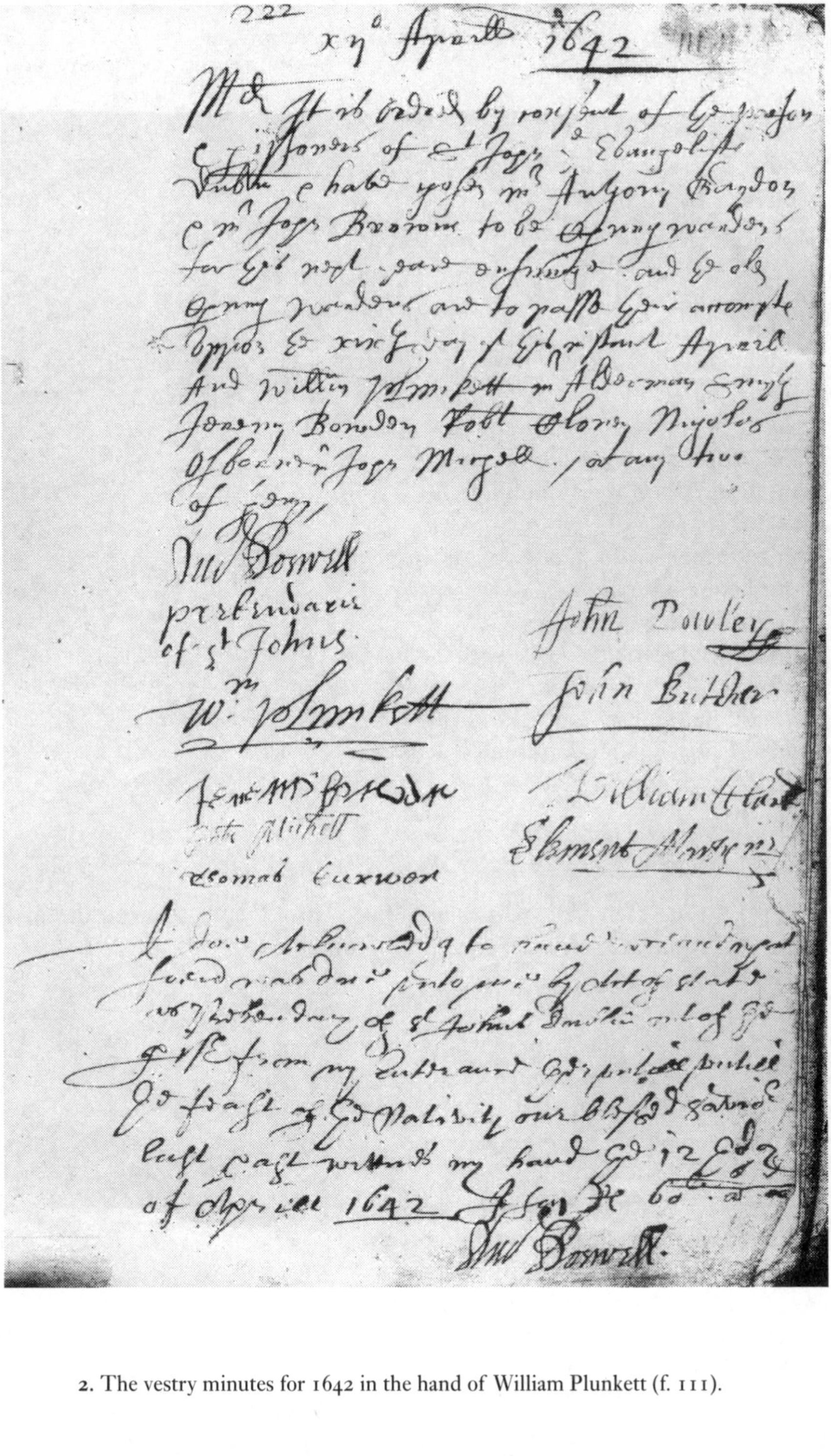
xvjo Aprill 1642

Mem. It is ordered by consent of the prebendary & parishioners of St John the Evangelist Dublin that we have chosen Mr Anthony [illegible] & Mr John Broome to be churchwardens for this next yeare ensuinge and the ould churchwardens are to passe their accompte upon the [illegible] day of this instant Aprill And William Plunkett, Mr Alderman Smyth, Jeremy Bowden, Robt Glover, Nicholas Osborne & John Mitchell, or any two of them

Jno Boswell prebendarii of St Johns

John Pawley

Wm Plunkett

John Butcher

[illegible]

William Clar[illegible]

John Mitchell

[illegible]

Thomas Luxwort

[illegible]

Jno Boswell

2. The vestry minutes for 1642 in the hand of William Plunkett (f. 111).

	li. s. d.
Imprimis paid at makinge Mr Cooke & my Accompt	4.0.
paid Bartholmew Jordane	2.0.0.
paid for a spade	1.6.
paid the longe Gable	3.6.
paid at severall tymes for wash[ing] Church lynen	10.6.
paid for a Board to carry the Corpse on	12.0.
paid ye glasier mending South windowes	3.6.
paid for wax Candles	3.0.
paid for Ringing the Bells	2.6.
paid for slating the Church	4.6.
paid for mending the windowes of the north sides of the Church	8.4.
paid two slaiters for 11 dayes worke a peece at 18d p[er] diem	1.13.0.
paid for slates, lyme, lathes and to two labourers	2.8.3.
paid for Ringing the bells	2.6.
paid for wyne for the Comunions	1.15.0.
paid for Bread	5.4.
paid a Carpenter for 3 dayes worke for mending the pews & B Jordaines seate	4.6.
paid for 2 p[ai]r of hindges	1.0.
paid for nayles to mend the pewes	3.0.
paid for a Bolt	1.4.
paid for mending two locks & keyes	1.6.
paid at Choosing new Churchwardens	1.4.4.
paid for 3li of Candles	1.10.
	12.11.9.

[f. 113] A note of the Burialls as hath been since Easter 1641 untill Easter 1642 in St Johns Church the Evangelist Dublin

	li. s. d.
Imprimis for Mr Coleman friends buriall	13.4.
Received for Mr Priderwoods Child	6.8.
Received for Mr Carpenters Child	6.8.
Received for Stephen Holt musition	3.4.
Received for Osbyes Child	3.4.
Received for Mr John Mitchells Child	3.4.
Received of Jeremy Sympson for Crosby	6.8.
Received for Mr Howards Child	6.8.
Received for Mrs Etheridges buriall	6.8.
Received for James Agards ten[an]t	6.8.
Received for Mr Mitchells friend	3.4.

Received of Mrs Fleminge	3.4.
Received for Mr Nowells Child	3.4.
Received for Mr Montgomerys Child	3.4.
Received for A[l]d[erman] Smiths two Children	6.8.
Received for Rice Williams Child	3.4.
Received for Mr Willm Plunkett Esquire [child]	3.4.
Received for Michael F[it]zgerralds Child	3.4.
Received for Mr Dunsterfield	3.4.
	4.16.8.

[f. 113v] A note of such monyes as hath been received for the parish Rents from Easter 1641 untill Easter 1642 as followeth

Received of the M[aste]r of [the] Taylors Company	1.0.0.
Received of Katherin Conran	4.0.0.
Received of Sir Thady Duffe knt	1.0.0.
Received of Nicholas Robucke	1.5.0.
Received of Thomas Conran	1.13.4.
Received of Widdow Smith	16.6.
	9.14.10.

xix° Aprill 1642
M[emoran]d[um] wee have examined ye accompts of Mr Clement Martine & Anthony Gayton, Church wardens of this Church, for one yeare ending at Easter last 1642 & wee fynd that they have Receaved of the Rents & Casualties of the said Church the some of thirtie six pounds sixteen shillings & three pence. And that they have disbursed as appeares by their accompts the some of twelve pounds eleven shillings & one penny soe as there is nowe remayning dewe uppon this accompt the some of twentie fowre poundes five shillings & two pence ster which is payd over into ye handes of Mr Anthony Gayton & Mr John Browne ye now Churchwardens.

Wm Plunkett
Joh Michell
Nicholas Ashbourne

[f. 114] xxx° May 1642
M[emoran]d[um] it is ordered by the consent of the parishioners of St Johns Dublin that Mr Alderman Smyth, Mr Willm Plunkett, Mr Clement Martine, Mr Benjemyne Rob[er]ts, Mr Edmund Leadbetter, Jeremy Boyeden, Mr John Michell, Mr Willm Cooke, Mr Matthew Nowell or any six of them to view & make the Cess of the parsons dewties for this yeare in pursuance of the Act of State.

Dud Boswell, prebendarie of St Johns

Wm Plunkett	Willm Smyth
Jeremy Bowden	Edm Leadbetter
Anth Gayton	Joh Michell
	John Browne

[f. 114v blank]

[f. 115] quarto die Aprill 1643
M[emoran]d[um] it is Ordered by Consent of the parishioners of St Johns Evangelist Dublin that Willm Plunkett Esq, Clement Martine, Mr Jeremy Boyden, Mr James Eager, Mr Thomas Dungan, Mr George Plunkett, Mr Anthony Gayden, Mr Bengamyne Rob[er]ts, Mr Willm Cooke & Mr Robt Clowny or any six of them to make & viewe the Cess for the parsons dewties for this next ensuing year in pursnance of the Act of State in that behalf.

Dud Boswell, prebendarie	Jas. + Eager mark
	Willm Smyth, maior dublin
	Wm Plunkett
George Plunkett	Anth Gayton
	John Browne
	John Hallowes

4 Aprill 1643
M[emoran]d[um] that it is ordered by consent of the parson & parishioners of St Johns Church Dublin that Willm Pettite, Willm Knight, Georg Hallys & Richard Ball shalbe sidesmen for this parish for this insuing yeare.

Dud Boswell	James + Eager mark
John Hallowes	Willm Smyth, maior of Dublin
George Plunkett	Wm Plunkett
	Anth Gayton
	John Browne
	Jeremy Bowden

[f. 115v] 10 April 1643
Memorand[um] It is Ordered by consent of the parson & parishioners of St Johns Evangelist Dublin that Mr Mathewe Nowell & Mr John Knott shalbe Churchwardens of the said parish for this next ensuing yeare & the old Churchwardens, Mr Anthony Geyden & Mr John Browne, are to passe their accompts on ffryday next being the 14th of this instant Aprill 1643 & Willm Plunkett Esq, Mr Clement Martine, Mr Jeremy Bowden, Mr Robt Clony, Mr John Michell, the newe Churchwardens, Mr Walter fflood or any three or more of them to be Auditors of the said accompt.

Dud Boswell, prebendarie of St Johns

Wm Plunkett	Willm. Smyth
George Plunkett	Anth Gayton
Clement Martan	John Browne
	Jeremy Bowden

I doe acknowledge to have received whatsoever was due to me by Act of State as prebendarie of St Johns Dublin out of ye parish from my entrance thereunto until ye Feast of ye Nativitie of our blessed saviour last past provided that this discharge shall not acquitt those whose names are given up by ye last churchwardens for such arrears as are due to me for ye last year. As witness my hand 10 Apr[il] 1643.

Dud Boswell

[f. 116 blank]

[f. 116v] Hereafter followeth the Cesse on the parishioners of St Johns parish Dublin due to the parson according to the Act of the State made and Cessed by us whose names are subscribed by the joint and unanimous consent & agreement of the said parishioners & Inhabitants of the said parish the 10th day of May 1643[88]

	li. s. d.
ffishamble Street	
The widdow Usher and her sonne Arlender Usher merchant	6.8.
Robert Dee, shoemaker	10.0.
Robert Dunne, shoemaker	6.8.
Thomas ffretley, Cutler, inmate	4.0.
Richard Kidd, Cutler, inmate	2.0.
John Hargrave, s[enio]r, Tayler, inmate	2.0.
John Knott, vitler	6.0.
John Hoggand, Musician	8.0.
Jane Eustace, vid[ow] inmate	10.0.
Peter Ryder	4.0.
Thomas {Lany}, cutler, inmate	6.0.
John Heney, tailor	8.0.
Richard ffloyd, vitler	4.0.
Widdow Bell	2.0.
Widdow Hastings, inmate dee	2.0.
Robert Sparke, gent, inmate hoggand	4.0.
Peter Mallady, inmate hoggand	2.0.
Henry Withers, inmate hoggand	2.0.
Widdow King	4.0.
Widdow Greene	4.0.

Robert Clowney, Chandler	12.0.
Thomas Lee, gent, Inmate	4.0.
Thomas Broaghall, pullterner	4.0.
Thomas Hill, Baker	12.0.
James Wilson, Taylor, Inmate	6.0.
[f. 117] Elizabeth Bolton Inmate	4.0.
The Swanne Taverne	[blank]
Wid Fullam, Baker & her Inmates	10.0.
John Trew	4.0.
Silvanus Glegge	8.0.
Sir John Dungans house lately Russell	8.0.
John Burrane, water bayliffe	10.0.
Doctor James	[blank]
George Hollys, shoemaker	8.0.
Widdow Birde	2.0.
William Rice	4.0.
John Colen, cooke	8.0.
John Chetyn	2.0.
Margaret Joanes	2.0.
Lieuten[an]t Lambert	6.0.
Symon Lewis	2.0.
Doctor Reeves	10.0.
Thomas Hill	4.0.
Arthur Chadsey, vitler	4.0.
Abraham Barker, Cooke	8.0.
Widdow Gwyn	6.0.
John Woodhouse	2.0.
Peter Ketling	2.0.
Francis Carthtoppe, Taylor, Inmate	2.0.
Mr Broughton	10.0.
Tho Corran, bricklayer	4.0.
William Wasley	4.0.
George Plunkett & <his Inmates>	6.0.
Peter Lemmon, Lieuten[an]t	14.0.
David Smith, vitler	4.0.
George Cheeneley, ffishmonger	4.0.
John Irland	10.0.
Robert Wade	8.0.
John Henry	2.0.
[f. 117v] John Hollys	8.0.
Wm Plunket, Esq	13.4.
Nicholas Osborne & Widdow Bedlow	8.0.
William Parker	4.0.

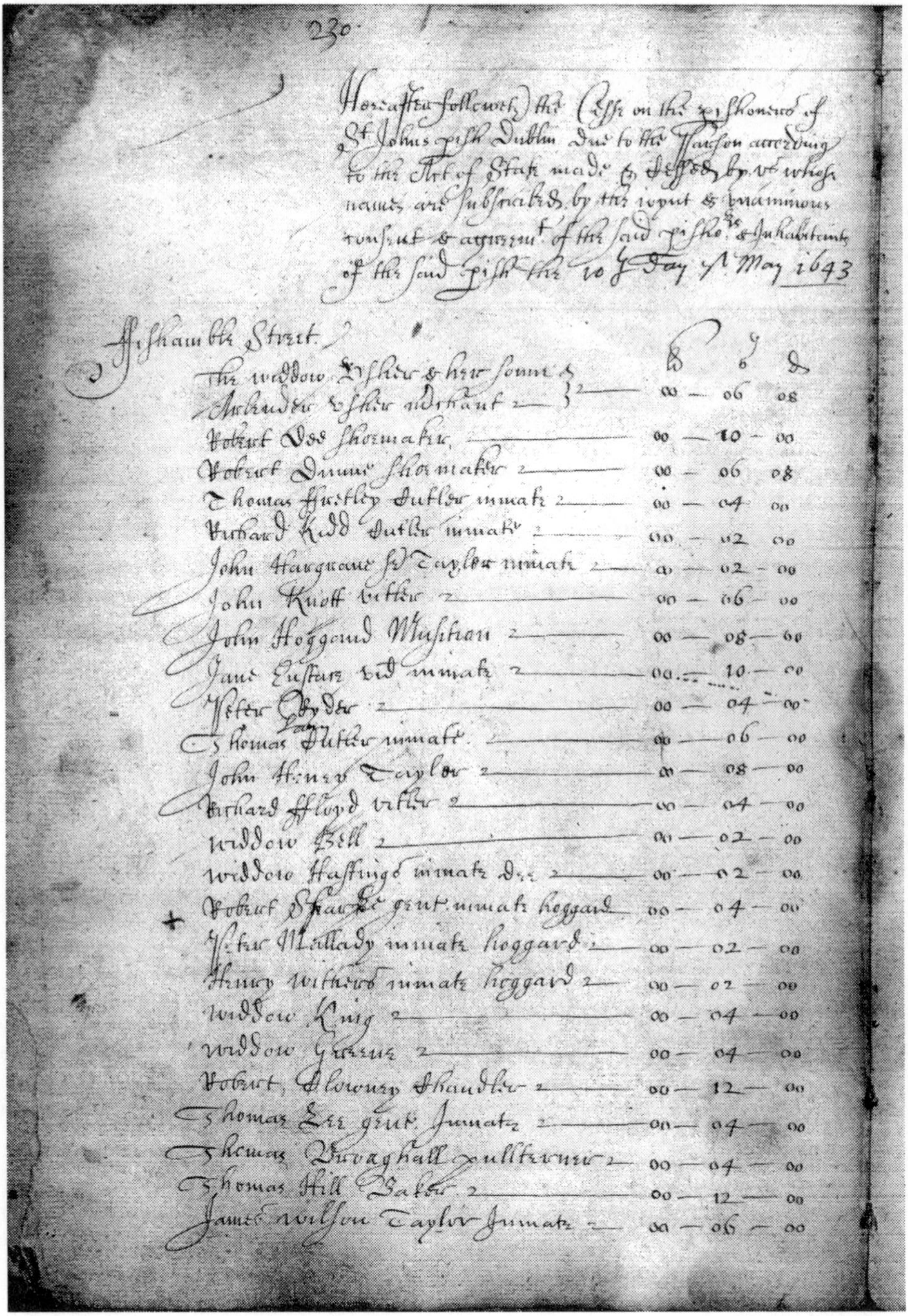

230

Hereafter followeth the Cesse on the parishioners of St Johns parish Dublin due to the Parson according to the Act of State made & assessed by us whose names are subscribed by the joynt & unanimous consent & agreement of the said parishioners & Inhabitants of the said parish the 10th day of May 1643

Fishamble Street

	li	s	d
The widdow Ussher & her sonne Arlander Ussher merchant	00	06	08
Robert Dee shoemaker	00	10	00
Robert Dunne shoemaker	00	06	08
Thomas Fleetley cutler inmate	00	04	00
Richard Kidd cutler inmate	00	02	00
John Hargreave Taylor inmate	00	02	00
John Knott cutler	00	06	00
John Hoggard Musitian	00	08	00
Jane Eustace widd inmate	00	10	00
Peter Ryder	00	04	00
Thomas Lacy Cutler inmate	00	06	00
John Henry Taylor	00	08	00
Richard Floyd cutler	00	04	00
widdow Bell	00	02	00
widdow Hastings inmate	00	02	00
Robert Sparke gent. inmate hoggard	00	04	00
Peter Mallady inmate hoggard	00	02	00
Henry Withers inmate hoggard	00	02	00
widdow King	00	04	00
widdow Greene	00	04	00
Robert Flowery Chandler	00	12	00
Thomas Lee gent. Inmate	00	04	00
Thomas Duvaghall poulterer	00	04	00
Thomas Hill Baker	00	12	00
James Wilson Taylor Inmate	00	06	00

3. The parish cess list for 1643 (f. 116v)

William Whitchett	6.0.
Gyles Robinson	4.0.
{Walter fflood	00.}
William Gates, Butcher	6.0.
Thomas Makam	6.0.
Tho Harper	4.0.
Tho Playsteed, merchant	6.0.
Richard Boarder, plumer	12.0.
Robert Stow	4.0.
Oliver Davorane	8.0.
John Mitchell, vintner	15.0.
John Jefferies & his Inmates	8.0.
Mrs Wiggins	4.0.
Edmond Leadbetter	8.0.
Rice Williams, stabler	8.0.
Bartell Jordan	10.0.
Widdow Whiting	6.0.
William Lamley	6.0.
Richard Ball	6.0.
Mr Scourefield	16.0.
John Tetlow, water bayliffe	4.0.
John Helym, smith	8.0.
John Boldrow, gent, Inmate	4.0.
Anthony Geaton	8.0.
Morris Cattvellider	2.0.
Robert Gille	2.0.
[blank] Reade	2.0.
[blank] Bridges	2.0.
Richard Moore	2.0.
[f. 118] Robert Prentice, warder	4.0.
Edward Hunt	12.0.
John Singleton, Gabbartmaker	4.0.
William Pettit	4.0.
Henry Jorgan	4.0.
John Cheevers	2.0.
John Darmell	8.0.
John Barrey, glasier	2.0.
Widdow Ashbourne	6.0.
Tristram Bolton	4.0.
Jeremy Bowden	6.0.
Oates Crowder	4.0.
Edmond Tyngham	4.0.
[blank] Mathews	4.0.

James Henley, gent	10.0.
Lady Derensy	6.0.
Mr William Kadogan, Mathew Castell	4.0.
Widdow Harcott	2.0.
Widdow Cooke	10.0.
[blank] Smith	4.0.
William Evans	6.0.
Stephen Holt	2.0.
Mrs Alderses	12.0.
Doctor Boate	1.0.0.
Sir Wm Reeves house	1.0.0.
Mrs Newman	12.0.
Sir Wm Sambage	16.0.
John Griffen	12.0.
Moses Thrappes	2.0.
Widdow Parker	8.0.
Mr Alexanders house	10.0.
Mrs Booth	10.0.
Jeffery Walsh	6.0.
[f. 118v] William Wooddall	4.0.
Robert Valentyne	8.0.
William Bell, Tho Croker & Richard Palfry	8.0.
George Prowdfoot, merchant	10.0.
Wood Key	
James Scott	2.0.
John Read, Gabbot man	4.0.
John Rasdell, vitler	2.0.
Capt[ai]n Tho Bartlett	8.0.
Alderman Smith	12.0.
Michael Purcell, merchant	8.0.
Tho fformby	4.0.
Peter Dale	4.0.
George Haley	4.0.
Widdow Begge	6.0.
Guy Sanders	4.0.
Philip Brangan	2.0.
Michael McCartey	2.0.
Edward ffynney	2.0.
George Boyde, sayler	8.0.
John Blacke, Gabb[ar]tman	6.0.
John Johnson, Gabb[ar]tman	6.0.
Wm Buy, sayler	10.0.
Widdow Maxwell	2.0.

Wm Dillon, Joyner	8.0.
Benjamyne Roberts, Cooke	10.0.
Wm Knight, merchant	8.0.
Wm Symons, merchant	6.0.
Richard Lutterell, Baker	12.0.
[f. 119] Clement Marten, Brewer	8.0.
John Hoare, Gabb[ar]tman	2.0.
Boland Tyrath	2.0.
John Browne, hot water	10.0.
Joseph Palyn, hot water man	6.0.
Wm Clarke, Inkeeper	13.4.
Tho Dixon, Chandler	4.0.
Robert Jerley, Chandler	4.0.
Jacob Ablyne, merchant	16.0.
Widdow Bough	4.0.
Luce Dobbin	2.0.
Tho Wayte, Chandler	4.0.
Henry Moore, Naylemaker	4.0.
Widdow Bennett	2.0.
John Warren	8.0.
Tho Hale, Inmate	4.0.
Randall Byas, Inmate	2.0.
Henry Quarrells	1.4.
William Hall, chandler	6.0.
James Johnson	6.0.
Henry Bowles	8.0.
John Montgomery	6.0.
James Egar & his Inmates	10.0.
George Woods	6.0.
Eddis Shoppe	6.0.
The old Crane	8.0.
Wine Tavern Street	
Tho Lyle	8.0.
The Spread Eagle voyd	8.0.
Widdow Dale	10.0.
Mathew Noell	10.0.
[f. 119v] Thomas Guire	2.0.
William Conrane, shoemaker	8.0.
The Kings Head, voyd	10.0.
Widdow White, shoemaker	8.0.
Widdow Chamberlaine	6.0.
Alben Levorett	10.0.
Patrick Moore, shoemaker	8.0.

Widdow Galbelley	6.0.
Thomas Dungan	8.0.
Thomas Walker, baker	6.0.
William Wafer	8.0.
Anthony Kyrk	4.0.
John Doggatts	10.0.
Patricke Lunders, taylor	10.0.
Nicholas Lutterell	8.0.
Michael ffitz Garrett	4.0.
Richard Taylor, cutler	2.0.
Michaell Hayes & Renell Hunte	16.0.
Thomas Jacob, baker	10.0.
An Preston, widdow	4.0.
Dorothy Browne, Inmate	4.0.
John Warren, tailor	4.0.
John Neale	2.0.
Edmond Shile, vitler	2.0.
Robert Browne & his Inmates	10.0.
Christopher Barnewell	2.0.
John Keyes	2.0.
Robert ffrench	2.0.
Richard Golden	10.0.
James Malone, merchant	16.0.
George Neugent, merchant	10.0.
Peerce Keating	2.0.
John Butcher	8.0.
Dane Donnogh	4.0.
[f. 120] Richard Talbott	4.0.
Joseph Newtowne, Miller	8.0.
George Crowder	10.0.
James Begge, smith	10.0.
Patricke Savage, Taylor	2.0.
James White, gent	4.0.
Robert Cadwell, wast	10.0.
Mr Joseph Con, The Maggazen	12.0.
Tho Johnson, Esq	12.0.
Stephen Garlen	10.0.
Widdow Shurlock	2.0.
Robert Dollard, chirurgion	8.0.
James Carvell, baker	8.0.
Nicodemus Gowby	8.0.
Widdow Duffe	4.0.
Peerce Moore	6.0.

Rosemary Lane	
William Bee, drummer	2.0.
John McWort	2.0.
John Oker	4.0.
Mr Worrall	6.0.
Alsome Humfry	2.0.
Robert Dorane	2.0.
Richard Blackestone	2.0.
William Settle	4.0.
William Beaghan	2.0.
Mary [blank]	6.0.

George Plunkett — Wm Plunkett
Robert Clony — Edm Leadbetter
Clement Martyn — Jeremy Bowden

[f. 120v] The accompt of Mr Anthony Gaydon & Mr John Browne late Churchwardens of St Johns Evangelists Dublin for one year ending at Easter 1643

Receaved of the severall tenents viz. of Robt Gilbert, Nich Robuck, Walter fflood, Georg Usher, Jo Crene, Math fford, Eliz Smyth, Jo Trewe, Master of ye Taylors & Sir Thady Duff, kt, as appeareth by the several pariculers <amounting to > & the monys Receaved remayning uppon the foot of the late Churchwardens accompt amounting to xlvj^{li} xij^{s} iij^{d}

More Received for buryalls for that year as app[eare]th by the p[ar]ticulars amounting to ix^{li} xiij^{s} vj^{d}

Sum lvj^{li} v^{s} ix^{d}

And disbursed & Layed out by the said accomptance for buylding the newe vestrye & repayringe the said church, ye old Clarkes wages, breade & wyne for severall Comunions etc as app[eare]th by ye p[ar]ticuar accompt the some of lxij^{li} ix^{s} 4^{d}

Soe as their remayneth dewe to the said accomptant the some of vj^{li} iij^{s} vij^{d}

Wm Plunkett
Jeremy Bowden
Robert Cloony

[f. 121] 240 Aprill 1644
M[emoran]d[um] It is ordered by & with consent of ye parson & parishioners of St Johns Evangelist Dublin that Mr Richard Palffrey & Mr Willm Knight shalbe Churchwardens of the said parish for this yeare. And the old Churchwardens Mr Mathew Nowell & Mr John Knotte are to passe

their accompts on Mundaye come seinght & Mr Willm Plunkett, Mr John Michell, Clement Martine, Jeremy Bowden, Mr George Prodfoote Mr Robt Dee & the nowe Churchwardens or any three or more of them are to be Auditors of the said accompt.

Dud Boswell, prebendarie of St Johns

Willm Smyth, Maior Dublin

Jeremy Bowden	Wm Plunkett
Robert Deey	Joh Michell
Gyles Robinson	Geo Prowdfoot
Richard Burder	Edm Leadbetter
Will Langham	
John Warren	
William Lewis	

I doe acknowledge to have received whatsoever was due to me by Act of State as prebendarie of St Johns Dublin out of ye parish from my entrance thereunto until ye Feast of ye Nativitie of our blessed saviour last past. Provided that this discharge shal not acquitt those whose names are given up by ye last churchwardens for such arrears as are due to me for ye last year. Witness mine hand

24° Apr 1644

Dud Boswell

[f. 121v] 24° April 1644
Memorand[um] It is ordred by consent of ye parsone & parishioners of St Johns Evangelists Dublin that Davye Murphie, Willm Lewys, Willm Clarke & Trestram Bolton are chosen Sydsmen for this parish for this insuing yeare.

Dud Boswell
Willm Smyth, maior Dublin
Wm Plunkett
John Michell
Jeremy Bowden
John Warren

vj° May 1644
Memorand[um] it is agreed by the parishioners of St Johns parish that Willm Plunkett Esq, Mr Jo Michell, Mr Georg Prodfoot, Mathew Nowell, Jeremy Boyden, Mr Clement Martine, Gyles Robinson, Georg Nugent & Robt Clowney or any six of them to make & viewe the Cess for the parsons dewties for this next ensuing year in pursuance of ye Act of State in that behalf.

Dud Boswell, prebendarie of St Johns
Wm Plunkett
William Knight

Rich Palfrey
Gyles Robinson
John Michell
Mathew Noell
Jeremy Bowden

[f. 122] The Accompt of such monies & yearly revenues belonging to St Johns Church received by Matthew Noell & John Knott Churchwardens for one year ending att Easter 1644.

	li. s. d.
Imprimis Received of Gyles Robinson for the house of Walter fflood in ffishamble street for 2 yeeres ending att Easter 1644	1.10.0.
Item of Mathew fford Esq for the house in ffishamble street where Geo Hollys now dwelleth for a yeere & halfe ending Michel[mas] 1643	2.10.0.
Item of John Boran waterbayliffe for the use of Geo. Usher for the house in ffishamble street where he now dwelleth for a yeere & a halfe ending att Michel[mas] 1643	3.10.0.
Item of M[aste]r of the Company of Taylers for one whole yeere for St Johns Chappell ending att Michel[mas] 1643	1.0.0.
Item of Jo Cruce and Katherine his wife for the house on Oxmontowne for one whole yeere ending att Michel[mas] 1643	4.0.0.
Item of the Widdow Smith for the house & Garden late in the possession of Morrice Smith deceased for halfe a yeere ending att Easter 1644	16.8.
Item of Capt Winkfield in p[ar]t of his Arreares for his house in Oxmontown the some of	1.0.0.
Item of Nicholas Robuck for the house where he lives in St ffrancis street for halfe a yeere ending att Easter 1643	12.6.
[f. 122v] Item of Hen Powell for the house late in the possession of Tho Conran in ffishamble street in p[ar]te of his Arrears	1.0.0.
Item of Richard Stiles for the house in ffishamble street late in the possession of Jo Glegg for two yeeres ending att Easter 1644	3.6.8.
Item of Mr Cosney Molloy for the house in Copper Alley late in the possession of the Earle of Corke & Sir Jeffrey ffenton, kt, for a whole yeere ending att Michel[mas] 1643	1.6.3.
Item of Sir Tady Duffe for one whole yeere ending att Michel[mas] 1643 for his house upon the woodkey	1.0.0.
Some	xxj^{li} xij^{s} j^{d}

Received by the said Churchwardens for Burialls in the said yeere upon their accompt.

Imprimis for the buriall of an Ensignes child	2.6.
Item for the buriall of Tho Howards wife	13.4.
Item for the buriall of Tho Howards child	3.4.
Item for the buriall of Thos Wilson	6.8.
Item for the buriall of Geo Plunkett	6.8.
Item for the buriall of the wid Osbornes child	3.0.
Item for the buriall of Mr Abraham Wright	10.0.
Item for the buriall of Mrs Coleman	10.0.
Item for the buriall of Mrs Conningham	9.4.
Item for the buriall of Capt Henries child	3.4.
Item for the buriall of the wid Reynolds child	3.0.
Item for the buriall of Wm Bells child	3.4.
Item for the buriall of Wm Evans child	3.4.
Item for the buriall of James Whites child, nothing	0.0
	iij^{li} xvij^{s} x^{d}

Total xxv^{li} ix^{s} xj^{d}

[f. 123] Disbursem[en]ts by the said Accomptants Mathew Noell & Jo Knott for the Church of St Johns from Easter 1643 to Easter 1644.

	li. s. d.
Imprimis for the service book	2.6.
Item for mending locke of the Church doore	1.0.
Item for putting in the p[re]sentm[en]ts	3.4.
Item for pointing Church towards the bells	4.8.
Item for lyme & sand	2.8.
Item payed to Mr Graton	6.3.7.
Item for burying the poor who were found dead in the streets	1.4.6.
Item for wine severall tymes for ye Comunion	2.5.0.
Item for Nursing a Child left on the parish for one whole yeere ending att Easter 1644	3.0.0.
Item for clothes for the Child	6.0.
Item for Bread for the Comunion	4.8.
Item for washing the Church Lynnen	10.0.
Item for Glazing the Church	10.6.
Item for Lyme & sand to point the Glasse windows & thear worke	5.6.
Item to the Smith for 3 iron barrs for the glasse windows	2.4.
Item for Carrying away the dirt from before the Church doore	6.9.
Item payd Mr Tadpoll[89] for <a q> {halfe a yeere} ending att Easter 1644	1.0.0.
Item for Holly, Ivy & Rushes	2.6.
Item for a warrant to Gather the Cesse	1.0.

[f. 123v] Item for putting in the p[re]sentm[en]ts	3.4.
Item payd for dozen of trees	15.0.
Item payd to Barthol Jordan	2.0.0.
Item for Long Cable	3.6.
Item for getting souldiers to distreine on Capt Winkfields Tenents	1.6.
Item for mending pewes	3.0.
ye Gallery built	
Item for building of the Ballconey	1.15.0.
Item spent att the Choosing of the new Churchwardens	1.5.0.
a warrant from ye L[or]d Lieu[tenant] & Council for ye poore cess	
Item for writing a booke of the Inhabitants names to Collect weekly meanes for the poore by v[er]tue of a war[ran]t of the Lord Lieatent & Councell	3.0.
Item spent att the making of this Accompt	6.1.
Item for drawing up the Accompt and entring the same in the booke	2.0.
Some	23.13.11.

vj° Maij 1644

Mem[oran]d[um] we have examined the Accompts of Mathew Noell & John Knott Churchwardens of this Church for one yeare ending at Easter1644. And we finde that they have received of the Rents & casualties of the said Church the some of Twentie ffive pounds Nine shillings & Eleven pence ster. And that they have disbursed as appeares by their Accompts the some of Twentie three pounds thirteene shillings & eleven pence. Soe as there is now remayning in their handes the some of one pound sixteene shillings ster which is nowe payd over into the hands of Richard Palfry & Wm Knight the now Churchwardens. All which we wittnesse being Auditors Assigned for the passing of this Accompt

Rich Palfrey — Wm Plunkett
Jeremy Bowden — Joh Michell
William Knight — Geo Proudfoott

[f. 124] 9° die <Aprilis> Maij 1644

Hereafter followeth the Cesse of the parishioners of the parish of St Johns the Evangelist Dublyn made by us whose names are hereto subscribed according the Joynte and unamimous consent and agreement of the said parishioners for the parsons duties of the said parish in p[ur]suance of the Act of State for the yeare aforesaid

	li. s. d
ffishamble streete	
The widdowe Usher & Arlenter Usher her sone	6.8.
Roger Brereton, Esq	10.0.
Robert Dee, shomaker	6.8.

Michaell Warde, Taylor	4.0.
Robert Dun	6.8.
Widdowe Bell	4.0.
John Hargrave thelder, Taylor	2.0.
the widdowe Betson	2.0.
John <Heldsam> Huggard	8.0.
William Beadie	2.0.
John Hayney, Taylor	8.0.
Mounseir Tulleir	8.0.
Mrs Lestice her house	[blank]
Mrs Kinge	4.0.
Daniel Crofts	2.0.
Robert Clowney, Chandler	12.0.
Thomas Lee	4.0.
Thomas Brohall, poulterer	4.0.
David Murphey	12.0.
Marke Cooper, Greenes ten[a]nt	4.0.
Mrs Dun	4.0.
Mr Beinghurst	4.0.
Giles Robinson	12.0.
Henry Powell	6.0.
Richard Stiles	8.0.
Martin Arden	6.0.
the other Ten[a]nts in Sir Jo Dunghams house	4.0.
John Burham, waterbaylie	10.0.
George Hollies	8.0.
[f. 124v] Arthur Chadsey	6.0.
Mr Stanlye	4.0.
Abraham Baker	8.0.
John Tetloe, water baylie	4.0.
Doctor Reeves	10.0.
David Morries	6.0.
John Woodhouse	2.0.
Mr Branghton	8.0.
Ten[a]nts in Mr Allenes house	10.0.
The 3 Tuns	16.0.
Edward Prescott, spurrier	4.0.
Thomas Curran	4.0.
William Langham	8.0.
Maurice Cadwallader	2.0.
Thomas Reede	2.0.
Robert Prentice	4.0.
Mr Hunts house	10.0.

Peter Rider	4.0.
Wm Plunkett, Esq	13.4.
Widdowe Osborne	6.0.
Richard Edgerton	2.0.
Widdowe Reignolds	3.0.
Widdowe Bedlowe	8.0.
William Witched	6.0.
William Yates, Butcher	6.0.
Walter ffludd	8.0.
Thomasin Gibbones, herbewoman	4.0.
Mary Robinson	2.0.
Richard Burder	12.0.
John Gamey, butcher	6.0.
Oliver Daverin	8.0.
John Mitchell	15.0.
Mr Cheenely	2.0.
Thomas Pooles house	8.0.
Edmond Ledbetter	6.0.
[f. 125] Doctor James Weaver	8.0.
Rice Williams, stabler	8.0.
Anthony Thompson, smith	2.0.
Mr Staffords house	6.0.
Widdowe Jordanie	8.0.
Thomas Wallis	8.0.
Patrick Kennell	4.0.
Richard Balls house	6.0.
Adam Bucke	2.0.
John Clinch	2.0.
Wood Key	
John Cheevers	2.0.
Mr Darnell	8.0.
John Barrey	2.0.
Michaell Antell	2.0.
Mr Smith	6.0.
Tristram Bolton	4.0.
Jeremy Bowden	6.0.
Oates Crowder	4.0.
Lady Derenzy	4.0.
Mr Hambleton	4.0.
Hugh Summerell	4.0.
Capt John Henrick	4.0.
Thomas Whitfilde	4.0.
Jeffrey Welch	6.0.

Mr Draper	10.0.
Mr Evanes house void	6.0.
Richard Martin, Jo Meighbois & Barrett	8.0.
Mr Evans	6.0.
Mr Lyn	10.0.
Sir Adam Loftus	1.0.0.
John Mapues	2.0.
Wm Warsdall	2.0.
Robert Wade	8.0.
Mr John Newman	10.0.[90]

[f. 125v] 10 Aprill 1645
Memorand[um] It is ordered by & with the Consent of ye parson & parishioners of St Johns Evangelist Dublin that Mr Willm Langame & Mr John Sheppard shalbe Churchwardens of the said parish for this next ensuing yeare. And the ould Churchwardens Mr Richard Palffree & Mr Willm Knight are to passe their accompts this day Monthe. And Mr Willm Plunkett, Mr John Michell, Mr Clement Martin, Mr Jeromy Boyden, Mr George Prodfoote, Mr Robt Dolland & Mr Richard Goulding or any three or more of them to be Auditors of the said accompt

Dud Boswell, prebendarie of St Johns

Gyles Robinson
Richard Burder
William Whiteshed
Patrick Landeres
Richard R Ganтterell his mark

Wm Smyth, maior dublin
Wm Plunkett
Joh Michell
Robert Dowlan
Jeremy Bowden
Richard Goulding
Geo Prowdfoot
James Baron
John Barrany

[f. 126] 10 Aprill 1645
M[emoran]d[um] It is ordered by consent of ye parson & parishioners of St Johns Evangelists Dublin that James Wylde, Willm Wichingdale, Patrick Landers & Nicholas Eddis are chosen Sydesmen for this parish for this next ensuing yeare.

Dud Boswell, prebendarie
Willm Smith, maier dublin
Wm Plunkett
Robert Donlan
Jeremy Bowden
William Langham
John Sheppard

Geo Prowdfoot
Gyles Robinson
Richard Burder
Lancelot Patent

[f. 126v] 10 Aprill 1645
M[emoran]d[um] It is ordered by & with the Consent of the parishioners of St Johns Evangelist Dublin that Willm Plunkett Esq, Mr Jo Michell, Mr Robt Dollard, Mr George Prodfoot, Mr Jeromy Boyden, Mr Clement Martine, Mr Richard Goulding, Mr Richard Palfree, Mr Willm Knight, Mr Willm Langame, & Mr John Sheppard to make & viewe the Cess for the parsons stipend for this next ensuing year in pursuance of the Act of State in that behalf provided. Or any six of the forenamed p[er]sons

Dud Boswell, prebendarie
Willm Smyth, maier dublin
Wm Plunkett
Robert Donlan
Jo [S]hippard   Geo Proudfoot
J Bowden
Will Langham
James Baron
Gyles Robinson
Richard Burder

[f. 127] The Accompt of such monyes & yearely revenues belonginge to St Johns Church receaved by Richard Palfrey & Wm Knight Churchwardens for one yeare endinge att Easter 1645

	li. s. d.
<Rec of> Mr Nowell and Mr Knott of the last Church wardens are to be charged with the moneys that was due upon the foote of their Acc[ompt] beinge	1.16.0.
Received of Martin Ardell for 2 yeares & a halfes rent endinge easter 1644	1.6.0.
Of John Burran for halfe yeare ending easter 1644	1.3.0.
Received by Mr Plunkett & charged in our disbursements	1.3.0.
Of the M[aste]r of the Comp[any of] Taylors	1.0.0.
Of Cosney Molloy for a yeare endinge Mich[aelmas] 1644	1.6.0.
Of Mr Robuck <ending> for a year endinge Easter 1644	1.5.0.
Of the widdowe Smith in p[ar]t paym[en]t	13.4.
by Mr Boswell of Mr Smith & charged upon our disbursements	6.8.

of Katherine Cruse 4 bar[ells of] herringes at 12^{s} p[er] barr[ell]	
in p[ar]t of a whole yeare endinge at Mich[aelmas] 1644	2.8.0.
for a peece of Ewe tree	3.0.
	12.10.0.

Received by these Churchwardens for buryalls in the said year

Received of the gentlewoman from Mr Plunketts house	10.0.
for Tristram Boultons Childe	2.6.
for Luke Doyles wife	5.0.
for Luke Doyles mother	5.0.
for Mr Dees wifes buriall	6.6.
	1.9.0.
	the totall 13^{li} 19^{s} 0^{d}

[f. 127v] Disbursed by the said Accomptants Richard Palfrey & Wm Knight for the said yeare endinge att Easter 1645 followeth

To the accomptes by the last Churchwardens upon the foote of their acc[ompt]	1.16.0.
Disbursed by Mr Plunkett of John Burrans rent	1.3.0.
Mr Tadpoole his yeares wages	2.0.0.
Mr Boswell laid out {of} Mr Smiths moneyes	6.8.
Loss in Katherin Cruse herringes	13.4.
badges p[er] poore	
for badges for the poore	1.8.
Spent when parsons Cesse was made	2.6.
A staffe for the beadle	1.0.
for bricks, lyme & sande for mendinge the Church wall & workmanshipp	5.0.
for a warr[an]t to leavie the parsons duties	1.0.
for Sparrs & boards, nayles, workmanship & hinges for mendinge severall pues & the beares	11.10.
formendinge the Church porch	1.0.
to the plummer for leade and worke	6.0.
for lyme, sand, lasts, nayles & 12 dayes worke in slating the Church	7.5.
for a hooke for ye Church yard dore	8.
for 2 presentm[en]ts	6.8.
ffor nursing the Child	3.0.0.
for necessaryes for her	4.0.
for washinge Church lynnen	10.0.

for buryinge the poore that have beene found dead in streets & 3 sheets for them	10.0.
for holly & Ivie	2.6.
for wyne for the whole yeare & other things att meetings	2.8.6.
for mendinge Candlestick	2.0.
for breade	4.6.
paid the Slater for lyme, sand, pynes, nayles, slates & workemanship	11.10.
	15.17.1.

paid	15 – 17 – 1
receieved	13 – 19 – 0
	1 – 18 – 1

[f. 128] M[emoran]d[um] wee have examined the Accompts of Richard Palfrey & William Knight churchwardens of this Church for one yeare endinge att Easter 1645 and we fynde that they have receaved of the rents & Casualties of the said Church the sume of thirteene pounds Nyneteen shillinges. And that they have disbursed as appeares by their Accompts the sume of fifteen pounds seaventeen shillinges soe as there is nowe remayning unto them to <pa> be paid by the nowe Churchwardens of the said parish the sume of one pound eighteene shillings. All which we wittnesse being Auditors [as]signed for the passing of this Accompt this Tenth day of June Anno Dm 1645

Wm Plunkett
Robert Donlan
Joh Michell
Jeremy Bowden
Geo Proudfoot

[f. 128v] ultimo March 1646
Memorand[um] It is ordered by and with ye consent of the parson & parishioners of St Johns Evangelist Dublin that Mr Richard Burder & Mr Nicholas Eddys shalbe Churchwardens for this yeare of the said parish. And the ould Church wardens Mr Willm Lanngam & Mr John Sheppard are to passe their accompts on Thursday come seinght. And Willm Plunkett Esq, Mr Jo Michell, Mr Jeromy Boyden, Mr Richard Goulding, Mr George Prodfoote & the newe Churchwardens or any three or more to be Auditors of the said Accompt

Dud Boswell, prebendarie of St Johns

Wm Plunkett
John Michell
Rich Palfrey
John Haydocke
James Malone
Richard Goulding
Jeremy Bowden
William Whitshed
Henry Jourdan

[f. 129] ultimo March 1646
M[emoran]d[um] It is ordered by consent of ye parson & parishioners of St Johns Evangelists Dublin that Henry ffinch, James Johnson, James Mallone & Willm Dillon are chosen & appoynted Sydsmen for this parish for this next ensuing yeare.

Dud Boswell
Richard Burder
Nicholas Eddis

Wm Plunkett
John Michell
James Malone
Jeremy Bowden
Will Langham
Henry Jourdan

[f. 129v] ultimo March 1646
M[emoran]d[um] It is ordered by & with ye consent of the parishioners of St John Evangelist Dublin that Willm Plunkett Esq, Mr John Mihell, Mr George Prodfoot, Mr Jeremy Boyden, Mr Clement Martyne, Mr Richard Goulding, Mr Willm Langame, Mr John Sheppard & Mr James Malone or any six or more of them to make the Cess for the parsons stipend for this next ensuing year in pursuance of ye Act of State in that behalf provided.

Wm Plunkett
John Michell
James Malone
Jeremy Bowden
Henry Jourdan

[f. 130] *1646*
The Accompt of such monys & yearely revenues belonginge to St Johns Church Receaved by Mr Willm Langeham & Mr John Sheppard, Churchwardens, for one whole yeare endinge att Easter 1646.

Received of Gyles Robinson for two yeares Rent ending at Easter 1646 for the house in ffishamble street belonging to Walter fflood	1.10.0.
Received of Henry Powell for the house wherein he dwelleth being p[ar]t of Mr Conrans howse in p[ar]t paym[en]t of his arreares the some of	1.0.0.

Received of Martin Arden for the howse wherein he dwelleth in ffishamble street belonging to Sir Jo Dongan in p[ar]t paym[en]t 3.10.
Received of John Barran for one year and a half Rent ending at Easter 1646 for the howse wherein he dwelleth in ffishamble street belonging to Mr George Usher 3.10.0.
Received of Nicholas Robuck for two yeares Rent ending at Easter 1646 for the howse in St ffrances street wherein he nowe dwelleth the some of 2.10.0.
Received of Sir Thady Duff, Kt, for one year & a half ending at Easter 1645 for his howse on the woodkey the some of 1.10.0.
Received of Jo Cruse & Katherine his wiff in p[ar]t paym[en]t of the Rent dewe for the howse wherein they nowe dwell in Oxmanton the some of 3.0.0.
Received of Mr Smyth in p[ar]t paym[en]t of <the> for Rent for the howses of Jo Poolley in Oxmanton 13.4.
Received of the Master of ye taylors for one whole yeare ending at Midsomer 1645 1.0.0.
[f. 130v]Received of Mr Cosney Molloye for one yeares Rent endinge at Mich[ale]mas last 1645 the some of 1.6.3.

S[u]m of ye Rents 16.3.5.

Moneys received for the Burialls in the said Church for ye year aforesaid

Received for a wydow out of Hiestret 5.0.
Received for Mr [William Smith] Mayor Child 3.4.
Received for ye buryall of a child out of Mr Powells howse 2.6.

S[u]m 10.10.

S[u]m total 16^{li} 14^{s} 3^{d}

Disbursem[en]ts made by the said accomptants Mr Willm Langhame & Mr John Sheppard for the yeare aforesaid

Imprimis payd to ye late Church Wardens dewe unto them uppon ye foot of their accompt 1.18.0.
Item payd to Mr Michell for arrears dewe to him for taking ye late Churchwardens accompt 16.1.
Item payd for Nursing the child 1.15.0.
Item payd for two pressenm[en]ts 5.8.
Item payd for ye making of 4 graves for ye poore 2.0.
Item payd for a warrant to ye mayors clarke 1.0.
Item payd for ye Comunion wyne for ye whole year & for loe Sundaye last 2.12.0.

Item payd for bread for ye Comunion	4.5.
Item payd to Clark of ye parish for his whole yeares stypend	2.0.0.
Item payd to ye Sheriff of Dublin for Langable	3.3.
[f. 131] Item payd to the Clark for wasshing the Church lynnen	5.0.
Item payd & disbursed about the heylers work in poynting & covering the Church cleane over & to the glaser etc as appe[ar]eth by the p[ar]ticulars the some of	7.4.11.
S[u]m tota[l]	17.7.4.

9° Aprill 1646.

Wee have examined the accompts of Mr Willm Langhame & Mr John Sheppard, late Churchwardens of this Church, for one whole yeare ending at Easter 1646 and we fynde that they have Receaved of the Rents & Casualties of the said Church the sume of sixteen pounds fourteene shillinges & three pence. And that they have disbursed as appeares by their accompts the some of seaventeene pounds seaven shillinges & four pence soe as theire is nowe remayning dewe to them to be payd by the nowe Church wardens the sume of thirteene shillings & one penny. All which wee wittnes being Auditors <being> assigned for taking & passing the said accompt the day and year aforesaid.

Jeremy Bowden
Richard Burder

Wm Plunkett
Joh Michell
James Malone

[f. 131v] The Cesse for the parishioners of St Johns Church made by us whose names are underwritten chosen to that purpose by the unamimous consent of the said parishioners for the parsons stipend of the said parish. In pursuance of the Act of State for the yeare of our Lord 1646

	li. s. d.
ffishamble street, east syde	
The widd Usher & her son Arlonter	6.8.
Roger Brearton, esq. inmate	10.0.
Nicholas Garlon, chirurgion	10.0.
The widd Brookes	4.0.
Michaell Ward	4.0.
John Miller inmate	6.0.
The widd Dun and the rest of her Tenants	2.0.
The widd Duns Tenants in her other house	[blank]
William Eustace	8.0.
John Huggard	2.0.

William Dradie	2.0.
Widd Kinge	4.0.
Robt Clowney	8.0.
John Ogdon inmate	8.0.
David Murphy	12.0.
William Whiteshead	8.0.
Widd Gibbons inmate	2.0.
Widd Robinson	12.0.
Henry Powell	6.0.
William Malone inmate	4.0.
Richard Stiles	8.0.
Martin Arden	6.0.
John Borran	10.0.
Peter Halfpeny	4.0.
Arthur Chadsey	6.0.
Thomas Winstanley inmate	4.0.
Captaine Billingsley	10.0.
[f. 132]Doctor Rives	10.0.
David Morris	6.0.
Mr Barrowne	10.0.
Mr Allen & his tenants	8.0.
Stephen Holt	4.0.
Mr Momford	4.0.
Robt Bingham, shoemaker	4.0.
William Langham	6.0.
The Signe of the Tobacco Rowle	4.0.
Nicholas Willoughby	4.0.
Richard Moore	2.0.
Patrick Kenan, inmate	2.0.
John Shepheard	10.0.
The west syde of ffishamble street	
John Clinch	2.0.
Thomas Williams	4.0.
Richard Doleman	2.0.
Widd Whiteing	1.0.
Mr Parnell	4.0.
Mr Leadbeater	6.0.
James Malone	6.0.
Lawrence Tuite	2.0.
Mr Michell	8.0.
Oliver Deavering	8.0.
Mr Burder	8.0.
John Haddock	4.0.

John Gany inmate	6.0.
Walter ffloud	6.0.
John Elderidge	4.0.
Thomas Broaghall	2.0.
Thomas Challener	6.0.
[f. 132v] Widd Osborne	6.0.
Widd Reynalls inmate	4.0.
William Pluncket, esquire	13.4.
Peter Riders house	4.0.
Stable Alley	
George Draper	2.0.
[blank] a couper	4.0.
Edward Prescod, smith	2.0.
Robt Dakers	2.0.
Robt Wade	8.0.
In Captain Cadogans house	
William Mosley	4.0.
Henry Jordan	4.0.
ffrom Copper Alley	
Sir Adam Loftus	1.0.0.
Mr Linn	10.0.
William Evans	6.0.
Robt the Spurrior	4.0.
George Hollis	6.0.
Mr Drapers house	10.0.
Mrs Newman	10.0.
Mr John Newman	10.0.
Mrs Sheley	10.0.
The Lady Derenzie	4.0.
Oates Crowder	4.0.
Walter Robinson	2.0.
Richard Symons	2.0.
Henry Finch	8.0.
Mr Boden	6.0.
Mr Bland	4.0.
[f. 133] John Smith	6.0.
John Barry	2.0.
Mrs Hasset	4.0.
Leonard Graves	2.0.
Widd Bentson	2.0.
Minor Christian	2.0.
Peter Langhorne	2.0.
William Bell	6.0.

William Wodard	4.0.
John Dill	4.0.
George Proudfoot	10.0.

Wood Key

Captn Thomas Bartlet	8.0.
Mr Wm Smith, maior	12.0.
Geo Winstanley	4.0.
Peter Dale, inmate	2.0.
Luke Doyle	6.0.
Robt Prentice	2.0.
George Boyd	8.0.
John Johnsons house	6.0.
John Blake	6.0.
William Boy	10.0.
William Dillan	6.0.
Beniamine Roberts	10.0.
Wiliam Knight	6.0.
William Morris	6.0.
Rich Luttrell	12.0.
Clement Martyn	10.0.
Rich Halfepeny	4.0.
[f. 133v] John Browne	10.0.
Jonathan Paly	6.0.
Vallentine Waite	10.0.
James Wilde	6.0.
John Mount Gomery	4.0.
Nicholas Eddis	8.0.
James Johnson	6.0.
Daniell Burtfield	8.0.
George Woods	6.0.
Tho Lyle	8.0.
Captn John Bartlet	10.0.

Wine Taverne Street

The Goulden Dragon	10.0.
Lawrence Holgan	2.0.
Tho Gwyre	2.0.
The Kings Head	6.0.
John Lawles	4.0.
John Magraffe	8.0.
Luke Borkes house that was	4.0.
Patr Moore	4.0.
Terence Murphie, baker	6.0.
Luke Burke	6.0.

Rich Palfrey	6.0.
Mary Vyan	4.0.
James Browne, inmate	4.0.
The corner house by St Michaells Lane	2.0.
Mr Settles house	4.0.
Patr Waren	8.0
Anth Kirke	4.0.
[f. 134] The house under Gate	4.0.
Patr Lounders	10.0.
The White horse	8.0.
Thomas Jacob	6.0.
Richard Kitching	8.0.
widd Kettle	2.0.
Rich ONeale	2.0.
Rich Goulding	8.0.
Widd Kerdiffe	4.0.
The Bricklayer in her house	2.0.
George Nugent	10.0.
Peirce Keating	4.0.
John Butcher	6.0.
John Wright	2.0.
Rich Talbott	4.0.
Eliz Bennet	2.0.
Widd Barrie	2.0.
The Sellor on the East side of the Gate	2.0.
James Begg, smith	8.0.
John Worrall	4.0.

Magazen

Mr Carpenter	10.0.
Mr Hutchenson	10.0.
The Kings Bench office	1.0.0.
Joseph Newton	4.0.
Jas Carvanes house that was	6.0.
Thos Kelley	8.0.

Wm Plunkett

[f. 134v blank]

[f. 135] vicesimo die Aprilis 1647

Memorand[um] it is ordered by and with the consent of the parson and parishioners of St Johns Evangelists Dublin that Mr Daniell Burfeilde & Mr Thomas Challinor shalbe Church wardens for this yeare of the said parish and the ould Churchwardens Mr Richard Burder and Mr Nicholas Eddies are to passe their accompts on this day fortneight. And <Mr John M> Wm

Plunkett Esquire, Mr Jo Mitchell, Mr Jeremy Bowden, {Mr}Richard Palfrey, Mr Wm Langham, Mr John Brown and the newe Churchwardens or anie three or more of them to be Auditors of the said Accompt.

Dud Boswell, prebendarie of St Johns

John Michell
John Browne
Jeremy Bowden
Rich Palfrey
Will Langham
Richard Burder
Nicholas Eddis
Oliver Daverin
the mark of D. D Murphy
James JJ Johnson his mark

[f. 135v] vicesimo die Aprilis 1647
M[emoran]d[um] it is ordered by consent of the parson & parishioners of St Johns Evangelists Dublyn that Thomas Lyslie, Thomas Pelley, Richard Kitchen and Edward Prescott are chosen & appoynted sidesmen for this parish for this next ensuing yeare.

Dud Boswell, prebendarie of St Johns

John Michell
John Browne
Jeremy Bowden
Rich Palfrey
Will Langham
Richard Burder
Nicholas Eddis
Oliver Daverin
Daniel Burtfelt

[f. 136] vicesimo die 20 Aprilis 1647
M[emoran]d[um] It is ordered by and with the consent of the parishioners of St John the Evangelist Dublyn that Wm Plunkett Esq, Mr John Mitchell, Mr Jeremy Bowden, Mr George Proudfoote, Mr Clement Martin, Mr Richard Gouldinge, Mr Wm Langham, Mr Richard Palfrey, Mr John Sheppard & Mr John Brown and the old churchwardens or anie six or more of them to make the Cess for the parsons stipend for this next ensuing year in p[ur]suance of the Act of State in that behalfe provided.

Dud Boswell prebebdarie of St Johns

John Michell
John Browne

Jeremy Bowden
Richard Burder
per me Rich Palfrey
Will Langham
Nicholas Eddis
Oliver Daverin
Richard Goulding
James JJ Johnson his mark
the mark D of David Murphy
Daniel Burtfelt

[f. 136v] The Accompt of such monyes & yearely revenues belonginge to St Johns Church Receaved by Mr Richard Burder & Mr Nicholas Eddies Churchwardens for one whole yeare endinge att Easter 1647

	li. s. d.
Receaved of Mr Powell for the house wherein he dwelleth being part of Mr Conrans house in p[ar]t paym[en]t of his arreares	1.0.0.
Receaved of Mrs Smith in p[ar]te paym[en]t of her Rent for the house she dwelleth in in Oxmonton	13.4.
Receaved of Richard Styles for the other part of Conrans house in p[ar]t paym[en]t of rent and arrears	1.13.4.
Receaved of Mrs Robinson for one yeares rent for the house wherein she now dwelleth endinge att Easter last 1647	15.0.
Receaved of John Burran for one yeares rent endinge this last Easter for the house wherein he nowe dwelleth belonginge to Mr George Usher	$2^{li}\ 6^{s}\ 8^{d}$
a house in Coperally least to the Earl of Cork[91]	
Receaved of Mr Cosney Molloy for the rent of the house lately held by Mr Gilbert under the Erle of Corke in Copper Ally for one whole yeare ending att Michaelmas last past	1.6.3.
Receaved of John Cruse & Katherin his wife in p[ar]te paym[en]t of rent and arreares	1.10.0.
Receaved of the Master of the Company of the Taylors endinge att Midsomer 1646	1.0.0.
Receaved of Nicholas Rubuck for his house in ffrancis streete for one half yeare endinge att Easter 1646	12.6.
Sum of the rent is	$10^{li}\ 17^{s}\ 1^{d}$

[f. 137] Moneys receaved for the burialls in the said Church for the year aforesaid

Received of Mr Evans for his Childe	2.6.
Received for the buriall of a young man from hothe	6.8.
for the buriall of the widdowe Murran	6.0.
for the widdow Creag in Cooke Stret	5.0.
for Ensigne Brownes Childe	3.4.
for Leiffetenante Donosones Childe	2.6.
for Mr Bells Childe	1.8.
for Mr Bowdens wife	5.0.
	1.12.8.
rent received	10.17.1.
Total	12.9.9.

Disbursem[en]ts made by the same Accomptants for the yeare aforesaid

Imprimis paid to the late Church wardens due unto them uppon the foote of their accompt	13.0.
To Mr Tadpole the Clarke for his stipend	2.0.0.
To Mr Mitchell which was spent att a meetinge of the parish	9.6.
for washinge the lynnen	10.0.
for the langable	3.3.
for a warrant	1.0.
for presentm[en]ts	3.4.
to the scrivenier for drawing ye [as]sessemt	1.0.
paid the glasier for mendinge ye windows	2.6.
2 hodgsheds of lyme	4.0.
2 loads of sand	6.
400 & ½ Slates & pynes	3.6.
for langhes	1.6.
for Nayles	1.3.
	4.14.4.

[f. 137v] for 200 of slates	1.0.
for nayles more	1.1.
for slates more 300	1.10.
for nayles more	1.4.
for lyme & sand	1.6.
for a laborer & bordes	2.0.
for 17 dayes & ½ to a slater	17.6.
for holly & Ivie	2.6.
to Mr Mitchell for wyne	2.7.7.
for breade for the Communion	5.6.

paid the plummer for leade and workemanship	1.11.1.
for mending 2 candle stickes	1.0.
to the plummer more for lead for the gutter and the vestrie	1.6.6.
the slater for lyme & sand	3.4.
for Slates & nayles	8.
for presentments	3.4.

Sum totalis 12. 2. 7.

received 12li 9s 9d
xp[ended] 12. 2. 2.
received to the parish 00. 7. 7.

4to May 1647
We have examined the Accompts of Mr Richard Burder and Mr Nicholas Eddis, late Churchwardens of this Church, for one whole yeare ending att Easter1647 and wee finde that they have receaved of the rents and Casualties of the said Church the sume of twelve pounds Nyne shillinges & Nyne pence and that they have disbursed as may appeare by their accompts twelve pounds two shillinges & two pence soe as nowe there is remayninge in their hands due to the parish seaven shillings seven pence and which they have paid over to the new Churchwardens. All which wee wittnes being Auditors assigned for takinge and passinge the said Accompt the day and year aforesaid.

Per me Richard Palfrey
Jeremy Bowden
William Langham
Daniel Burfelt
Thomas Chaloner

[f. 138–8v blank]

[f. 139] 4o April 1648
M[emoran]d[um] it is ordered by and with the consent of ye parson and parishioners of St Johns Evangelists Dublin that Mr Oliver Daverin and Mr David Morphew shalbe Churchwardens for this yeare of the said parish and ye old Churchwardens Mr Daniel Barfield and Mr Thomas Challenor are to passe their accompts on this day forteneight. And Alderman Wm Smyth, Wm Plunkett esquire, Mr Richard Palfrey, Mr Jeremy Bowden, Mr Wm Langham, Mr John Browne and the newe Churchwardens or anie three or more of them to be Auditors of the said accomptes

Dud Boswell, prebendarie of St Johns
Willm Smyth
Wm Plunkett

John Michell
Jeremy Bowden
Samuel Weston
Will Langham
Richard Burder
John Sheppard
Daniel Burtfell
George Carmicke

[f. 139v] 4° Aprilis 1648
M[emoran]d[um] it is ordered by consent of the parson and parishioners of St Johns Evangelists Dublin that [blank] Plunkett, [blank] Phillipps, John Ogden and John Sanderton are chosen and appoynted Sidesmen for this parish for this next ensuing yeare.

Dud Boswell, prebendarie of St Johns

Willm Smyth
Wm Plunkett
Jeremy Bowden
John Michell
Will Langham
Richard Burder
Daniel Burtfell
Thomas Challoner
Ol Daverin
Samuel Weston
John Sheppard
George Carmicke

[f. 140] 4° Aprilis 1648
M[emoran]d[um] It is ordered by consent of ye parson and parishioners of St Johns Evangelists Dublin that Mr Alderman Smyth, Wm Plunkett esq, Mr John Mitchell, Mr Daniell Burfield, Mr Thomas Challenor, Mr Richard Palfrey, Mr Jeremy Bowden, Mr Richard Burder, Mr Nicholas Eddies, Mr John Sheppard and Mr Wm Langham or anie six of them to make ye Cesse for ye parsons stipend for this next ensuing yeare in pursuance of ye act of State in that behalf provided. Which shalbe done the eleaventh of this present

Dud Boswell, prebendarie of St Johns

Ol Daverin
Samuell Weston
George Carmicke

[f. 140v] A note of all such rents and buryalls money receaved by Daniel Bursfeld & Thomas Challioner since Easter 1647 untill Easter 1648

Receaved of Henry Powell for Mr John Trew his house in fishamble street for half a yeares rent at Easter 1647	16.8.
Receaved of the M[aste]r of the Company of the Taylors	1.0.0.
Receaved of Rawbuck ye butcher for Easter 1647	12.6.
Receaved of the widdowe Smith for Easter 1647	6.8.
Receaved of John Borran for Michelm[as] 1647	1.3.4.
Receaved of Mrs Weston for Michelm[as] 1647	7.6.
Receaved of John Cruse in p[ar]te of Rent	1.0.0.
Receaved more of John Cruse Two barrells of herrings at 17^s	1.14.0.
Cosney Malloy[92]	
Receaved of Mr Cosney Mulloy for Easter 1647 the some of	13.1.
Receaved of Rawbuck the butcher for Michelmas 1647	12.6.
Receaved of the widdowe Arden in p[ar]te payment of arreares of Rent	7.6.
Receaved of the widdowe Smith for Michelmas 1647 the some of	6.8.
Receaved of ye Churchwardens when we came into our office	7.7.
Receaved of Mrs Weston for Easter 1647	7.6.
9.14.6.	
Receaved of Mr King for a buryall	4.0.
Receaved of Mr Howard for the buryall of his child	3.6.
Receaved for the buryall of Sr Wm Rives	5.0.
Receaved of Thomas Edward for the buryall of his child	2.0.
[f. 141] Receaved of Captene Johnes for a buryall	6.0.
	10.15.0.
Disbursed out of the said sumes	10.10.9.
The parish rest	00. 4.3.

A not of all such disbursed by Daniell Burfield & Thomas Challoner since Easter 1647 till Easter 1648.

paid Mr Tadpoll the Clerk	1.0.0.
paid the healier for mending the roof of the Church	5.0.
paid for washing the Church Lynnen	5.0.
paid Morrice for mending the seat that was broken in the Church	1.0.
paid more to the healier for mending ye roofe of the Church	5.0.
paid for burying a child that was left uppon the parish	2.0
paid for returning the presentments	2.0.
The first of No[vember] 1647 paid the smith for mending the locks of the Chest & making Two keyes & mending the lock of the Church doore	2.0.
More paid the healier for mending the roofe of the Church	3.6.

The first of December 1647 paid ye healier for mending Mr Boswells study & p[ar]t of the Church.	7.2.
paid for one hogshead of lime, sand & haire	3.0.
2d of January 1647 paid Mr Harris the heallier for mending the roofe of the Church	12.0.
[f. 141v] paid more to Tadpoll Clerk	1.0.0.
paid more to the heallier	6.6.
The first of ffebr[uary] 1647 paid the Carpenter for mending the roof of the Church	6.0.
The 5th of ffebr[uary] 1647 paid more to ij healliers for meding the roof of the Church & Mr Boswells studdy	10.0.
paid for a Bell rope	1.0.
paid for Carryeing the hearinges over ye water	1.0.
The 9th M[a]rch 1647 paid to the plummer for leading over Mr Boswells studdy & mending the gutter of the Church	9.0.
paid the heallier for mending ye ruffe	4.0.
paid the ould heallier for lime, haire & sand & plaistering about the Churches of the windowe & for mending a place over the roofe	10.2.
paid for Carrying away the dung before the Church doore	1.6.
paid more to Mr Tadpoll for washing the Church Lynnen	5.0.
paid to Mr Michell for our expences when the newe Churchwardens weare chosen	1.4.4.
paid Mr Michell for wine for ye Communion	1.10.8.
paid ye baker for bread for the Church	8.3.
10. 4. 9	
Rest due on the other side	10. 4.9
disburst for expenses the first day wee came into our office	0.6.0.
	10.10.9.

[f. 142] Wee have examined the Accompts of Mr Daniell Burfeild & Mr Thomas Challinor, late Churchwardens of this Church, for one whole yeare endinge att Easter 1648 and we finde that they have receaved of the rents & Casualtyes of the said Church the just sume of Ten pounds ffifteen shillinges and that they have disbursed as may appeare by their Accompts Ten pounds ten shillinges & nyne pence soe as nowe there is remayninge in their hands due to the parish fower shillings & three pence which they have paid over to the new Churchwardens. All which wee wittnes being Auditors assigned for the takinge & passing of the said Accompt this 18th day of Aprill as wittnes our handes 1648

Wm Plunket
per me Rich Palfrey
Ol Daverin

[f. 142v] 27° M[ar]tij 1649
Memorand[um] That it is ordered by Consent of the parson & parishioners of St John the Evangelists Dublin that Mr Nathaniel Neville & Mr John Odgen shalbe churchwardens for this yeere of the said parish & the ould Churchwardens Mr Oliver Daverin & Mr David Murphey are to passe their accompts on this day forthnight. And Alderman William {Smyth}, William Plunkett Esquire, Richard Palfrey, Jeremy Bowden, Thomas Challinor & the newe Churchwardens or any three or more of them to be Auditors of the said accomptes. And it is likewise ordered by their said consents that John Rasdall, Anthony Robinson, Leonard Graves & John Alexander are chosen and appointed sidesmen for this parish for this next ensuing yeere.

Dud Boswell, minister   Willm Smyth
Wm Plunkett
Jeremy Bowden
John Michell
Rich Palfrey
Thomas Challoner

[f. 143] 27 M[ar]tii 1649
Memorand[um] That it is ordered by consent of the parson and parishioners of St John the Evangelist Dublin That Mr Alderman Smyth, Willm Plunkett, Esquire, Captaine Mitchell, {Mr Sheapherd, Mr Waterhouse} Jeremy Bowden, Richard Palfrey, Thomas Challoner & the ould churchwardens or any <five or> six of them to make the Cesse for the parsons stipend for this next ensuing yeere in pursuance of the Acte of State in that behalf p[ro]vided which shalbe done the 5th of <this> Aprill next ensuing.

Willm Smyth
Wm Plunkett
John Michell
Rich Palfrey
Jeremy Bowden
Ol Daverin
Thomas Challoner

[f. 143v] An accompt of such monyes and yearely revenuyes belonginge to St Johns parish receaved by Oliver Daverin and David Murphey Churchwardens for one whole yeare endinge att Easter 1649.

rents
receaved of John Borran for Mr ffords house in fishamble street in p[ar]te of arreares of rent 1.0.0.
more receaved of the said John Borran for a house wherein he liveth for a yeares rent endinge at Michaelmas 1648 2.6.8.

Received of Mr Samuell Weston for one yeare ending att Easter 1649	15.0.
Received of Sir Thad Duffe in p[ar]te of arreares	1.0.0.
Received of Nich Robuck for yeare endinge att Mich[aelmas] 1648 for a house in St ffrancis street	1.5.0.
Received of the Company of Taylors	1.0.0.
Received of Mrs Smith in p[ar]t of Arrears for a house in Oxmonton	13.4.
	8.0.0.

Burials

	s. d.
ffor the buriall of Mr Clement Martin	6.8.
ffor the buriall of Mrs Laxton	3.0.
ffor the buriall of Mr Bowdens Childe	2.6.
ffor the buriall of Thomas Broughalls Childe	1.0.
	0.13.2.
Tot rec[eived]	8.13.2.

Disbursed by the same accomptants for the yeare abovsaid

Disbursed for slatinge, tyling & other necessaryes about the Church	2.0.0.
ffor wyne for the Communion for the whole yeare as appeares by p[ar]ticulars	2.2.11.
ffor breade for the whole yeare	8.0.
ffor the Clarkes stipend	2.0.0.
ffor washing the Lynnen	10.0.
ffor a lock for the balcony	2.6.
ffor hollwee & Ivie	2.6.
ffor the Langable	3.3.
7–9–2	
[f. 144] ffor expenses att Church meetinges	1.5.2.
to the Carpenter for a dayes worke	1.6.
1.–.6 –8.	tot disburst 8.15.10.

M[emoran]d[um]we have examined the accompts of Mr Oliver Daveryn and David Murphy late Churchwardens of this Church for one whole yeare ended att Easter 1649 and wee ffinde that they have receaved of the rents & casualties of the said Church the just sume of eight pounds thirteen shillinges and two pence and that they have disbursed as may appeare the sum of eight pounds ffyfteen shillinges & ten pence soe as there is nowe remayning due unto them from the parish <with them> two shillings eight pence which the newe Churchwardens <have> {are to} pay[93] to them. All which wee wittnes being Auditors assigned for taking and passing the same Accompt this tenth day of Aprill 1649

Willm Smyth
Wm Plunkett
Rich Palfrey
Thomas Challoner

[f. 144v]16° Aprilis 1650
Memorandum. That it is ordered by consent of the parson & parishioners of St John the Evangelist Dublin That {Mr} William Martin and Mr Robert Wade are chosen churchwardens of the said parish for this yeere ensuing and that Mr Nathaniell Nevill and Mr John Ogden the ould churchwardens of the said parish have time given them {to passe their accompts} till this day three weeks. And it is further ordered that William Plunkett Esquire, Alderman Hutchison, Captain Mitchell, Ensign Palfrey, William Langham & the newe Churchwardens or any Three or four of them {are}to audit the same said churchwardens accomptes. And it is likewise ordered that the undernames persons vizt. Rice Phillips, Thomas Pickering & William {Galton}be appointed sidesmen of the said parish for the next year. It is ordered likewise that the said William Plunkett, Alderman Hutchison, Captaine Mitchell, Ensign Palfrey, William Langham, Thomas Challoner, Jeremy Bowden, John Shephard, John Waterhouse & the ould churchwardens or any <five> {six} of them be appointed Sessors for the yeaere next ensuing

Dud Boswell	John Michell	Wm Plunkett
minister	Ol Daverin per me	Dl Huchinson
Thomas Chaloner	Rich Palfrey	Will Langham
		John Waterhouse
		Jeremy Bowden

[f. 145] An Accompt of such monyes & yearely Revenues belonginge to Johns parish receaved by Nathaniell Nevill & John Ogden churchwardens for one whole yeere ending at Easter 1650

Rents

Receaved out of Mrs Borran for Mr ffoords house in ffishamble streete {in p[ar]t arrears}	2.12.6.
More receaved of the said Mrs Borran for a house wherein she liveth for a yeares rent ending at Michelmas 1649	2.6.8.
More of Samuell Weston for one year ending at Easter 1650	15.0.

More for Sir Thady Duffes house in p[ar]t arrears	1.0.0.
More of Nicholas Robuck for one half yeares rent & ye other half yeare in arrear	12.6.
More of the Company of Taylors	1.0.0.
More of Mrs Smith in p[ar]te of arreares for a house in Oxmantowne	13.4.
More of Patrick Browne baker for Sir John Dongans house fishamble streete for three yeares arrears ending at Easter 1649	1.2.6.
Sum	10.2.6.

Buryalls

ffor Mr Eddis his child	3.3.
ffor Mary Vyans	4.0.
ffor Captaine Cole	6.2.
ffor Robert Lawrence, seaman	6.8.
ffor Symond Skelding	5.0.
ffor Mr Astons child	2.6.
ffor Mr Lyle	6.8.
[f. 145v] ffor Mrs Gouldsmiths buryall	4.0.
ffor John Butcher	6.0.
ffor his wife	6.0.
ffor Mr Parnes	5.0.
ffor Mr ffloyde	6.8.
ffor Mrs ffloyde	6.8.
ffor Mr Brownes child	3.3.
ffor Anthony Robinsons child	3.4.
ffor Mr Booker	5.0.
ffor Mr Broghall	6.0.
ffor the lame butcher	6.0.
ffor Mrs Jones	5.6.
ffor Lieutenant Lebybone	3.0.
ffor Mr Desmeneers child	2.6.
	5.3.2.
Suma totalis	15.5.8.

Disbursed by the said Accomptants for the year aforesaid

Disbursed for slateing, tyleing, mending of the said church and for latts, nayles, lime, sand & workmens wages & other necessaryes aboute the said church	3.1.2.
ffor wyne {& bread} for the Comunion for ye whole year	2.6.6.

ffor Glaseing the church windows	14.2.
ffor the plumer	8.0.
ffor mending Two locks	2.6.
[f. 146] ffor dying the blackcloth and dressing of it	3.6.
ffor mending the church bible and ye clasps hereof	5.6.
ffor mending a seat in ye chancell	1.8.
ffor Evy & holly	2.6.
ffor the Langable	3.3.
ffor making of one beare and mending of another	16.6.
ffor burying a poore man	6.
disburst about other affaires of the church	4.5.
ffor the clerks stipend	2.0.0.
ffor washing the Lynen	5.0.
payed to ye ould churchwardens to ballance their Accompts for the precedent year.	2.8.
ffor expenses at church meetinges	2.6.0.
tot disb[ursed]	13.3.10.

Having examined the Accompts of Mr Nathaniell Nevill & Mr Ogden, churchwardens of St Johns, for the yeare ending {at Easter} 1650 wee finde that they have receaved of the Rents & casualties of the said church the Just sume of fifteen pounds five shillinges & eight pence and that they have disbursed as appears the sume of thirteen pounds three shillinges & Ten pence soe that there remaines in their hands the sum of Two pounds one shilling & ten pence which sum is <to be> payed over to the new churchwardens. All which wee witnes being auditors assigned for the said Accompt this 14th day of May 1650

Robt H Wades mark	Will Langham	Wm. Plunkett
	Jeremy Bowden	John Michell
		John Sheppard
		Ol Daverin

[f. 146v] This12th of November 1650
It is ordered by the consent of the parishioners of the parish of St Johns that the Churchwardens of the said parish shall make & seale a lease of a house late in poss[ess]ion of Patrick Browne, Baker, for 41 years to John Ogden att 20s rent the first 10 yeares & 40s the last 31 yeares, he Covenannting to repaire & uphold said house with other ordinary Covenants. The said house being out of repair and nowe ready to fall down.

Dl Huchinson	Timothy Gilbert
John Sheppard	John Alexander
the mark of Benaimen B Roberts	Tho Wilks

James Johnston
James W Wilde
Arlenter Usher
Rich Palfrey

the mark of Thos B Barton
the mark of George +Humphreys

[f. 147] A true and p[er]fect rentall of the rents & Revenues of St Johns the Evangelists Dublin aswell in its own right as in the right of St Tullocks united to the said Church taken the 25th day of <Ja> December 1650

Thomas Conrans houses in Anno 1633 were given & graunted unto the deane & Chapter of Christchurch under the yearely rent of 3^{li} 6^{s} 8^{d}. To have & to hold to them & their successors in trust for the minister of the said parish for the tyme which the said deane & Chapter did by deed assign over unto <the said> Atherton & his successors under the said rent iij^{li} vj^{s} $viij^{d}$

Walter Fludds house nowe in the poss[ess]ion of Mr Samuell Weston.

I cannott find anie lease thereof. It were necessary that he or his landlord should shewe what terme of yeares is yett to come & what rent. I find by the rent Roll the rent to be xv^{s}

Walter Usher & his assignes hath the lease of the house that Mr Tadpole ye Clarke lives in. It beares date from Easter 1597 for 99 yeares att 2^{li} 6^{s} 8^{d} ster. There is yett to come of the lease 46 yeares there is arreares since ye Rebellion. The Churchwardens reentyred it being much out of repaire which the said Tadpoole lives in 2^{li} 6^{s} 8^{d}

[f. 147v] Docter Usher and his assignes hath a lease of the house wherein Mrs Carmock liveth for 61 years it beares date in 1593 att 1li 13s 4d p[er] ann[um]. It is very necessary to send for her to see the lease for I conceave there is not above 4 yeares to come in the lease $xxxiij^{s}$ $iiij^{d}$

Walter Dungans house is by Indenture dated 1650 granted to one John Ogden for 41 years the first ten yeares 20^{s} p[er] ann[um] & the remaynder of the terme att 40^{s} p[er] ann[um] xx^{s} 10 yeares xl^{s} 31 yeares.

The Master & Company of Taylors for their geald in St Johns Chapple p[er] ann[um] xx^{s}

The priests Chamber is that grounde upon which our church house stands soe that rent which was formerly paid by one White being 5^{s} p[er] ann[um] is extinct 0.0.0

James Bath in 163<8>4 took a lease of the parish of a plott & p[ar]cell of grounde in Oxmantowne for 41 yeares att the yearely rent of ls ster there is

10 yeares rent in arrears. The possession or interest thereof is come to the hands of the Lady Culme or alderman Huchinson or one of them. 1^{s}

[f. 148] John Anderson for 2 gardens in Oxmantowne. The parish in Anno 1614 granted a lease to the said John Anderson for 60 yeares att 40s p[er] ann[um] there is above 10 years arrears. Noe tenant to clayme noe distresse to be had the parish re-entered {20li arrears due by Capt Wingfield}. Catherine Carroll als Kelly took a lease of the parish in 1638 of a messuage, tenement & back side in Oxmanton whereon the thatched house stands at 4^{li} p[er] ann[um]. She is much in arreare as by this book will appeare & the house lyeing void & <in> the parish hands to perform the same & the other 2 gardens the parish did under divers trustees to viewe the premeses & by their consents the Churchwardens did grant a lease in 1650 to one Thomas Cooper of the above p[re]mises att 3^{li} p[er] ann[um]. $3^{li}\ 0^{s}\ 0^{d}$

Catherin Taylors house & Maurise Smith hir house by Indenture dated in 1626[94] are granted by the parish to the said Maurice Smith for 61 yeares under the joynte rent of $33^{s}\ 4^{d}$ & not severall if the rent be eight weeks behind there is a Nominae pene of $33^{s}\ 4^{d}$ ster & if wee distres her the lease to be void. There is above 10li arreares for which <the said> Mrs Smith is sued $1^{li}\ 13^{s}\ 4^{d}$

John Goods house in ffrancis Streete hath a lease for 61 yeares to begin immediately after the expiracon of a lease of 61 years bearing date 37 year of Henry the 8th. The lease will determine in 1668 att Easter there will be 17 years to come rent is $33^{s}\ 4^{d}$ Irish & paid hetherto $1^{li}\ 5^{s}\ 0^{d}$

[f. 148v] The lord of Corke for one house in the holding of one Sir Jeffrey ffenton in Copper alley at $26^{s}\ 3^{d}$ p[er] ann[um] ster about 4 yeares rent behinde the booke will make it appeare that there is $5^{li}\ 5^{s}$ arrears $1^{li}\ 6^{s}\ 3^{d}$

Mr Goulding for a windowe in the Churchyard 9 yeares arrears att 4^{d} p[er] ann[um]. 0.0.4.

Sum total of these rents $19^{li}\ 15^{s}\ 11^{d}$.

[f. 149] The rents belonginge to St Johns the Evangelist in right of St Tullocks Sir Thaddy Duffes executors for the house upon the wood key <for> att 20^{s} p[er] ann[um]. There is att easter 1651 fower yeares arreare 4^{li} 1.0.0.

George Proudfoote for 8 years arreares for a house in fishamble st ending att easter 1650 9.10.

There are severall other leases & estates as appears by the old rent Roll but what hath been a long tyme made of them I cannott finde.

[f. 149v] The 31th day of March 1651
a house at 5^{li} *p[er] A[nnum]*
Whereas the parishioners of the said parish did give order and consent that divers trustees should see in what condicion the houses and lands belonging to the said parish were in and likewise that they should lett, sett & dispose of such of them as they should thinke good of for the good of the said parish and wheras the Churchwardens Robert Wade and William Martin by the advise & consent of the said trustees have lett a lease & p[er]fected the same unto one Thomas Coop[er] of two gardens in Oxmantown, late in John Andrewes poss[ess]ion and a thatched house hereby late in poss[ess]ion of Catherin Carroll, widdowe, for the terme of forty one yeares under the rent of three pounds ster & under divers other Covenants as in the same is expressed.[95] And whereas the said Churchwardens by the consent and directions afore said have likewise joined with Mr Carr, our minister,[96] in the granting of a lease of thirty one years <to one> of the house wherein one Henry Powell lately lived unto one Edward Dermott att the rent of ffive pounds ster with Covenants to repaire & other wise to p[er]forme as in the said lease is expressed.[97] If which said acts of theirs the said Churchwardens whereby allow of and <will> {have} ratifie and confirme the same by setting our hands to these presents.

Thos Browne	Richd Palfrey	Dl Huchinson
The mark of DDavid Murphy	Arlenter Usher	John Browne
James Johnson	William Langham	
Jo Ogden		
Theodorus Barlowe		

[f. 150] This 31th day of March 1651
It is ordered by the consent of the parson and parishioners of the parish of St Johns that Mr Thomas Browne & Mr James Johnson shalbe Churchwardens for this yeare of the said parish and the ould Churchwardens are to passe their accompts by this day <month> forthnight and Alderman Huchinson, Alderman Smith, John Browne, Samuell Weston, David Murphy, Richard Palfry & John Ogden & the new Churchwardens or anie three of them to be auditors of the said accomptes. And it is likewise ordered that Lewis Williams, Jonathan Paylye & John Creshfeild to be sidesmen for the said parish for the year

Pa Ker	David D Murphie his mark
Willm Smyth	Timothy + Gilbert his mark
Dl Hutchinson	Morgan + Burne his mark
John Browne	John Crutchfeild

Rich Palfrey
Arlenter Usher
Samuell Weston
John Ogden
Lewis LWWilliams his mark

[f. 150v] 31th March 1651
It is ordered by consent of the parishioners of the parish of St Johns Dublin that Alderman Smith, Alderman Huchinson, John Browne, Samuell Weston, Richard Palfrey, Robert Wade, William Martin, John Odgen, David Murphy & the 2 newe Churchwardens or any six of them shall make the Cesse for the parsons stipent for this next ensuing year

Arlenter Usher	Willm Smith
	Dl Hutchinson
	John Browne
	Rich Palfrey
	Samuell Weston

13° April 1651
It is agreed that the above named Cessors shall have power to make a Cess in the parish of St Johns for the some of Twelve pounds which is to be levyed by the Constables & payd to the church wardens to be by them disburst to ye skavengers & for other necessary uses for the good of the parish.

Pa Ker	Dl Hutchinson
James Johnson	John Browne
Tho Browne	Wm Martyne
	Robert H Wade
	his mark

[f. 151] The Accompt of such monies and yearly revenues belonginge to St Johnes Church Receaved by Robert Wade & William Martin Churchwardens for one year ending att Easter 1651

	li. s. d.
Receaved of Mr Ogden the old Churchwarden	2.1.10.
Receaved of the widdow Birne & Carmick for rent of the house wherein Mrs Carmick liveth	2.6.8.
Receaved of the Company [of] taylors	1.0.0.
Receaved of Mr Weston for one yeares rent for his house	15.0.
Receaved of one Hillary Oldmeadowes for the tyme he lived in the house wherein Mr Tadpole liveth	8.0.
Receaved for one quarters rent which the woman of the shop was to pay out of Powells house	1.5.0.

Receaved of the executors of Nicholas Robuck for a yeares rent {& halfe}endinge att Mich[aelmas] 1650	1.17.0.
Receaved of the executors of Mr Jeremy Bowden which he left to the Church by his will	2.10.0.
In tot	12li 3s 6d

[f. 151v] Moneys receaved by the aforesaid Churchwardens for Burialls in the said church for the yeare foresaid

ffor Mr ffinch his wife & Childe	15.0.
ffor Alderman Smiths wife & Childe	9.8.
ffor Mrs Braughells Child	3.0.
ffor a woman & 3 Childrens att Rice Williames	9.0.
ffor Mr Welsh & his Childe	6.6.
ffor Mr Kitchens son & daughter	10.0.
ffor William Boyes father & mother	10.0.
ffor Dent Daniells wife	5.0.
ffor Alderman Hutchinsons 4 men	1.1.6.
Received of Mr Osborne	6.6.
ffor Richard ffranncies Childe	3.0.
ffor Mathew Browne & his wife	12.0.
ffor Capt Mitchell & 4 Children	16.0.
ffor burialls att Mr Borranes	10.0.
ffor Anthony Robinson & wife	11.0.
ffor Mr John Brownes 3 Children	9.0.
ffor Jo Desmineires wife & Child	7.0.
ffor Jo Waterhouse 2 Children	5.0.
ffor Mr Browne for a youth	3.0.
ffor Lieft Burfield Child & man	14.0.
ffor Mr Coopers boy	2.6.
ffor Mr Bayly & Rich Bell	12.0.
In tot	10li.0.8.
	12.3.6.
	22.4.2.

[f. 152] An acc[ount] of the disbursement by the said Churchwardens for the parish in the yeare aforesaid

Spent att several meetinges	1.5.0.
ffor breade & wyne for 3 Communions	11.0.
ffor altering minister & Clarks seates	12.0.
ffor buringe 8 poore [at the] begining of the sickness	17.6.

ffor mending the wheeles & ropes belonginge to the Church	1.3.4.
ffor Langable	3.3.
ffor 3 keys	3.0.
ffor mending the staires of the gallery & a seate	5.0.
ffor pavinge the Midle ally	6.0.
ffor mendinge the Roofe of the Church att twice	1.9.6.
ffor mending the ministers house	1.13.0.
paid to Mr Tadpoole by the parish order the yeare	4.0.0.
ffor washinge the lynen	4.0.
ffor burnishinge the plate	1.0.
mending ye Galleries[98]	
ffor mendinge the 2 galleryes & for Carpenter & plasterer & Colloring worke	1.13.6.
To Rich Palfrey for fferrye Councell sendinge mesenger into the country to serve & to sue M[istr]ies Smith.	1.0.0.
Spent att the Choosinge of the newe Churchwardenes	1.9.4.
in tot	16^{li} 17^{s} 1^{d}

[f. 152v] 1° May 1651
Wee have examined the accompts of Robert Wade & William Martin, the ould Church wardens, and we finde remayning in their hands of the parish monyes the sum of ffive pounds six shillings & Nyne pence which they have paid over unto Mr Thomas Browne & Mr James Johnson the new Churchwardens. The p[ar]ticulars appears in the accompt aforewritten.

Pa Ker — Dl Hutchinson
John Browne
Rich Palfrey
James Johnson
Tho Browne

[f. 153] The 19th April 1652
It is ordered by consent of the <parson> {minister} & parishioners of St Johns parish Mr Lewis Williams & Jonathan Paylye shalbe Churchwardens for this yeare ensuing of the said parish and that the old Churchwardens are to passe their accompts by this day seighnight and Alderman Huchinson, ald[erman] Smith, Sheriffe Browne, Richard Palfrey, John Waterhouse, Theodorus Barloe, Rice Williams, John Shephard, Samuell Weston, John Odgen & the two newe Churchwardens or anie three them to be auditors of the said accompts. And it is also ordered that the abovesaid p[ar]ties or any six of them are likewise ordered to make a Cesse for the ministers stipent the <next> yeare {ending att Christmas next}. And lastly it is ordered that James Hancock, Morgan Burne, George Hollis, and Thomas Grimes are to be sidesmen for the siad year.

Pa Ker

Willm Smyth
Dl Hutchinson
John Browne
Rich Palfrey
John Waterhouse
Theodorus Barlow
Tho Browne
John Ouldfield
Timothy Gylbert
Thomas Guire

[f. 153v blank]

[f. 154] An accompt of what Monyes James Johnson and Thomas Browne Churchwardens of St Johns Dublyn have laid out for the use of St Johns Church since Easter 1651.

Spent att two meettings with the gentlemen of the parrish	1.7.0.[99]
paid for Rushes att severall tymes	4.0.
paid for the wine att 3 Comunions	1.0.0.
paid for breed to the Comunion	1.0.
paid for Nayls towards repaireinge	14.0.
paid for more Nayls	9.4.
paid for timber	13.6.
paid for Lime & Carpenters wagges and claye & other necessaryes for ye Church	7.7.6.
paid Mr Weston for timber	2.18.4.
paid the Plumer	1.4.4.
paid Mr Grymes for timber & workmanship	7.14.0.
paid the Smith for Iron	15.0.
paid Mr Vanhoven for timber	5.17.0.
paid Mr Harrison for laths & Nayles with other matterialls	26.10.0.
paid more for Claye & sand	1.17.6.
paid more for mendinge ye Church portch	13.6.
paid more for two Sumances to Mr Smith	5.0.
paid Mr Tatpoule	1.0.0.
paid att severall tymes to Carrie earth to the Church	10.0.
paid Ald[erman] Smith for timber	10.0.
paid for my owne expences with the workmen att severall tymes	10.0.
paid for two Comunions since	12.10.
paid Mr Border	1.4.0.
<paid Michael Roggers for tyleing for>	
[f. 154v] paid Michaell Roggers for tyleing for ye pavinge of the Church for three weekes wagges at 2^s 6^d p[er] diem	2.5.0.

paid for the Labourers which wrought with him	1.16.0.
paid Thomas Woodarte the whiteliner for 11 dayes at 2^{s} 6^{d} p[er] diem	1.7.6.
paid another workman att 2^{s} p[er] diem	1.2.0.
paid for one Labourer for there imployment att 1^{s} 6^{d} p[er] diem for 11 dayes	12.10.
paid beere & bread which the workemen were allowed	13.6.
paid Nicholas the Sexton	6.6.
paid for Lime	1.8.0.
paid Walter to make morter	1.6.
paid for Haire	1.6.
paid for lether to make glue	6.
paid John Somes for the remaynder of the sand & clay which wee have used about the Church	1.3.5.
paid att taverons att tymes when wee were about the parish busines	4.0.
paid for another Comunion for breed and wine	10.0.
for making sun diall	11.0.
the totall due to them as Churchwardens 60^{li} 7^{s} 5^{d}	
	75.18.0.

[f. 155] A noate of the receats that the said Churchwardens for the said yeare 165<1>2

Receaved for the breaking of the wyndows for Mr Sergeant	6.0.
Receaved of Mrs Camuck for a years rent endinge att Mich[aelmas] last	2.6.8.
Receaved of Mr Leash for a yeares rent endinge Mich[aelms] 1651	1.5.0.
Receaved of the Master of the taylors	1.0.0.
Receaved of Ald[erman] Smith for Sr Thaddy Duffes rent endinge Easter 1651	4.0.0.
Receaved of the old Church Wardens	5.6.9.
Receaved of the widdow Smith for rent	1.6.8.

15–11–1

M[emoran]d[um] the12 th of May 1652 we have Examined the accompts of James Johnson & Thomas Browne the old Church wardens and we ffinde that there is resting due & owing unto them from the parish the sum of sixtye pounds seaven shillinges five pence and the new churchwardens are desired to {only} pay over unto the said old Churchwardens such moneys or yearely revenues of the Church as they shall receave in p[ar]te satisffacion of the moneys due to the said old Churchwardens the Church being kept in repair.

Willm Smyth
Dl Hutchinson
Rich Palfrey

Joseph Whitechurch
Theodorus Barlowe

the 19th of Aprill 1653. Receaved of Jonathan Paley & Lewis Williams in p[art]t payment of the sixtie pounds seven shillings and five pence above mentioned the some of Three pounds four shillings as witness our hands the day above written.

James Johnson
Tho Browne

[f. 155v] Accompt with Mr fford & there is due <him from the parish> from him to the parish six pounds ffourteen shill & two pence att Mich[aelmas] dated June 1652.

$6^{li}\ 14^{s}\ 2^{d}$

Mr Tadpole to allowance in accompt to the Church $4^{li}\ 13^{s}\ 4^{d}$

Willm Smyth
Rich Palfrey
Dl Huchinson

8th of June 1652
The order for adding 40^{s} *p[er] Ann[um] to the Clarkes stipend*
by consent of the parishioners it is ordered that the Clarke shall have forty shillings p[er] annum added to his former stipent <du> to continue duringe the parish his pleasure

Willm Smythe
Dl Huchinson
Rich Palfrey

Jonathan Paley
Lewis LW Williams his mark
churchwardens

[f. 156] This 4th day of ffebruary 165[3]
Whereas the parish of St Johns dublyn have a peece of grounde in Oxmantowne that lyeth voyde & waste & noe benefitt made thereout and fforasmuch as some of the same parishioners have desired that the same might be viewed. It is ordered by the consent of the s[ai]d parishioners that Robert Wade, William Martin, Nathaniel Nevill, Jonathan Payle and Thomas Browne <doe>or anie four of them or more doe view the said ground and witi[nes]se unto the same parishioners the length & breadth thereof and what condicion the same is now in by this day siegnyght to the end that the parishioners <be> may be the better Informed howe to lett or dispose of the same.

Willm Smyth
Rich Palfrey
John Sheppard
Nath Nevill
Tho Browne
James Johnston
Jonathan Paley
Churchwardens
Lewis LW Williams his mark

[f. 156v] 14th Aprill 1653
It is ordered by the consent of the Minister & parishioners of St Johns parish that Mr Samuell Weston & Mr Jonathan Pallien shalbe Churchwardens for this yeare ensuing of ye s[ai]d parish and that the old Churchwardens are to pass their Accounts by Twesday next in the after none and the wo[rshipful] Daniel Huchenson, Maior, Alderman Smith, Mr Samuell Weston, Mr Jonathan Pallyen, Mr Jo Shephard, Mr Rich Palfery, Mr Nathaniell Newell, Mr Roger Breerton, Mr Walter Plunkett or any fower of them to be Auditors for ye saide accounts; and it is also ordered that the abovesaid p[ar]ties or any six of them are likewise ordered to make a cess for the Ministers stipend the yeare ending at Christmas next. And lastly it is ordered that William Ben, Thoms Guier, Ralph ffenton, and James Rea to be sidesmen for the said yeare.

Pa Ker

Dl Hutchinson
Willm Smyth
Thos Browne
Arth Hendy
William Dixson
fa farrell
James Boye
John Garrott

[f. 157] An account of such monyes and year[ly] revenues as belongeth to St Johns parish by Jonathan Pallyn and Lewis Williams Church wardens for one whole year ending att Easter 1653.

	li
Receaved of Thomas Cooper for a yeares rent ending att Christmas 1651	3.0.0.
Received of ye M[aste]r of ye of Taylors	1.0.0.
Received of Walter Leith for halfe a yeares rent endinge att Mich[aelmas] 1652 {for Robucks house}	12.6.
Received of Mrs Cormick for a yeares rent ending att Mich[aelmas] 1652	2.6.8.
Received of ye Widdow Smith in p[ar]t of her rent	13.4.

Received of Mrs Ogden for 2 years rent	2.0.0.
	9. 12. [6]
More received by ye said Accountants	
from Mrs Cormicke for ye breaking of ye ground for hir Child	3.4.
from Mr Theodor Barlow for ye breaking of ye ground for his child	2.6.
from Mrs Browne for breakinge of ye ground for hir husband	6.8.
	0.12.0.
	9.12.0.

Receaved in all by ye said Churchwardens <Twentie> Ten pounds five shillings 10.5.0.

[f. 157v] The accompt of the disbursements of ye within menconed Churchwardens for the parish in ye year afores[ai]d

	li. s. d.
ffirst for bread and wyne for 2 sacraments	16.0.
paid Mr Harrison for slating ye Church	1.3.9.
Item given to ye workmen in bread & beer	1.6.
Item paid more to Mr Harrison for work done to ye Church	2.1.0.
Item paid for nails, lyme and sand	5.0.
Item paid for Langable	3.3.
Item paid for bread and wyne for 3 sacraments	1.4.0.
Item paid for Removing Mr Plunckets stone and for lyme and sand for ye Church use	6.0.
Item paid for bread and wyne for one sacrament	8.6.
Item paid for making a new key for the Church dore	6.
Item for nailes att severall tymes	2.6.
Item paid Mr Ja Johnson and Mr Thomas Browne	3.4.0.
Totall of ye disbursements	9.18.10.

[f. 158] We have examined ye Accounts of Jonathan Pallyn and Lewys Williams ye old Church wardens and we find remayning in their hands of ye parish monyes ye sum of seaven shillings which they have paid over unto Mr Samuel Weston and Mr Jonathan Pallyen the <old> {new} Churchwardens. ye day above written xvij^{s}

p[er] me Rich Palfrey
Willm Smyth
Samuel Weston
Jonathan Paley

[f. 158v] this 28th of March 1654
It is ordered by the consent of the Minister & parishioners of the parish of St Johns that Mr George Hollis and Mr Rice Williams shalbe Churchwardens for this present yeare ensuing of this parish and that the old Churchwardens are to pass their accounts by this day seinghnight and ald[erman] Wm Smith, <Samuell Weston>, Richard Palfery, Lewis Williams, William Martin, John Gamye and Morgan Birne or anie three of them to be auditors for taking that the saide accompts and it is also ordered that ald[erman] Wm Smith, Richard Palfery, Wm Martin, John Shepard, Lewis Williams, Richard Burder & the old churchwardens or any six of them are likewise ordered to make a Cess for the Ministers stipend for this ensuing yeare. And it is lastly ordered that James Coffney, Robert Eaton, John Higgeson & Henry Bushell to be sidesmen for the said yeare.

	Pa Ker
Willm Smyth	the marke of Thos TB Barton
Rich Palfrey	Morgan MB Birne
Wm Martyne	Danil Byrn
Samuell Weston	
Jonathan Paley	
the mark of Lewis LW Williams	
John Gary	

[f. 159 blank]

[f. 159v] An Accompt of such moneys as hath bin Receaved p[er] us the undernamed Samuell Weston & Jonthan Paley in the time of our Churchwardenshipp

Receaved of the ould churchwardens	7.0.
Receaved of Mrs Cormeck for a yeares rent ending at Mighellmas 1653	2.6.8.
Receaved from Samuell Weston for 1 yeres rent	15.0.
Receaved from Walter Leech for one yeares rent ending att Mighellmas 1653	1.5.0.
Receaved from Mrs Ogden for one yeares rent ending at Mighellmas 1653	1.0.0.
Receaved from widdow Smith in part of her rent	13.4.
Receaved from Mr Tho Cooper in part of two years rent which ended at Christmas last 1653	4.0.0.
Receaved from Walter Leech for halfe a yeares rent endinge att Easter 1654 & is	12.6.
Receaved of Ald[erman] Dee for breakinge of ground for Mrs Waldrum	6.8.
Receaved of Theodorus Barlloe for breaking of ground for his Child	3.4.

Receaved from the M[aste]r of the Taylors for one yeares rent for there geld in St Johns Church which ended at <Mighellmas> {Midsomer} 1653 & is received	1.0.0.
Receaved from Mr Tadpoole the sume of 4li 13s 4d which was to him paid by Mathew foord att Mighell[mas] 1652	4.13.4.
Receaved of Mr Tadpoole more for one yeares rent due att Mighellmas 1653	1.13.4.
Receaved from Mr Tadpoole for half a yeares rent due att Easter 1654 for Mr Michel ffoards house where the said Tadpoole now dwelleth	16.8.
Summa	19.12.10.

Rich Palfrey

[f. 160] An Accompt of moneys paid p[er] us the undernamed Samuell Weston & Jonathan Paley in the time of our Churchwardenshipp

paid to Mr. Lynnegor for slating the Church	6.0.0.
paid p[er] Carpinter for his worke	16.0.
paid for bread & beer for the workmen	1.6.
paid for wine for six sacraments paid	2.8.6.
paid for Bread for ditto sacraments	3.0.
paid for wine for two sacraments paid	18.8.
paid for bread only for ditto sacraments	1.0.
paid for glasing of the windows in the north gallery paid	2.0.
paid for mending the seats in ye west gallery	8.
paid for mending the slate worke over the pulpitt	6.
paid for a warrant from the Maior and is concerning Mr Boyds house I say paid	6.
paid for Langable	3.3
paid for mending a lock & a Keay for the Church doore	10
paid Mr Tadpoole According to a former order of the parish at 4^{li} p[er] Annum for his stypent for this two yeres past the sume of	8.0.0.
paid for An atachment that Issued out from the ould Churchwardens against the parishioners[100] the sume of	7.6.
paid for a Keay for the vestery doare	6.
paid expenses {of} the Minister & newe Church wardens.	8.5.
Totall	19.12.10.

Rich Palfrey

[f. 160v] The 26th Aprill 1654
Wee have examined the Accompts of Mr Samuell Weston and Jonathan Paley the Old Church wardens and we finde that there is nott Any of the

Parish money Remaining in there hands for that they have receaved the some of nineteen pounds twelve shillings and ten pence and have disburst the some of nineteen pounds twelve shillings and ten pence as the Accompt before written apeeares

Wm Martyne
Willm Smyth
Morgan MB Birne his mark
Rich Palfrey

[f. 161] We have examined ye Accompts of Mr Samuell Weston and Jonathan Paley the old Churchwardens and we finde that there is nott Any of the Parish mony remaineing in there hands.

[f. 161v] this 23th of Aprill 1655.
It is ordered by consent of the Minister & <Ch> parishioners of the parish of St Johns parish that Mr John Sanderton & Mr George Hewlett shalbe Churchwardens for this present yeare ensuing of this parish and that the old Churchwardens of this parish are to pass their accompts by this day senghnight and that ald[erman] William Smith, John Shepard, Sam Weston, Lewis Williams, William Martin, Richard Palfry, John Gamye, Mr James Barloe & the <newe> {old} churchwardens or anie six of them be appoynted for makying the Cess for the Minister <and> for the ensuing year and <three> {fowre} also for taking the old Churchwardens accompts. And that George Humphrys, <Thomas> John Givaker, <James Caffrey> George Lowther and Edmund Daniell be the sidesmen for this ensuing year.

Pa Ker
Jonathan Paley
Henris B Bricklan his mark
George W Humphries his mark

Rich Palfrey
Wm Martin
Ralph Hall
Ja Barlow
Theodorus Barlowe
John Pullen
John Alexander
Morgan MB Birne his mark

[f. 162] Monyes Received for the use of ye parish of St Johns for the year 1654 by George Hollie and Rice Williams.

	li. s. d.
Received of Mr Harris for Ogdens house for one year & a halfes Rent	1.10.0.
Received of Mr Carmick for Burrowes his house for one yeare & ½ Rent	3.10.0.

Received of Mr Cooper in p[ar]te of his Rent & arrears for ye houlding in Oxmantowne	3.0.0.
Received of Mr Leech for Robuc{k}s house in ffrancis street for one years Rent	1.5.0.
Received of Widd Smith in p[ar]te of her rent & arrears for ye house in Oxmantone	13.4.
Received of Mr Moulsworth for breaking of grounde for his wife	6.8.
<*quere what has become of Mr Proudfoots lease*>[101]	
Received of Mrs Proudfoot in p[ar]t of her Rent & arrears of Rent	2.0.0.
Received of John Tadpole for Rent of Mr ffoords house	1.13.4.
Received of Mr Theodore Barlow for breaking of grounde for his childe	3.0.
	14.1.4.

[f. 162v] Monies paid by George Hollis and Rice Williams for the use of the parish of St Johns in ye year 1654

	li. s. d.
June 12th	
paid James Wilde for a cushion	1.12.9.
paid to Lewis Williams for Iron work in ye gallary	11.10.
Paid Mr Grimes for his Carpentery worke	4.0.
July 23th 1654	
Paid to Mr Huelett for wine for one sacrament	9.0.
Paid Mr Weston for nailes	2.0.
Paid Mr Huelett for wine for another sacrament	8.0.
Paid for Longe Cable	3.3.
paid Mr Hulet for wine for 3 sacraments	1.4.6.
paid Mr Harrison for repairing ye Church	4.15.0.
paid Mr Tadpole	4.0.0.
paid for beeing attached att Mr Price & Lieut Halls suite	2.6.
{paid to Mr. Hulet for 3 sacraments	1.2.6.}
paid for beere for ye workmen att the Church	1.0.
paid for bread for 3 sacraments	1.6.
paid for a copy for the Bill of Mr Price & Leiut Hall & ye appear[ance]	3.2.
ffor ye ffees of the Attachm[ent]	7.6.
ffor engrosing the Answere	6.
Given the clerke for entering these acompts in ye book	1.6.
	15.10.6.

This 5th of June 1655
Wee have examined the Accompts of the Old Churchwardens and we ffinde that there is due to them over and above what they have layde out the sume of one pound Nyne shillings which the now churchwardens are to pay over to them when they shall have receaved the same out of the revenues of the parish:

Rich Palfry	Ge Hewlet
Ja Barlow	John Sanderton

[f. 163] An accompt of Mr Ker his receipts from the several Churchwardens since hee came unto the parish, sixty pounds a yeare being promised him.

Imprimis for the year 1650 hee was fully paid by Mr Martin and Mr Wade beeing then Churchwardens	nothing due
Item from Christmas 1650 unto 1651 James Johnson and Tho Browne beeing Church wardens received only fifty one pounds nyne shillings & six pence, due	8.10.6.
Item from Christmas 165<2>1 unto 165<3>2 Jonthan Palin and Lewis Williams beeing Church wardens receaved sixty pounds five shillings	0.0.0
Item from Christmas 1652 unto 1653 Mr Weston & Jonathan Palin aforesaid being Church wardens I received fifty five pounds tenn shillings and fower pence due	4.9.8.
Item from Christmas 1653 to 1654 George Hollis & Rice W[illia]ms beinge Church wardens received[102] ffiftie seaven pounds Twelve shillings seaven pence. Rests due	2.7.5.
for the tyme that Mr Carr hath been mynister of this parish there is resting due unto him of his stipend of sixty pounds p[er] ann[um] ending at Christamas 1654 according to the Accompt above said the some of fifteen pounds seaven sh[illings] seaven pence	15.7.7.

G. Hewlett	Rich Palfry
John Sanderton	Ja Barlow
Rice R Wms mark	George Hollis

[f. 163v] the 21th of June 1655
by consent of the Minister <and parishioners> & Churchwardens and parishioners {of St Johns} it is ordered that Mr Ardagh[103] be authorised to appeare for the said parishioners to the suite nowe against them in the Court for Administration of Justice in Ireland, att the suit of John Price and Marye, his wife, Raphe Hall and Jane, his wife & <to> in the name of the parishioners to confesse, adress or judgement <to th> for 57^{li} 3^{s} 5^{d} to be satisfied out of the parish rents and revenyes and alsoe out of the Arrears due

to the Church. And also it is ordered that until that <the> said Price & Hall and their wives be satisffied the said decree what charges shalbe towards reparacion of the Church or anie other necessary disbursements shalbe from tyme to tyme <be> receipted by way of Cesse upon the said parishioners. And this wee consent unto[104]

Willm Smith
Rich Palfrey
Dl Hutchinson
Rice R Williams his mark
Jonathan Paley
George Lowther

[f. 164] this 15th of April 1656.
It is ordered by the consent of the Minister & parishioners of the parish<ioners> of St Johns that Mr James Barloe and Mr Thomas Cooper shalbe churchwardens for this present year of this parish and that the old Churchwardens are to pass their accompts by this day fortnight and that Alderman Smith, <ald> Richard Palfery, Samuell Weston, Mr John Shepard, Mr Robert Wade, Mr Theodore Barlowe and the newe churchwardens or anie fower of them are appoynted to take the old Churchwardens accompts. And it is also ordered that the aforenamed ald[erman] Smith, Richard Palfery, Samuell Weston, John Shepard, Robert Wade, Theodore Barlowe, William Martin, Rice Williams, Lewis Wiliams and the old churchwardens or anie six of them be appoynted for the making of the cess for the Minister. And it is also ordered that Mr Wm Daniell, Mr <Wm> Richard Westropp, Mr Thomas Browne and Mr Brickland <for ye> be sidesmen for this ensuing year.

Pa Ker	Rich Palfrey
Theodorus Barlow	John Bexwicke
John Bolton	Jonathan Paley
George Hollis	Wm Martyne
M Potts	Robert H Wade his mark
John Crutchfeild	

[f. 164v] Monyes Receaved for the use of the parish of St Johns for the yeere 1655 by Mr John Sanderton and Mr George Hewlett Churchwardens.

	li. s.d.
Imprimis Receaved from Mr Cooper, <for> {in p[art]t} for <one yeeres> {arrears}Rent due at Christamas 1655 for howse ni oxmanton	3.0.0.
Received from Walter Leech for one yeeres Rent due at Easter 1656 for a howse in francistreet & 5s Allowed for ye Cess	2.0.0.
Received from Mr Weston for one yeeres Rent due at Easter 1656 for a howse in fistreet	15.0.

paid for Cess 6^s 10^d

Received from Mr Cormock for one yeres Rent ending at Easter last for a howse in fishstreet	19.10.
Received from Mr Harris for a howse in fishamble street for one yeares rent Ending at Easter 1656	1.0.0.
Received from the widow Smith for a howse in oxmanton being in p[ar]te of arrears of Rent	1.5.0.
Received for ye buriall of one Mr Blake for breaking the ground	6.0.
Received for breaking the ground for Ja Boys Child in ye Church	3.4.
Received for breaking the ground for Mr Jones Child in the Church	3.4.
Received for the buriall of Alderman Smiths Child	3.4.
Received from the M[aste]r of the taylors[105]	1.0.0.
Received of Mr Tadpole for Mr foordes howse in fishamble street	1.13.4.
Proudfoots rent	
Received of Mr Proudfoote in p[ar]te of arrears of Rent	1.6.8.
	13.15.10.

[f. 165] Moneys laid out by Mr John Sanderton and Mr George Howlett Churchwardens for the use of St Johns parish ye yeere 1655

	li. s. d
Imprimis to Mr Ardagh, Attorny for the parish for fees disburset by him for the parish	12.10
More to him for his fee	5.0.
To Mr Harrison for slating the Church	6.3.6.
Item to John Jones for mending the Comunion Table & Railes	5.0.
for bread and wine for ye Comunion this yeere	3.7.0.
Remaineing due to Mr Hulett the last yeere for wine	7.2.
for Langable	3.0.
Paid unto Mr Tadpole for his yeers Sallary	4.0.0.[106]
	15.3.6.

22th of May 1656
Wee have examined the Accompts of the ould Churchwardens and doe finde that there is due unto them which they have laid out more then they have receaved the sume of Twenty seaven <pounds> shillings and Eight penc which the new Churchwardens are to pay over unto them when they shall have receaved the same out of the Revenues of the parish

John Sheppard
Theodorus Barlow
Robert H Wades mark
Ja Barlow
Thos TC Coopers mark

[f. 165v] 22th January 1656

M[emoran]d[um] that there is due unto Mr Carr for arrears due unto him this last yeere the Sume of Three pounds sixteen shillings and six penc, besides the some of fifteen pounds seaven shillings seven penc formerly due in arrear unto him since he was minister. In all amounting unto the some of nynteene pounds fower shillings & one penny endnig at xprimas 1655

$19^{li}\ 04^{s}\ 01^{d}$

Ge Hewlett
John Sanderton
John Sheppard
Ja Barlow
Robert H Wades mark

[f. 166] The 30th March 1657

It is ordered by the consent of the Mynnister <&> Churchwardens and parishioners of the parish of St Johns parish Dublin that Mr <James Boye and John Boulton> {John Boulton & Mr James Boye}shalbee Churchwardens for this present year for the said parish, begining at Easter 1657 & ending at Easter 1658. And that the ould Churchwardens are to pass there accompts by this day fortnight and that Mr Alderman Smith, {Mr Rich Palfry}, Mr John Sheppard, Mr Samuell Weston, Mr John Price, Mr Rice Williams and the new Churchwardens or any fower of them are appoynted to take the ould Churchwardens acc[omp]ts. And it is further ordered that the aforenamed Mr Alder[man] Smith, {Mr Rich Palfery}, Mr John Sheppard, Mr Samuell Weston, {Mr Wm Martyn} Mr John Price, Mr Rice Williams,Theodor Barlowe, {Mr Arthur Henly} and the ould Churchwardens or any six of them be appoynted for the making of the Cess for ye Mynnister. And that Mr Thomas Loe, John Alexander, James Bishopp & [blank] Hill are appoynted sidesmen for the said parish for the said year.

Pa Ker	John Hendy
John Peppard	Lewis LW Wms mark
John Price	Hen ffahayton
Rice R Williams [mark]	Tho Lowe
Ja Potts	Jas + Coveney mark
Christopher Lovett	

[f. 166v] this13th of April 1657

It is ordered by consent of the parishioners of the parish of St Johns that alderman William Smith, Mr Wm Martin, Mr Jonathan Paley, Mr Rice Williams, Mr John Sheppard, Mr George Hollis or anie fower of them, takinge to their assistance the old Churchwardens or one of them, to viewe over the arrears of dues to the <parson> Minister since he came to this parish, and to certifie the defaults of such as are in arreare and what the same may amount unto that maybe gotten in for the arreares that the parish due to the Minister, whereby <it> there maybe a course taken for the Ministers satisffacion. And it is further ordered by consent aforesaid that in case that soe much of the arrears may not be gotten in or may satisfie the minister then what shalbe wanting hereof shalbe by consent afores[ai]d layde on the parishioners by way of addicon to the <the> Ministers <rent> stipent for the ensueing yeare.

	Willm Smyth
	Dl Hutchinson
John Price	Rich Palfrey
John Sheppard	Wm Martyn
Chas Andrewes	the mark of Rice R Williams

[f. 167] this13th day of Aprill 1657

It is ordered by Consent of the {minister &}parishioners of St Johns Parish that Mr Thomas Cooper shall have a lease made unto him for forty one yeares from Michaelmas next of a p[ar]cel of wast land in Oxmantowne belonginge to the <lan> parish adjoyninge to the lands of Hore of Balsheelan att the rent of fforty shillings p[er] annum <qarterly> half yearly, free of anie deducion or taxe whatesover on the rent or land and that said Mr Cooper shall be att all charges in the gayning poss[ess]ion thereof and in mayntayning the same during the said term of 41 years.

Pa Ker	Willm Smyth
John Price	Rich Palfrey
John Sheppard	Wm Martyne
John Bolton }	Cha Andrewes
James Boy } {newe}Churchwardens	

I Thomas Cooper doe accept of and agree to this order of the parish & shall p[er]form the same accordingly

The mark of Tho TC Cooper

[ff 167v–8 blank]

[f. 168v] Monyes Receaved for the use of St Johns parish for the yeare 1656 by James Barlow & Thomas Cooper Churchwardens of the said parish

Receaved <from> of widow Nolan for Mr Cormocks howse for one yeere ending at Easter 1657	2.6.8.
Received of the M[aste]r of the taylors for the said yeere	1.0.0.
Received of widow Smith for p[ar]t of Arrears	13.4.
Received of Walter Leach for one yeers Rent ending at Easter 1657	1.5.0.

Received of Thomas Coop[er] for rent & arrears of rent for & untill Christmas 1656.	5.0.0.
Received for the burialls following	
Alderman Smiths Child	0.3.4.
James Boyes Child	0.3.0.
Samuell Gibbs Child	0.3.0.
Thomas Howards Child	0.3.0.
Theod. Barlows 2 Children	0.6.0.
a stranger	0.7.6.
Note that this is in ye p[ar]t of ye parish[107]	
Received for standings ag[ains]t ye wall	0.6.3.
	11.17.1.

[f. 169] The paym[en]ts made by the said Churchwardens for the said yeere.

To Mr Tadpole	1.0.0.
For slating the Church	1.16.5.
To Mr Coop[er] for bread & wine	3.13.4.
allowed ye widow Nolan for Cess	4.8.
Allowed Mr Coop[er] for Cess	1.9.3.
Paid Mr Price in p[ar]t of such moneys due out of ye Rents in the behalf of the Executors of James Johnston & Thomas Browne	7.11.1.
	15.14.9.

20th of Aprill 1657
Wee have Examined the above accompt of the said Churchwardens and doe finde that there is due unto them which they have paid more than they Receaved the sume of Three pounds Seaventeen shillings and Eight pence which is to bee paid unto them by way of Cess on the severall Inhabitants of the said parish.

Willm Smyth
Wm Martyn
Theodorus Barlow
John Bolton
James Boy

[f. 169v] April 20 1657
Received then of Mr James Barlow the sume of seaven powndes Eleaven shillings and one penny in part of a sume recovered by decree from ye parrish of saint Johns Dublin as Executor to James Johnson and in the right of Mr Ralph Hall. I say received £ 07–11 –

John Price

March 18th 1658
Received of Mr John Boulton & Mr James Bwoy the sume of five poundes five shillings and eight pence being by vertue of theire Receipts as church wardens in part of a decree above mentioned. I say received £05li 05s 8d
John Price

from Walter Leech to Easter 1658	£1.5.0.
From Wm Harris to East[er] 1657	£1.0.0.
the like to Easter 1658	£1.0.0.
from Wid Newland to 1658	£2.0.8.
	5.5.8.

[f. 170] 16 Apr[il] 1658
It is ordered by the consent of the Minister, Churchwardens and parishioners of St Johns parrish Dublin, Mr James Potts & John Alexander shalbee Churchwardens for this present yeere begining at Easter 1658 & Endnig at Easter 1659. And that the ould Churchwardens are to pass their Accompts by this day fortnight and that Mr Alder[man] Smith, Mr Richard Palfery, Mr John Sheppard, Mr Wm Marten, Mr Rice Williams, James Barlow, George Hollis and the new Churchwardens or any fower of them are appoynted to take the ould Churchwardens Accompts. And it is further ordered that ye s[ai]d Ald[erman]Smith, Mr Palfery, Mr Sheppard, Mr Marten, Mr W[illia]ms, Jas Barlowe, George Hollis, Robert Wade and the ould Churchwardens or any six of them be appoynted for makeing the Cess for the Mynister {ye ensueing year}. And that Georg Humfry, Gawen Duglas, Jeramy Smith and Edmond Daniell are appoynted sidesmen for the said year.[108]

Pa Ker minister of the said p[arish]
Rich Palfrey
Wm Martyn
Rice R Williams [his mark]
J Barlowe
Edmond [MS damaged]
Robert [MS damaged]

[f. 170v] Att a meeting of ye parrish December ye 28 1658
It is this day ordered that the old Church wardens {Mr Jo Bolton & Mr James Boy} doe give their accompts unto ye new Churchwardens of all their Receipts and disbursements upon Tuesday next at nine a Clocke in ye morning. It is allsoe ordered that the sexton doe give notice unto all those poore that now receive ye Almes of ye parrish that they be here uppon Tuesday afforesaid at ye same time.

Ordered that Mr Carr doe then also bring in accompt of what is due to him in arrear of his stypend.[109]

	Willm Smyth
Jas Potts	Dl Hutchinson
John Allexander	
Churchwardens	Thos Howard
[MS damaged] Whitchurch	Wm Martyn
John Price	Andrew Lloyd

[f. 171 bank]

[f. 171v] 1657

Moneys Received ffor the use of St Johns Parrish by John Bolton & James Boy Churchwardens.

Received of ye Widdow Newland for one yeares Rent ending at Easter 1658	£2.6.8.
Received ffrom Walter Leech for one yeares Rent ending at Easter abovesaid	£1.5.0.
Received ffrom Mr William Harrys for Ogdens house 2 yeares rent ending as above	£2.0.0.
Received ffrom the Master of ye Taylors	£1.0.0.
Note that what is & shalbe due for ye butchers standings due to ye parish[110]	
Received ffrom the Butchers for standing in the lane	£1.12.6.
Received for burialls etc.	
Ald[erman] Smiths Child	£ 0. 3.4.
The Child out of Skynner Rowe	£0. 3.4.
	£8.10.10.

[f. 172] 1657
Disbursements in the same year by the said Churchwardens

Paid to Mr Harryson for Repairing of ye Church	£2.5.6.
Paid to Mr John Price treasurer	£5.5.8.
Allowed for the Cesse of Widdow Newlands house	£0.6.0.
Paid ffor 2 locks for the use of ye Church	£0.3.2.
Paid for a Casement for the Church	£0.2.4.
Paid Mr Harvie for paving before ye Church dore	£0.4.6.
Paid for the long Cable	£0.3.6.
	£8.10.8.

Paid to the new Church wardens for the ballancing of their Accompt [MS damaged]

The 22th day of March 16[58]
We whose Names are subscribed [have examined] the above Accompt and doe find [Ms torn] Resting in the hands of the fo[rmer Churchwardens and] is now paid over to Mr Jam[es Potts and Mr John] Alexander. Witnesse our [handes this day above] written

Wm Martyne [MS damaged]

[ff 172v–3v blank]

[f. 174] Tho MaGlew of Cloghran Swords sayth hee will bringe & leave a chyld of ab[ou]t 2 yers old by Tho Mason, In some house in this parish, ye 24th March 1667.

[ff 174v–5v blank]

APPENDIX 1

This undated fragment of St John's rental was transcribed *c.*1690 by a person who also made extensive notes of baptisms, marriages and burials from the Dublin parish registers. The latest date in these notes is 1697. It does not correspond to any of the rentals in the churchwardens accounts so may be a fragment of a missing account or a separate survey of the rents. It is after 1621 when James Ussher became bishop of Meath but before the death of Nicholas Carmick in 1630.

Trinity College, Dublin, MS 851

[f. 106v] Rents ex of St Johns	
fishamble street	
Tho Conran for an house late in ye pos[session] of Jo Trew	3. 6. 8
Walt flood, merchant, one house in ye pos[session] of fran Anesly, mil	0. 15. 0
Jac Ush[er], ep[iscopus] Mid, {1 house} in pos[session] Math ford	1. 14. 4
Walt Ush[er], merchant, 1 house in pos[session] Nicholas Carmick	2. 6. 8
Walt Dungan, gent, 1 house rent Jo Baker	0. 7. 6
Corporation of Tailours for ye guild in ye chappel of St Johns	1. 0. 0
Tho White for a place nere ye church in St Jo[hns] lane cald ye preists chamb^{er}	0. 5. 0
Oxmantowne	
Mr [blank] Bath for a place in Oxmanton	2. 10. 0
Cath Connor 1 house pos[session] of Jac Right	4. 0. 0
Cath Tailour 1 h[ouse] <pos>	1. 0. 0
Math Smith, gent, 1 h[ouse] pos[session] Jo Allen	0. 13. 4
John Anderson for his h[ouse] pos[session] Paul Hearing	2. 0. 0
Jo Good Butch[er] 1 h[ouse] in Castlestr[eet]	1. 5. 0
Ld of Cork 1 h[ouse] pos[session] Jeffry fenton in castle street	1. 6. 3
Ald[er]man Bradocks house in franc[is street]	[blank]
Judge Keating h[ouse] oxmanton	10. 4. 0
St Tulocks <Rents> chappell in oxmant[own] united to St Johns	
Thad Duffe Ald[erman] 1 h[ouse] on ye wood key, Dub[lin]	1. 0. 0
Ald[erman] Younge for a brewhous on ye wood key	1. 5. 0
Xpr Bysse, gen[t], for a place	0. 10. 0
Sr Ja Ware, kt, for his house in Castle str[eet]	0. 19. 3
Xpr Greaves in right of his wife wid[ow] Tailour for ye preists chamber	0. 9. 10
Richard Quinn, merchant, 1 h[ouse] in Oxmant[own]	0. 7. 6
ye Lands of Brownstown & Horeston in ye county of Meath	0. 15. 0
A garden without Damesgate pos[session] Nicl Quitriot	0. 3. 0

APPENDIX 2

A number of cess lists survive for Dublin covering the period February 1648 to July 1649 but with a gap between May 1648 and March 1649. The cess was collected to support the parliamentarian army of Col. Michael Jones which was quartered in the city. It was levied at a rate of £463 per month but this was abated to £400 a month from March 1648. This text provides the first and last of these cess lists for the parish of St John.

Dublin City Archives MR/16

[p. 6] The Sess for 1th February 1647[8]
St Johns Parish

	li. s. d		li. s. d
Roger Brereton	10. 0	James Browne	2. 0
Widdow Usher and her sonn	12. 0	John Rasdall	1. 0
William Daniell, Baker	1. 0	Nicho Dongan	1. 0
Widdow Brooks Inmate	1. 0	Widdow Ardan	2. 0
Widdowe Dunne	2. 0	Andrew Bruton	2. 0
Wm Drady Inmate	2. 0	John Barran	4. 0
Barnard Basssano	1. 0	Peter Halpenny	2. 0
Henry Fryar	1. 0	Thomas Cotton	4. 0
Lawrence Haverick	2. 0	Patrick Halpenny	2. 0
Wm Widdnall	3. 0	Ro Scudmore	8. 0
Widdow Egerton	1. 0	Edward Chadshee	1. 0
Widdow King	1. 0	Richard Winstanly	2. 0
Robt Clowny and his daughter	4. 0	David Morris	2. 0
John Ogden	4. 0	Patrick Stone	2. 0
Tho Lauson, Buttonmaker	1. 0	Patrick Luttrell	2. 0
David Murphy	15. 0	Daniell Curragh	5. 0
For Mr Foord	10. 0	Richard Burder	2. 0
Wm Wragg	1. 0	George Marten	2. 0
John Alexander	1. 0	Christopher Rooth	2. 0
Wm Whitshed	12. 0	Mr Bully, marchant	10. 0
Wm Whitshed to be allowed by Mr Foord out of his rent	10. 0	George Draper	1. 0
		Thomas Drake	4. 0
Daniel Brady Inmate	2. 0	Wm Langam	1.0. 0
Thomsin Gibbons	3. 0	Patrick Keman	1. 0
Samuel Weston	1.10. 0	Richard Moore	1. 0
Henry Powell	1. 0	John Sheppard	1.10. 0
Patrick Long, fisher[man]	2. 0	Edward Lewis	4. 0

	li. s. d		li. s. d
John Biby	2. 0	Widdow Benson	2. 0
John Wallis	4. 0	Wm Bell	2. 0
Francis Quiby	2. 0	Wm Woodworth	6. 0
Mr Bolton	10. 0	John Dill	1. 0
Arthur Chadsey	1. 0	George Prowdfoote	5. 0
Wm Bastin	2. 0	Morgan the Gabbertman	4. 0
Ed Ledbetter	1. 0	Ro Prentice	1. 0
James Malone	3. 0	Captn Tho Barttlet	4. 0
Widdow Malone	2. 0	Alderm[an] Smith	1. 0. 0
Captn Michell	12. 0	George Winstanly	2. 0
Oliver Daverin	4. 0	Peter Dale	2. 0
Wm Knight	6. 0	Martin Wat	1. 0
Widdow Haddock	1. 0	Thomas Kelly	1. 0. 0
John Genny	10. 0	George Boyd	6. 0
Morgan Byrne	3. 0	Francis Courtopp	1. 0
Walter Flood	5. 0	John Blake	4. 0
John Lowman	4. 0	Wm Boy	4. 0
John Etherige	8. 0	Wm Dillon	10. 0
Rich Langfoord	2. 0	Benjamin Robarts	1. 5. 0
Robart Neale	5. 0	Jonathan Palin	1. 0
Thomas Braghall	5. 0	Wm Norris	2. 0
Widdow Osburn	2. 0	Rich Luttrell	1. 0. 0
Thomas Challynor	4. 0	Clement Martin	1. 4. 0
Wm Plunkett, esq	1.10. 0	John Browne	10. 0
Martin Burst	1. 0	Valentine Wayte	10. 0
Robart Tompson	1. 0	James Wilde	2. 0
Robert Wade	1. 0. 1	Roger Warren	2. 0
Wm a smith	1. 0	Nicholas Eddis	15. 0
George Hallis	1. 0	James Johnson	10. 0
[p. 7] Wm Taylor	6. 0	Daniel Burfeild	12. 0
Thomas Lee	2. 0	Tho Lyle	10. 0
Richard Doleman	15. 0	Otes Crowder	10. 0
Mr John Newman	1. 0. 0	Wm Woodworth	3. 0
Jane Shilly	4. 0	John Waterhouse	12. 0
Richard Styles	1. 0. 0	Lawrence Halgan	2. 0
Henry Finch	12. 0	Thomas Maguire	2. 0
Walter Robinson	3. 0	Sarieant Morgan	4. 0
Richard Symons	6. 0	Patrick Moore	2. 0
John Singleton	3. 0	Terence Murphy	2. 0
Jeremy Bouden	4. 0	Thomas Maguire	2. 0
James Rea	4. 0	Rich Palfrey	12. 0
John Clinch	1. 0	Mary Vials	1. 0
Michael Mc Carty	2. 0	Alexander Worrall	6. 0
George Bennett	2. 0	John Meagh	1. 0
Wm Totty	2. 0	Widdow Lunders	10. 0
Leonard Graves	4. 0	Mr Pluncket	1. 0

→

	li. s. d
Rich Kitchin	6. 0
Widdow Kerdiff	4. 0
Abraham Crafford	2. 0
Lieftent Walsh	1. 0
John Egar	1. 0
John Butcher	1. 0
James Handcock	4. 0
Rice Williams	6. 0
John Worrall	1. 0
Edward Phillips	1. 0
Daniell Hutchison	4. 0. 0
Joseph Newton	2. 0
In toto	46^{li} 14^{s}0^{od}

[p. 213] 1649 A week ending 27 July

St Johns parish	li. s. d.
Thomas Lyle	2. 0
Rice Phillips	3. 0
Daniel Burfield	6. 0
James Johnson	6. 0
Nicholas Eddys	12. 0
James Crutchley	2. 0
James Wilde	2. 0
Valentine Wayte	8. 0
John Browne	7. 0
Richard Luttrell	8. 0
William Martyn	10. 0
Jonthan Palyn	1. 0
Benjamin Roberts	5. 0
And out of Mr ffagan of ffeltryms rents	10. 0
William Dillon	6. 0
William Boy	1. 0
John Blake	3. 0
George Boyd	6. 0
Mr Owen Jones	1. 0. 0
John Annyon at Mr Jones	5. 0
Mr Alderm[an] Smyth	5. 0
Mr Baily at Ald[erman] Smyths	1. 0. 0
Thomas Browne	1. 0
Thomas Cooper	4. 0
William Morris	2. 0
Thomas Pickering	3. 0
Leonard Graves	2. 0
Symon Skelding	1. 0
Henry ffinch	6. 0
Walter Robinson	1. 0
Jane Singleton	2. 0
Jane Sheely	3. 0
Jeremy Bowden	1. 0
Robert Wade	8. 0
John Waterhouse	12. 0
Lawarence Halgan	1. 6
John Desimires	1. 4. 0
Thomas Gwire	1. 0
George Gilbert	1. 0. 0
Daniel Huchinson Ald[erman]	4. 0. 0
Rice Williams	1. 0
Anthony Robinson	5. 0
Richard Palfrey	12. 0
Widow Lounders	1. 0
Richard Kitchen	1. 0
Roger Brerton, esq	5. 0
William Daniell	6. 0
Lawrence Haverick, esq	1. 0
John Alexander	1. 0
David Murphy	10. 0
William Whitfield	6. 0
Thomasin Gibbons	0. 6
Mr Samuel Weston	2. 0. 0
John Rasdall	1. 0
Richard Burder	2. 0
William Langham	12. 0
[p. 214] John Shepheard	2. 0. 0
John Barran	1. 0
George Winstanley	1. 0
Widow Bibby & her brother	1. 0
Oliver Davoren	2. 0
Timothy Gilbert	2. 0
John Gainy	2. 0
John Mitchell	10. 0
Morgan Byrne	1. 0
Thomas Braghall	1. 0
Thomas Chaloner	4. 0
William Plunkett, Esq	1. 0. 0
Arthur Chadsey	1. 0
Mr Seaman	8. 0
William Taylor	4. 0
Nathaniell Pimloe	2. 0

APPENDIX 3

Representative Church Body Library P328/10/1

[f. 3v] June 14th 1659
It is Agreed by Consent of the Parishioners of the parish of St Johns Dublin that Ald[erman] William Smith, Ald[erman] Daniell Hutchinson, Mr Richard Palfrey, Mr William Martine, Mr John Price, Mr John Sanderton, Mr Joseph Whitchurch, Mr Andrew Loyd, Mr Rice Williams, And the two Churchwardens ffor the time being or Any six of them shall make the Asseeam[ent] ffor the Ministers stypend ffor one yeare Ending at Christmas next the summe being sixty pounds. And by Consent as afforesaid sixty pound more is to be {asseased} ffor the Repaire of the said Parish Church

Dud Loftus
Nicholas Awnsham
Andrew Lloyd
Wm Martyne
Willm Smyth
Rich Palfrey
John Whitchurch
Humphery Jervis
ffrancis Williams
Simon Hill

	£.	s.	d
[f. 4] [Woodkey ward]			
Thomas Mercer Att ye sign of bristoll		4.	0
Henry Powell		10.	0
Paule Palmer		10.	0
Thomas Haward		12.	0
Robert Cartwright		6.	0
Thomas Wicker		4.	0
Henry Blacke		6.	0
ffrancis Will[iams]		10.	0
John Critchfeld		6.	0
Nicholas Aunsham		4.	0
William Martin		16.	0
William Warring		6.	0
John Langley, ffrancis fenton &		2.	0
Mr Daggaroll, inmates		4.	0
Arthur Studard & John Barber, inmates		4.	0
now Geo Birne		2.	0
Benjamin Roberts		16.	0
William Woodall		8.	0
James Boy		8.	0
William Bettson		4.	0
Thomas Michell		4.	0
Samuel Gibbs		12.	0
William Bell &		12.	0
Hugh Pearse, inmates		2.	0
James Morison		4.	0
Perce ffowks		4.	0
Alderman Wm Smyth	1.	8.	0
John Joyles		4.	0
Richard Treadgould		4.	0
Thomas Payne		4.	0
Robert Hill		6.	0
Morgan Hendley &		4.	0
Arthur Grymes, inmates		2.	0
Widdow Primfine		2.	0
William Edwards		2.	0
James Wray		8.	0
Elizabeth Bythill & Mr Sutton, inmates		12.	0

→

	£.	s.	d
Widdow Horsley & James Warrington, inmates		6.	0
Sargeant Berry		4.	0
Sr Mathew Derinza house	[blank]		
Major Cadogan or tenant	1.	0.	0
A waste house	[blank]		
Mr Leigh	[blank]		
Dorothy Pooley & James Camell, inmates	[blank]		
George Hollis		10.	0
Capt Lewis & Abell Leigh, inmates	[blank]		
Mr Harbart In Cadogans Alley		6.	0
Mr Bonnell 2 howses in that Alley		10.	0
Mary Grasson A poore woman	[blank]		
Richard Borne		<4.0>	
John Evans &		10.	0
Robert Werrall, inmates		2.	0
Widdow Mc Adames		2.	0
Edward Moory		4.	0
William Gill, stabler		8.	0
Thomas Lawrence, smyth		2.	0
Robert Wade		16.	0
John Sherard		6.	0
[blank] Blanchard		4.	0
Dr Duddley Loftus	1.	8.	0
Christopher Lovett &	1.	4.	0
Joseph Whitchurch, inmates		16.	0
Charles Andrews house wast	[blank]		
Humphray Jarvis	1.	0.	0
Wiliam Elicocke		4.	0
Richard Symons		12.	0
Widdow Brassell		1.	0
Edmund Stephens		3.	0
Symon Hill		12.	0
Richard Swan & William Williams, inmates		8.	0
James Potts		10.	0
Dennis Allen		8.	0
Stephen ffoxtwift & Mrs Roe, a poore widdow, inmates		4.	0
Gawen Dugglas		18.	0
William Berbans & John Blackewell, inmates	[blank]		

	£.	s.	d
Thomas Cooper	1.	0.	0
John Gest	1.	0.	0
William Holland		2.	0
Mr [blank] Glasier		6.	0
Richard Parsons		6.	0
& William Thrupp		4.	0
John Price		14.	0
John Berfine		10.	0
Anthony Parker		4.	0
[f. 4v] Winetaverne streete Ward			
Benjamin Gosmore		4.	0
William Sparkes		4.	0
Thomas Gilpatricke		8.	0
Thomas Gwyer		6.	0
William Yates &		4.	0
Richard ffreind, inmates		2.	0
Lewis Williams		8.	0
Richard Paulphray		8.	0
{Mr Andrew Lloyd		10.	0}
James ffarrell		2.	0
William Mallone		8.	0
Thomas Bacon		4.	0
Phillip March		2.	0
Bryan ffeney		4.	0
Morgan Roberts		4.	0
Capt Mather Jones his house is <lyin> wast		0.	0
Ensign Sicklemore		8.	0
Mrs Kitchins		16.	0
Joseph Bancks		4.	0
Rowland Bishop		4.	0
Walter Dowlin		4.	0
[blank] Duddley at ye tennis courte		12.	0
Arthur Hendley		6.	0
Thomas Potter		2.	0
Mrs Sanderland		2.	0
William Wood Atturney		0.	0
John Gilpatricke		2.	0
John Whit<head>		2.	0
William Evans		2.	0
Oliver Whelch		10.	0
James Coveney		8.	0
James Woodward &		6.	0

→

	£.	s.	d
Mr Story inmates		4.	o
Mathewe Hawley		4.	o
Thomas Robinson		4.	o
Rice Williams	1.	o.	o
Johnathan Paley		6.	o
Alderman Daniell Huchison	1.	8.	o
Mr Buttler		6.	o
Adam Gould		18.	o
John Sanderton		12.	o
Jeremy Smyth		8.	o
Jer Berstawe		10.	o
<ye Magesine seller>			
ffish streete ward			
Widdow Gouldsmyth		4.	o
Mr [blank] ffleetewood		2.	o
Nicholas Clarke or his tennant		2.	o
James Handcocke		8.	o
John Boulton		16.	o
John Blacke		10.	o
George Handley		4.	o
John Batter		6.	o
Ambros Whitthead		6.	o
Nicholas Holliwood		8.	o
Robert Sheppley		4.	o
Mr [blank] Bucke		12.	o
Robert Sherwin & tenants		8.	o
Tymothy Gilbert		8.	o
Widdow Birne		4.	o
Thomas Tarlington		10.	o
Edward Dannell		8.	o
James Barlowe		12.	o
John Taverner		4.	o
Richard Styles		8.	o
John fuller		8.	o
Thomas Smarte		10.	o
John Thomson		10.	o
John Bishoppe		10.	o
Arlender Usher		14.	o
George Hulett	1.	o.	o
Mr [blank] Knight & ten[ants]		12.	o
Richard Paffley		2.	o
Richard Denistrapp		10.	o
Robert Nele		18.	o
Thomas Potter		2.	o
Widdow Lynch		2.	o
William Challener		6.	o
George Whittey		2.	o
William Lutterall		6.	o
Thomas Cliere		4.	o
Mr Sam Weston	1.	8.	o
Edward Dermote		10.	o
John Alexander		10.	o
Wiliam Millborne		10.	o
Widdow Moeland		10.	o
George Humphreyes		6.	o
Patrick Lutterall		2.	o
Widdow Winstanley & Mr Harden		6.	o
[f. 5] fishstreet ward			
Thomas Grymes		6.	o
John Cullen		2.	o
Wiliam Beenne		12.	o
Widdow Border		10.	o
George Rowh		2.	o
William Langham	1.	4.	o
Robert Eaton		4.	o
Andrew Donne		4.	o
John Sheppard	1.	8.	o
John Welsh		8.	o
Mr Jewit		6.	o
Henry Bushell		8.	o
in all	70.	16.	o

Willm Smyth
John Price   Dl Huchinson
Wm Martyne

APPENDIX 4

Representative Church Body Library P328/10/1

[f.3] A note what Church goods where delivered By Mr Pattricke Carr late minister of St Johns into the hands of James Potts and Thomas Haward Churchwardens for ye yeare 1659

1 The Comunion Silver <Cup> {Challice}, cover and the box where it tis keept
2 one pottle pewter pott and A three pint pewter pott, two pewter dishes
3 two napkins and A diap[er] Table Cloath <and one black Cessian cloth> rotten & worth nothing[111]
4 one ould hearse Cloth & A greene Carpitt for ye Comunion Table
5 Three greene Cussions of raysed sattin and one greene brodcloth Cussion
6 one watchatt Taffata Cussion, one blue velvet Cussion
7 one watchatt pulpitt cloth & A watchatt Cloth for the Comunion Table
8 A Red damaske coveringe for ye pulpitt & Cussion of A darke red Collo[ur]
9 two vellum Registers bound in leather & A chaire in ye Inner vestry with a cussion {brought to ye outward}[112]
10 Two covered stoules and two Joynt stoules. 1667 one of ye Joynt stooles broake.
11 Two Tables ye one in ye Inner ye other in the outer vestry
12 Two Chest in ye outer Vestry & one chaire with A Trunke. broke & gon p[er] ord[er][113]
13 A little Chaire in ye Inner Vestry, one Carpitt of stript stuffe. this carpitt worne out & a new greene one bought in ye roome thereof[114]
14 one grate in the outer Vestry, one ould mape of ye world
15 ffoure wood shutters for windowes, fforttie Bucketts {but twenty seven bucketts to be found} And Two Lathers <1 bucket lost 1667>
16 Thirtteene shelves In the Vestry, Two ffire hooks with Chaynes (1 shelf lost 1668)
17 A Comunion Table, one houre glasse, A p[ar]sell of ould Brasse Cont[ains] 15 peces
18 A Table in the Lower Vestry

The above s[ai]d goods were delivered Aprill 15th 1662 unto Mr Nicholas Ansham & Mr John Vanperseen Churchwardens theise utinsells of ye church were delivered July 9 1663 unto ye new church [wardens] Mr Chr Lowet & Mr John Qualsh

John Prudockes lease
Wm Harris his lease
James Bathes lease
August 26th 1667 Ald[erman] Smiths lease
Mr Maurice Smiths lease

19 one new Tinn standish[115]
20 Two bibles one whereof old
21 fower Comon prayer bookes two wherof old
22 one parish booke covered with parchment. theise & the above goods d[elivere]d Capt Cokayne & Mr Williams June 17th 1781 thery being Churchwardens for s[ai]d year.[116]
23 one newe dale Chest
24 two accompt bookes & one dowble alphabett for said book lettred A:B

These utensills of the Church above mentioned were d[elivere]d unto Wm Anion & Mr Tho Leeson Church wardens July 30th 1791
9ber: 8th 1680 These above utinsels were d[elivere]d to Mr Richard Gray & Mr Richard Reeves Churchwarden for this present year.

NOTES TO THE TEXT

The following abbreviations have been used:

Robinson, 'Ancient deeds'	J.L. Robinson, ' On the ancient deeds of the parish of St John, Dublin' in *Proceedings of the Royal Irish Academy* xxxiii (1916), pp 175–224. Deeds are cited by number.
Anc. rec. Dub.	J.T. and R. Gilbert (eds), *Calendar of the ancient records of Dublin* (19 vols, Dublin, 1889–1944).

1 Despite the fact that Christ Church was the diocesan cathedral of Dublin diocese the diocesan administration was based at St Patrick's cathedral throughout the early modern period.

2 The text of most of this entry has been lost but the conditions of the lease are preserved in a later deed, Robinson, 'Ancient deeds', no. 200.

3 Barnaby Bolger became prebendary of St John's in 1602. He may also have been prebendary of St Michan's in 1607. He was also prebendary of Killamery in Ossory from 1591 and became dean of Ossory in 1613 and was deposed from St John's by the archbishop in 1613 for non-residence. He died in 1647.

4 Robinson, 'Ancient deeds', no. 179.

5 Robinson, 'Ancient deeds', no. 182.

6 Robinson, 'Ancient deeds', no. 186.

7 John Bullock was clerk of the parish. He was also a vicar choral of Christ Church from 1586 to his death in 1618. For his will, National Library of Ireland, MS GO 290, p. 23.

8 The tailors guild had their chapel in St John's church, H.F. Berry, 'The merchant tailors gild' in *Journal of the Royal Society of Antiquaries of Ireland* xlviii (1918), p. 52.

9 Robinson, 'Ancient deeds', nos 173, 174, 176.

10 Edward Hill, graduate and former fellow of Trinity College, Dublin, was elected prebendary of St John's on 23 November 1613. He was also a minor canon of St Patrick's. He was described in the 1615 visitation as 'a very sufficient preacher'. He died in January 1639 and was buried in St John's. Sir James Ware's diary notes that he had foretold his own death a few days before and was 'suspected to have used magic' (Trinity College, Dublin, MS 6404, f. 108v.).

11 Langable, which appears in various forms throughout the church wardens' accounts including 'Long cable', was a property tax payable to the corporation and calculated on street frontage of the parish property. Its origins lay in the grant of the property from the city to an owner.

12 The king's days were the king's birthday (19 June) and the date of his accession (24 March).

13 According to the seventeenth-century pagination there are twelve pages missing here. The document, which begins in mid sentence is a decree from the court of Exchequer.

14 William Methold, chief baron of the exchequer 1612–21, F.E. Ball, *The judges in Ireland, 1221–1921* (2 vols, London, 1926), i, p. 324.

15 John Blennerhasset, baron of the exchequer, 1609–17, chief baron of the exchequer, 1621–25, Ball, *Judges in Ireland*, i, pp 243–4.

16 The order, which set the incumbent's income at £6, is in Representative Church Body Library, MS C6/1/26/2, no.9.

17 Christopher Clements, one of the churchwardens, died in January 1621 and was buried in St John's.

18 Bartholomew Jordan was parish clerk from the death of Bullock in 1620. He had also been a stipendiary in the choir of Christ Church until 1617.

19 Albone Levert was Athlone pursivant of arms, one of the heraldic offices attached to the office of Ulster king of arms.

20 It is not clear why the bells should have been rung on 5 August.

21 Anniversary of the gunpowder plot in 1605.

22 The date of James I's succession to the throne.

23 The duke of Buckingham and Charles, prince of Wales had gone to Spain in February 1623 in a secret attempt to negotiate a marriage for the prince. This proved hugely unpopular. The negotiations failed and they returned to Portsmouth on 5 October 1623.

24 Henry Carey, first Viscount Falkland who was sworn in on 8 September 1622.

25 The purchase of a ladder is probably to conform to the Dublin corporation order of 1620 by which parishes were to have buckets, ladders and hooks for fire fighting, *Anc. rec. Dub.*, iii, p. 129. For further purchases below ff 47–7v, 83v and appendix 4.

26 Charles I was proclaimed in Dublin on 10 April 1625.

27 What is probably referred to is the making of a new lease of Boyle's holding of church property and clearing his arrears as described in his diary for 27 May 1624, A.B. Grossart (ed.), *Lismore paper*s (1st ser, 5 vols, London, 1886), ii, p. 128.

28 Mending the seats seems to imply burial in church. For his background, Colm Lennon, *The lords of Dublin in an age of reformation* (Dublin, 1989), p. 252.

29 For the new grant Robinson, 'Ancient deeds', no. 188

30 No account was forthcoming from Graves and Ussher and the wardens for the following year accounted for two years, see below f. 32.

31 'Cloney' added in a later hand.

32 This seems to be a mistake. Patrick Bathe was master of the tailors' guild in 1625–6, Berry, 'Merchant tailors guild', p. 59.

33 5 November.

34 Mending the seats seems to imply that he was buried within the church. For his will, National Library of Ireland, MS GO 290, p. 130.

35 John Atherton, an Oxford graduate from Somerset, was installed as prebendary of St John's on 22 April 1630 until December 1635 when he became chancellor of Christ Church. He became bishop of Waterford and Lismore in 1636. On his career Aidan Clarke, 'The Atherton file' in *Decies* no. 11 (May, 1979), pp 35–54. On his burial note 87 below.

36 'Sealed up in a bagge' added in the same hand which wrote the audit certificate.
37 This seems to be John Cunningham who was master of the tailor's guild from 11 December 1627 to 24 June 1628, Berry, 'Merchant tailors gild', p. 59.
38 'Their remaynes ... viij^{d} ster' added in the hand which wrote the audit certificate.
39 The names are added in a different hand to the rest of the heading.
40 Probably the birth of the future Charles II on 29 May 1630
41 For the background to this see ff 50–1 below.
42 The remainder of this account is in a different hand.
43 For the increase in business, *Anc. rec. Dub.*, iii, pp 279–80.
44 *Anc rec. Dub.*, ii, p. 174.
45 Why William Stoughton, who was elected churchwarden with Leadbetter, is not named in this account is not known. He died in 1642 and was buried in St John's.
46 Robinson, 'Ancient deeds', no. 182.
47 Marginal note in a later hand.
48 Rolf Loeber, *A biographical dictionary of architects in Ireland, 1600–1720* (London, 1981), pp 108–9.
49 Marginal note in a later hand.
50 Marginal note in a later hand.
51 Marginal note in a later hand.
52 Marginal note in a later hand.
53 'for pullissing ye East windowe' added in a different hand.
54 Marginal note added in a later hand.
55 '& so give a discharge' added in a different hand.
56 Marginal note added in a different hand.
57 For the legal documents, Raymond Gillespie (ed.), *The first chapter act book of Christ Church cathedral, Dublin, 1574–1634* (Dublin, 1997), pp 193–9.
58 Robert Eustace was churchwarden in 1620–1. There is no account in the volume for his period in office but an amount was recorded in the account for 1621–2 as being paid over by him. This entry must relate to some settlement made as a result of failing to file an account.
59 The total added in another hand.
60 Added in another hand.
61 St Audoen's church, the adjoining parish to the west of St John's.
62 Added in a different but contemporary hand.
63 Added in the same different but contemporary hand.
64 Added in the same hand as the makers of the marginal notes.
65 This entry added in a different hand.
66 It seems that St John's already had a beadle for the poor before this order since in 1629 they bought a coat for their beadle (f. 40v above).
67 'receaved of Mathew fford ... ffishamble street 3.0.0' added in a different ink but in the same hand.
68 Hugh Cressey, an Oxford graduate from Yorkshire, was chaplain to Lord Deputy Wentworth. He was elected as prebendary of St John's in December 1635. He became dean of Leighlin in 1637 and a canon of Windsor in 1642. He converted to Catholicism in 1646, seeing the wars of the 1640s as a judgement for schism. He became a Benedictine monk at Douai. He returned to England after the Restoration and died in 1674.

69 Marginal note in a different hand.

70 The text referred to is missing from the book in its present form and must have been part of the pages at the beginning of the book. For a copy of the text, Representative Church Body Library, MS C6/1/26/2, no 9.

71 The framework of this account seems to have been copied from an older document and the money amounts updated since James Ussher had been promoted from Meath to the archbishopric of Armagh in 1625.

72 A dosett is an ornamental cloth, usually embroidered, which was hung behind the altar.

73 Edward Dunsterville succeeded Hugh Fisher as curate of St John's in 1638 and remained there until 1640. In the 1640s he was known as a violently anti-Irish preacher in Dublin.

74 Robinson, 'Ancient deeds', no. 176.

75 Marginal note in a later hand.

76 'Patrick Dowde … 2.0' added in a different hand.

77 Dudley Boswell was a graduate of Trinity College, Dublin (M.A. 1630) who was installed prebendary of St Johns on 18 July 1638 and remained there until his death from plague in Dublin in 1650. He was previously prebendary of St Michael's and in St Patrick's prebendary of St Auoden's. For his will National Library of Ireland, MS GO 290, p. 33.

78 Each of these entries has the corresponding signature of the benefactor in the left hand margin.

79 Robinson, 'Ancient deeds', no. 190.

80 Robinson, 'Ancient deeds', no. 189.

81 What this refers to is not clear. It may be some form of reredos.

82 John Bramhall, bishop of Derry (1634–1661). The context of this entry is probably Bramhall's enquiries into the ownership of church lands in Dublin diocese which began seriously in 1639.

83 For the resulting communion cup Tony Sweeney, *Irish Stuart silver* (Dublin, 1995), pp 19, 30.

84 For this register James Mills (ed.)., *Registers of the parish of St John the Evangelist, Dublin, 1619–1699* (Dublin, 1906, reprint 2000), pp iv–v.

85 Marginal note added in a later hand.

86 Richard Osbaldston, died September 1640.

87 John Atherton, bishop of Waterford and Lismore, was convicted of sodomy and executed in Dublin on 5 December 1640. The register of St John's indicates he was buried the same day. For the funeral sermon, Nicholas Bernard, *A sermon preached at the buriall of … John Atherton the next night after his execution in St John's Church* (Dublin, 1641).

88 The date is added in a different ink.

89 John Tadpole became parish clerk on the death of Bartholomew Jordan. He was also vicar choral at St Patrick's (1639–69) and Christ Church (1644–69). He died in December 1669 and was buried in St John's.

90 This cess list is clearly incomplete and lacks the cessors signatures. There does not seem to be any page missing from the volume itself and the problem seems to lie in the transcription into the volume.

91 Marginal note added in a later hand.

92 Marginal note added in a later hand.
93 'pay' altered from 'paid'.
94 Robinson, 'Ancient deeds', no. 188
95 Robinson, 'Ancient deeds', no.186.
96 Patrick Carr or Kerr was rector of Dunaghy and vicar of Glynn, county Antrim in the 1630s. He officiated in St John's after Boswell's death in 1650 but how he was appointed is not clear. His irregular appointment may be behind the appointment of Thomas Harrison to St John's in 1655. The appointment does not seem to have taken effect although in 1658 Carr was forbidden to preach in St John's because he had no legal title to his position. In 1658 he was appointed to Dartry (Monaghan) and Galloon (Fermanagh) as a minister of the gospel. He was succeeded at St John's by Edward Baines before the restoration of the Church of Ireland in 1660.
97 Robinson, 'Ancient deeds', no.191.
98 Marginal note in a different hand.
99 The figures in this account are all in a different ink to the entries in the account and seem to have been added later.
100 For the case see below f. 163v and note 104 below.
101 Marginal note in a different hand.
102 From here to the end of the account is in a different hand to the earlier part of the account.
103 Robert Ardagh. For his fee of 12*s.* 10*d.* f. 165 below.
104 For the case to which this refers, Robinson, 'Ancient deeds', no. 193.
105 This entry and the following one are in a different ink but in the same hand.
106 'Paid unto … 4.0.0' in a different ink but the same hand as the main account.
107 marginal note in a different hand.
108 In this entry the main text appears to have been copied into the book and the names added later.
109 'Ordered that … his stypend' in a different hand.
110 marginal note in a different hand.
111 'rotten and worth nothing' in a later hand.
112 'brought to ye outward' in a later hand.
113 'broke … per ord[er]' in a later hand.
114 'this carpitt … roome thereof' in a later hand.
115 The remainder of the list is in a different, later, hand.
116 'Thiese … year' in a different hand.

INDEX

Surnames and place-names have not been modernised in the text or the index. Variant forms of the same name have been brought together in the index wherever positively identified. Where individuals termed only 'Mr' in the text have been positively identified the index entry supplies the relevant Christian name.